Let the Records Show

Let the Records Show

A Practical Guide to Power of Attorney and Estate Record Keeping

LINDA A. ALDERSON, B.A., C.A.

AND

DOUGLAS ALAN ALDERSON, M.A., LL.M.

iUniverse, Inc.
Bloomington

LET THE RECORDS SHOW
A PRACTICAL GUIDE TO POWER OF ATTORNEY AND ESTATE RECORD KEEPING

iUniverse books may be ordered through booksellers or by contacting:

iUniverse
1663 Liberty Drive
Bloomington, IN 47403
www.iuniverse.com
1-800-Authors (1-800-288-4677)

ISBN: 978-1-4620-0670-0 (sc)
ISBN: 978-1-4620-0671-7 (ebk)

Printed in the United States of America

iUniverse rev. date: 10/31/2011

Contents

To our parents, Alan and Jacqueline, exemplars of faithful stewardship and trust

Preface

The purpose of this book is twofold. First, it will offer the non-accountant a step-by-step guide, providing the tools necessary to efficiently and confidently perform the financial record-keeping duties of either

a) an attorney acting under a continuing power of attorney for property (or similar document), or

b) an estate trustee (executor) acting under a will (or an estate administrator acting in the absence of a will).

Second, it will provide brief and practical explanations of many of the legal aspects related to the accounting duties of an attorney/estate trustee, without the legal terminology that can often lead to exasperation and unnecessary worry.

With over 50 years of experience between us in accounting and legal practice, we have had many opportunities to assist people in understanding the record-keeping responsibilities that come with looking after someone else's money, either because they are an attorney under a power of attorney or an executor under a will. In our respective practices, we have kept a practical focus on assisting clients with estate planning and management issues leading to and ensuring client-centred solutions.

The need for this book became apparent after being engaged numerous times to prepare and present formal schedules of financial activity ("accounts") for submission to the court during estate litigation. There were a number of similarities between the cases with respect to the accounting challenges that had to be overcome in order to prepare accurate and comprehensive accounts to satisfy the court. For example, missing documentation, conflicting information supporting the whereabouts and treatment of some assets and liabilities, and/or questionable activity in numerous bank accounts not owned by the person for whom financial affairs were being maintained—all provided points of contention during the course of litigation. Indeed, most of the litigation was fuelled, if not caused, by a lack of proper record keeping, which would have provided timely, accurate and transparent information without the need to resort to the costly and time consuming process that is estate litigation.

Estate litigation teaches many lessons, and one of the most fundamental lessons is that there is a gap between the *requirements* provided by the legal statutes governing both power of attorney and estate trustee financial record keeping and the *practical* aspects of maintaining these financial records. In other words, the law *requires* that you keep certain records, but it does not tell you *how to* go about keeping those records.

Moreover, specific record-keeping requirements contained in various statutes and regulations governing this area appear to make little sense to the average, non-legally and non-financially trained individual. However, upon a closer look at what is really required, one discovers that essentially what is being asked for are itemized lists and the proper management and recording of the items on those lists. As most of the items on these lists are of a financial nature, generally accepted bookkeeping practices must govern the creation, maintenance and presentation of these lists no matter in which province one lives.

Again, the average lay person finds that they are in a world where the terminology, both accounting and legal, is outside their usual vocabulary—such words as debits, credits, financial instruments, dispositions, adjusted cost base, transparency and fiduciary are all terms that do not make up everyday conversations.

There is also a notable deficiency of tools available offering practical guidance on how to maintain financial records that will help them meet the legal requirements of completeness and presentation. Although some information is available in a number of legal texts dealing with estate management, one must either painstakingly extract it from detailed discourses on the legal requirements or be fortunate enough to read the appendixes first and come across, at the very most, a checklist. At first glance the checklist appears to be very comprehensive, but at best it ends up being general and tells you what your duties are. This of course is important, but the checklist does not tell you how to deal with the practical aspects of recording and keeping account of the financial information required to properly fulfill your duties.

This book will provide the reader with the how to of their financial record-keeping obligations, demystifying and simplifying accounting terminology and the related work processes associated with creating a complete and proper information trail that will satisfy both legal obligations as well as responding to any requests for information from appropriate parties. At the same time, this book will also provide a concise, legal context aimed at clarifying the basic obligations related to the financial record-keeping duties of an attorney and/or estate trustee to help the reader better understand the importance of those duties.

Ultimately, it is hoped that anyone reading this book will find the necessary instructions and encouragement to perform financial record-keeping duties in such a way that the costly and stressful event of estate litigation never occurs.

A Note about Jurisdiction

Canada is a country that, in addition to its national government, has as many legislatures as it has provinces and territories, all passing laws that regulate powers of attorney and estate matters. In addition, there are two legal systems responsible for the regulation of these matters, the Common Law and, in Quebec, the Civil Law. Thus, while this book is written primarily from the Common Law tradition and with the details of Ontario law in mind, the accounting principles and methods it uses are universal and applicable across Canada regardless of the legal peculiarities of provincial and territorial legislation. Readers must seek out appropriate legal advice given their province/territory of residence and the particular circumstances in which they find themselves.

Disclaimer regarding Legal Advice

Not only does the existence of multiple legal jurisdictions require seeking appropriate legal advice, for that legal advice to be appropriate, it must be focused on the particular factual circumstances in which readers will find themselves. This means that this book should not be used as an alternative to proper advice. Because we are dealing with "the big picture" of financial record-keeping requirements, we have had to keep our discussion of the law at a general level. It is important to bear in mind that general statements are always subject to exceptions and qualifications based upon both jurisdictional differences and the factual circumstances of each case. Although this book contains information about the law in general terms, it is not a substitute for, and should not be used as an alternative to, proper legal advice which is the application of the appropriate law to the reader's specific circumstances. Accordingly, the authors make no representations or warranties about the outcomes resulting from following the suggestions made in this volume, or the use to which the information contained in this book is put, and they are not assuming any liability for any claims, losses or damages arising out of the use of this book. Readers should seek appropriate legal advice to address their own specific circumstance.

Acknowledgements

Writing a book such as this, we are keenly aware of John Donne's observation that "No man is an island, entire of itself," and whatever merit this book now possesses would have been greatly diminished but for the time and expertise of the following who generously commented on earlier drafts of the manuscript: Craig Colraine and Stanley Landau of Birenbaum, Steinberg, Landau, Savin and Colraine, LLP, for their respective litigation and solicitor expertise; Glenn Lott, C.A., of Lott & Company Chartered Accountants, for his accounting and income tax proficiency; Richard Alderson and Sandra Leonard for their respective legal input; Linda Quirk for her insights into the Canadian publishing business; and Carol Bauhs, Kevin McAleese, Alan Alderson and Jacqueline Alderson for being our "John and Jane Q. Public" and providing feedback from the non-professional's perspective. In acknowledging and thanking them for their contribution, it must be clearly understood that although they share in making this a better book, we remain solely responsible for any shortcomings the reader may find herein.

Introduction

What Is This Book?

This book is designed primarily as a "how to" book addressing the financial record-keeping concerns of anyone who agrees to undertake the duties under a continuing power of attorney for property (CPOAP) or under a will as an estate trustee. Secondary to providing a practical guide as to how to keep financial records on behalf of someone else, it also contains brief explanations of many of the legal aspects related to the duties of an attorney/estate trustee as they might impact on financial record-keeping obligations. These explanations are (hopefully) without the legal terminology that can often lead to exasperation and unnecessary worry. Though primarily referring to the role of attorney for property, it should be noted that the ten steps given in Chapter 5 are universal in application to anyone who is looking after someone else's financial affairs—whether it be under a formal guardianship, trustee or power of attorney document. As there are a number of books available that comprehensively address the legal issues and considerations of an estate trustee and guardian (some of which are listed in the reference section of this book), this book focuses primarily on the role of power of attorney for property. However a chapter has been included addressing specific differences in financial record-keeping obligations between an attorney and that of the estate trustee.

At first, the prospects of acting as an attorney under a continuing power of attorney for property or under a will as an estate trustee might appear intimidating or taxing. Once informed of all the duties required, you might not be sure whether an honour has been bestowed or whether someone is getting even with you! Many of us will have a barrage of questions flitting through our heads: Where do I start? What questions should I be asking? What kind of record keeping do I really have to do? Do I have to accept the task? Am I going to be expected to make good on any of their debts? How much time is this going to take? How can I do this in an efficient manner to effectively carry out the trust of the person who has chosen me?

Acting as an attorney or estate trustee, however, need not be as complicated or daunting as one might believe, at least as it relates to financial record-keeping matters. This book provides practical instructions on such matters as what specifically has to be done to meet record-keeping requirements, where to obtain the required information, how to communicate with different financial institutions, how to document the financial activities associated with that information and how to fix common mistakes and errors in record-keeping activity.

New areas of learning are often more frustrating than they need to be due to a lack of knowledge of the common language used by the experts in the field. We have tried to minimize this frustration by providing, immediately before Chapter 1, a glossary titled, "Accounting and Legal Terms in Plain English." This list is not exhaustive, but we have tried to be as comprehensive as possible in providing clear explanations of words and phrases that are part of the common language of attorneys and estate trustees, especially in regard to record-keeping activities.

Chapter 1 addresses 10 important questions one should ask before agreeing to act as attorney. Considering the answers to these questions will enable newcomers to the role of attorney to determine whether they want to accept this task, and if so, to better understand some of the record-keeping ground rules that are expanded on in other sections of the book. Even if you have already begun to act as someone's attorney without realizing you had a choice, the questions posed and answers given are designed to fill in some gaps of your basic understanding and provide a firm foundation for moving on to Chapter 2.

Whereas Chapter 1 presents answers to some key questions, Chapter 2 takes the uninitiated into the legal fundamentals that need to be understood from the beginning. It still adheres to a question-and-answer format, providing the reader with brief explanations of many of the legal aspects related to the duties of an attorney. It is unencumbered by strict legal terminology that can often lead to confusion and frustration on the part of the attorney due to unfamiliarity with these topics. Some of the topics might appear to have little to do with keeping financial records *per se*. However, the completeness and integrity of the accounting records can only be achieved if attorneys are aware of the basic ground rules and legal context in which they will be operating. Taken together, Chapters 1 and 2 will provide the reader with a clear context for understanding why it is important to keep proper records as well as why and how these records are kept.

As noted above, legal rules governing the conduct and tasks to be completed when looking after the financial affairs of another are fairly consistent across Canada, although there can be differences in the language and procedures used in the different legislation governing these matters, as illustrated in Table 1. This table also provides a reference to the websites that provide access to the legislation for each province and territory in Canada.

Chapter 3 takes a look at the specific legal requirements for record keeping with a brief discussion of the importance of adhering to privacy law issues. Again, though not strictly financial in nature, an understanding of privacy issues is essential to properly appreciate the need to keep accurate financial records and to do so consistently and in a timely manner.

The principles of bookkeeping are the same regardless of circumstances, but there are practical considerations related to record keeping when the attorney is assisting someone who is still capable and involved with the management of their financial/property affairs. Chapter 4 addresses these practical considerations.

Chapter 5 turns to the situation where the grantor, the person who has made the power of attorney, is no longer managing their affairs. It sets out a practical, ten-step guide showing how to fulfil the legal requirements with respect to the financial documentation required to be maintained when the attorney has taken over the management of another person's property. Following these steps in the order presented will ensure the attorney starts off on the right foot; asking the proper questions and establishing an effortless discipline that will ensure this task is completed with efficiency, in a legally appropriate manner and with the least amount of stress possible for all parties involved. Whether the attorney is situated in Whitehorse, Yukon Territory, or Sydney, Nova Scotia, the practical dos and don'ts of financial record keeping are the same.

Of particular importance is "Step 2—Making an Inventory." Often the attorney simply does not know where to look for some of the information or what questions to ask the grantor.

Chapter 6 is devoted to a comprehensive discussion of the most common assets and liabilities a person is likely to have. Included for each asset or liability identified is a detailed description and where the most likely place for the information regarding this item might be found.

While *Let the Records Show* is primarily focused on assisting the attorney, many of the steps and principles are relevant for an estate trustee managing a deceased person's estate. However, there are differences, which are highlighted and discussed in Chapter 7. To further assist the attorney in accomplishing complete and transparent financial record keeping, Chapter 8 identifies common errors and suggests ways to fix them. Chapter 9 provides a consideration of a number of important steps to be taken should litigation commence due to perceived mismanagement of the property with which you have been entrusted. Final thoughts are offered in Chapter 10 together with a summary of the most important points from each chapter and advice on how to successfully navigate your way through the processes of financial record keeping on behalf of another. The book concludes with appendices presenting excerpts from legislation (Ontario) that will provide an easy reference for those readers who wish to see the exact legal text referred to throughout this book. A complete set of checklists and pro forma schedules, with samples of how they should be completed, is also included.

Who Will Find This Book Useful?

Most people will find many of the elements of this book useful and a worthwhile investment. However, it might be helpful to be specific about those who will find the information contained here invaluable.

> ➤ People who are maintaining, or assisting to maintain, the property and/or financial affairs of a relative or friend, regardless of whether they are acting under a formal CPOAP. Following much of the guidance will ensure that should a formal document be effective at some time, or when an estate trustee steps in, the record keeping has been maintained in such a way that there will be no awkward questions or suspicions that cannot be dealt with easily and effortlessly to the satisfaction of all.

> ➤ People who have just been made aware that they are an attorney under a CPOAP, are named as an estate trustee under a will or have the potential to be appointed as an estate administrator by a court order will appreciate this book as a source of valuable information in deciding whether they want to accept the responsibilities and obligations of being either an attorney or estate trustee. At the very least, once reading through the introduction and the first couple of chapters, if they decline to act, they can use this resource to organize their own financial affairs for the inevitability of their own incapacity and ultimate death.

> ➤ People who are contemplating making a CPOAP or a will can find this book useful to gain a better understanding of the type of information that the person they are thinking of appointing as their attorney or estate trustee will require in order to perform this task.

> ➤ People who are acting as an attorney for personal care or who have been appointed by the court as guardian of the person will also find this book useful, because it

will explain why the attorney for property must have certain information and the importance of why the attorney for personal care or guardian must be willing and able to provide that information in a timely and accurate manner.

➢ People who are acting as an attorney or estate trustee with others will find this book invaluable to help all attorneys or estate trustees understand their legal record-keeping obligations regardless of whether acting jointly (together with another) or acting jointly and separately (acting independently). Ensuring that all the attorneys or estate trustees involved with the same estate have access to this book will increase the likelihood that they are maintaining their part of the financial transactions consistently. This will ensure that all the records can be reviewed efficiently and their completeness and accuracy determined easily.

➢ Lawyers who prepare CPOAPs and provide estate administration advice to attorneys and executors will find this an invaluable tool. Catering to all levels of sophistication, this book demystifies accounting and legal terminology, presenting in layman's terms the accounting obligations of an attorney acting under a CPOAP or an estate trustee.

➢ People who have recently acquired the honour and duty of being an estate trustee will find this book useful because it provides a step-by-step approach to identifying and obtaining all the required information to assist them in executing their legal and fiduciary obligations with respect to record keeping and accounting to beneficiaries and potentially the court.

➢ Finally, anyone who will eventually die (and alas, that is all of us) will find this a useful book. It will identify what information your surviving relatives or friends will need in order to wind up your affairs and distribute your estate as you have indicated in your will. You will leave behind grateful family members should you yourself, while still in full capacity of your senses, gather some if not all of the necessary information that your estate trustee will require.

The material covered in this book is presented to allow the reader to identify the sections most relevant to them and proceed accordingly. However, for those of you who have already commenced acting as attorney or estate trustee and may be tempted to skip Chapter 1 because it addresses pertinent questions that you may have already asked, it is recommended that you do not. Chapter 1 introduces a number of important themes that one should have a firm understanding of to ensure a stress-free experience in keeping records as an attorney or estate trustee.

Glossary

Accounting and Legal Terms in Plain English

adjusted cost base (ACB): An income tax term that refers to the change in an asset's book value (i.e., the original purchase price) resulting from improvements, new purchases of the same asset (e.g., shares in a company), sales, payouts or other factors. When an asset is sold, the ACB is deducted from the selling price to determine the gain or loss that is reported on an individual's or a company's tax return.

administrator: A person assigned the task of administering the estate of a deceased person when there is no will. Sometimes referred to as an "estate trustee without a will."

assets: A term used by accountants and other business people to describe items of value that are owned by a person or company—whether fully paid for or not. For example, a car being driven by a person is considered an asset, although there may be a loan outstanding, representing money borrowed to purchase the car.

attorney: The person who has been named in the power of attorney (POA) document as a person who is given the power to act on behalf of someone else.

cash flow statement: A record of the money coming into a bank account and the money going out over a specified time period—that is, the flow of cash. It can be based on historical data showing what has happened. However, usually the statement is used to forecast what the cash requirements of a person or company are going to be in the medium to long term. A combination of known information and anticipated activities are used to determine the cash requirements of a person or company.

continuing power of attorney: Called "continuing" because the document specifically states that it continues to be legally valid even though the person who made the POA is no longer competent to manage their own affairs. Such a document may give a general authority to manage financial matters, although it can contain restrictions or specific instructions.

donee: The person who receives the authority given by the donor; that is, the attorney in the case of a power of attorney.

donor: The person who gives or grants the POA (also known as the grantor).

elder abuse: This can involve any number of types of conduct, alone or in combination, including: physical, mental, sexual, emotional or financial abuse of an elderly person, whether or not they are disabled or frail. In particular, elder abuse of a financial nature involves the financial or material exploitation of an older person using their resources without their consent for someone else's benefit. This exploitation typically occurs through: the misuse of the older person's personal cheques, credit cards or accounts; the theft of cash, income cheques or household goods; the forging of the older person's signature; or identity theft.

estate beneficiaries: Persons, organizations or companies that are identified in a will to receive money or specific property from the estate of a deceased person.

estate trustee: The person appointed to look after the estate of a deceased person, either under a will or by court appointment. Sometimes referred to as an "executor," "executor and trustee" or "personal representative".

estate trustee with a will: In Ontario, a person who has been identified in the will of a deceased person as the individual who is responsible for seeing the deceased's estate distributed according to the instructions in the will. Used interchangeably with the term "executor".

estate trustee without a will: In Ontario, a person who has been appointed by the courts to administer the estate, distributing its assets in accordance with the *Succession Law Reform Act*. Used interchangeably with the term "administrator".

evidentiary record: Records in a format that prove the transactions performed as part of the management of an estate, whether that estate belongs to a live person or one who is deceased.

executor/executrix: A man or women respectively, who has been identified in the will of a deceased person as the individual who is responsible for seeing the deceased's estate distributed according to the instructions in the will. Used interchangeably with the terms estate trustee, trustee or personal representative.

fiduciary: Refers to the type of relationship that exists between the grantor or estate beneficiaries and the person assigned as attorney or estate trustee. The Canadian legal system recognizes a multitude of special relationships in which one party is required to look after the best interests of the other in an exemplary manner. Fiduciary relationships entail loyalty, trust and confidence and require that fiduciaries act honestly, in good faith and strictly in the best interests of the beneficiaries of such relationships.

financial instrument: A general term used by the accounting and financial professions to describe financial assets and liabilities—more specifically, where there is an agreement between two or more parties with a right to the payment of money. Examples are bank accounts, accounts receivables, investments, insurance policies, trade payables and promissory notes.

grantor: The person who initiates and signs the power of attorney document; also known as the donor.

guardian: A person appointed by the court to take over the administration of a person's property and/or personal care in situations of mental and/or physical incapacities, as defined within Ontario's *Substitute Decisions Act, 1992.*

Guaranteed Investment Certificate (GIC): These are issued by banks and trust companies. They are similar to term deposits but are usually purchased when the investor is looking at having their money invested for a long period of time.

income trust: An investment that holds assets that pay income to investors. An income trust often pays out income monthly, but there is no guarantee that income will be earned.

liabilities: A term used by accountants and other businesspeople to denote the existence of obligations to compensate (pay) another party. Often used interchangeably with the word "debt." Common examples for individuals are credit card balances, mortgages and personal loans (used to buy a car or other large asset).

mortgage-backed securities (MBS): A type of security that is secured by a mortgage or collection of mortgages on residential or commercial properties. If represented by a single mortgage, the mortgage principal and interest paid by the property owner (commercial or residential) is the principal and interest paid to the MBS holder. If represented by a collection of mortgages, the investor buys an interest in the pool and receives their proportional share of mortgage principal and interest collected.

mutual fund: Managed by a professional who invests in a mix of investments (stocks, bonds, short-term money market instruments [e.g., treasury bills, commercial paper and bankers' acceptances] and/or mortgages) using money received from many individuals. The investment is in the form of "units" that can be bought and sold with limited restrictions on quantity and/or investment period. Some funds may require a minimum holding period before allowing units to be redeemed, or they charge an early redemption fee if sold before a stated time period has passed.

notarized copy: A photocopy of an original document that has been certified (i.e., confirmed) by a notary public to be a true and accurate copy of the original document.

notary public: A person who can administer oaths and statutory declarations, witness and authenticate documents and perform certain other acts depending on the jurisdiction in which they reside.

passing of accounts: The legal term used to describe the process of presenting for the approval of the court a formal record of the financial management of either the grantor's estate or a deceased person's estate.

personal representative: Often used interchangeably with estate trustee, although when used in the context of a live person, it can refer to the guardian of an incapacitated person or minor. The Canada Revenue Agency refers to this person as "legal representative" and extends this title to mean any of: attorney, estate trustee, guardian and administrator.

power of attorney (POA): A legal document in which a person (the grantor), gives to another (the attorney), the authority to act on the grantor's behalf in matters related to the POA.

property: Anything related to the finances and ownership rights of an individual, including liabilities as well as assets.

representative: The term used by the Canada Revenue Agency (CRA) to describe any individual (or firm) who has been authorized by another (you) to discuss income tax matters specific to your income tax return. A form T1013 must be filed with the CRA, signed by you or your personal representative if you are unable to sign. This authorization remains in place until such time as another T1013 form is filed indicating that specific authorizations are to be cancelled.

return of capital: A return to the investor of some or all of the money invested in a specific investment. Any such amount is not considered income and thus does not get included in the annual tax return. The value of the investment is decreased when amounts are paid back to the investor.

reverse mortgage: A loan available to seniors whereby a portion of the value of their home is released to them as one lump sum, with the obligation to repay the loan and accrued interest deferred until the owner dies and the home is sold or the owner moves into a care facility. Reverse mortgages are not for every situation; careful consideration and advice from a specialist in this area should be sought before deciding to obtain such a loan.

T1 Return: Formally called T1 General Income Tax and Benefit Return. This is the annual filing required by the Canada Revenue Agency from everyone who earns sufficient income during a calendar year that will result in them having to pay taxes. It is due April 30 each year for income earned the previous calendar year (i.e., January 1-December 31). The most common exception to this due date is for self-employed individuals, who have until June 15 to file their return, although all taxes owing for the calendar year being reported are due by April 30.

T3 Return: Formally called T3 Trust Income and Information Return. This is the annual filing required by the Canada Revenue Agency from every trust that earned income and/or had distributions of capital (i.e., money paid to beneficiaries) during the period. It is due within 90 days of the trust's year end. A trust is automatically triggered upon a person's death, regardless of the value of assets remaining. The first tax period of the trust begins on the day after the person dies and ends at any time you select within the next 12 months. Choosing a December 31 year end is convenient and makes the preparation of successive T3s more efficient, but it requires the payment of tax sooner.

tax clearance certificate: A certificate issued by the Canada Revenue Agency certifying that there are no taxes still owing by a person/estate.

term deposit: A term deposit is similar to a GIC but is usually used in situations where the investor does not want to tie up the funds for a long time. The interest earned is usually received upon maturity.

testator/testatrix: A man or women respectively, who makes a will.

Chapter 1

Just the Facts: Questions to Consider
before Acting as Attorney

You have an important decision to make when presented with the opportunity of becoming an attorney under a continuing power of attorney for property or an estate trustee: Do I really want to do this? Although you have been named as an attorney or estate trustee, you still have a choice as to whether or not to accept the honour and responsibility. Before you commit yourself to any acts that would constitute acceptance, ask the following important questions. Be aware that an action taken that would normally form part of the duties you are being asked to undertake, even before a formal response of "yes" or "no" is given, could be construed as an acceptance. Once acceptance is implied or stated, it can be time consuming and awkward to remove yourself from either the role of attorney or estate trustee. Though many of these questions are simple and straightforward; their answers are not. The reader is therefore cautioned that the answers that follow are general in nature, and that the reader's specific circumstances may require seeking out detailed legal advice.

Why is it so important to maintain clear and appropriate records?

Apart from the legal requirement to do so, there may come a time when there is a need for an evidentiary record of your stewardship of the grantor's affairs when you are called upon to account for your management of those affairs or the deceased's estate activities. This is most likely to occur when there is litigation threatened or instigated, when there is a tax audit by the Canada Revenue Agency, when you cease to act as an attorney or upon the wind-up of the estate.

For a more in-depth discussion of this topic, see the section entitled "Why care about doing this right?" in Chapter 2.

Do I need to use an accounting software program to keep the financial records?

No, you do not need to use a software program to keep the financial records, although using one can make life much easier and the job less time consuming when it comes time to sit down with the grantor or the beneficiaries of an estate. Whether you choose to do so will be based on such factors as how much activity there is and how comfortable you are with basic bookkeeping tasks. Most people may find a spreadsheet package such as *Excel* meets their needs.[1]

See the section "Where do I keep all the paper/documentation related to the record keeping?" in Chapter 2 for a more in-depth discussion.

How are the financial records of one person maintained when there are two or more persons appointed as attorney under the power of attorney for property?

If the tasks required to look after the property of the grantor are split between two or more attorneys, it will be necessary to ensure that they timely and accurately combine records into one central file. This will also provide an opportunity to review the transaction and property records for completeness and to verify that what was understood to be happening from ongoing verbal communication has indeed been happening.

Something that might influence how sophisticated your financial record-keeping procedures are will be the governance structure specified in the CPOAP, e.g., majority rule or one attorney having ultimate authority. Moreover, you need to confirm whether the appointment is "jointly" or "jointly and severally". If it is a "joint" appointment, then all decisions must be made together with the other party or parties who are also appointed. The ability to act "jointly and severally" means that you can act alone. However, care should be taken to ensure that your actions are consistent with other actions being taken and that all actions are made in the best interests of the grantor. At a minimum, this means that as far as record keeping goes, one set of records are maintained in an accurate and timely manner.

Are there differences between financial record-keeping responsibilities of a power of attorney for personal care and a power of attorney for property, and if so, what are they?

In Ontario, Regulation 100/96 made under the *Substitute Decisions Act, 1992,* stipulates the exact requirements with respect to the content of the records that must be kept for either a continuing power of attorney for property or a power of attorney for personal care. Although the record-keeping duties and principles are the same for both personal care and property attorneys, the content of those records differ. In other words, given the difference in the nature of the decisions being made by an attorney for personal care versus those being made by an attorney for property, a greater amount of financial record keeping is required for the latter. Therefore, it is important for both attorneys to understand their role in relationship to one another. Neither one should attempt to carry out their role in isolation. Working in isolation when there is a common goal (that being the ultimate well-being, both physically and financially, of the grantor) can be disastrous in the long run, resulting in much aggravation and stress for all parties, e.g., the introduction of lawyers and formal Court requirements.

Non-financial record-keeping requirements specific to being an attorney for personal care are outside of the scope for this book. Should you require information in this area, the reader is advised to contact a lawyer with their specific questions.

---

[1] *Excel* software is part of many standard operating systems such as Windows XP. It can also be purchased separately directly from Microsoft or at most business software supply outlets.

Do I really need to keep things separate, or is it okay for me to pay expenses of the grantor (i.e., the person's whose affairs I am looking after) from my own bank account?

Under no circumstances should an attorney settle debts or receive income of the grantor into their own accounts. If this does occur, rectification should be made as soon as it is realized and appropriate notes made so that the information trail remains clear as to the source and reasons for the transaction(s).

Chapter 8, "What to Do When Things Go Wrong," discusses in some detail what action would be considered appropriate should the attorney inadvertently pay an expense of the grantor.

As an attorney or an estate trustee, am I responsible for the debts of the person whose affairs I am managing?

First let's define what debt is. Some people think of debt as any amount owing, such as the monthly telephone bill, credit card statement, car loan and mortgage. Others consider only the big items as debt, such as a car loan or mortgage. The law gives a wide definition to this term and is quite clear about the fact that any debt—that is, any money owing to another (regardless of size)—existing at the time you take over managing or helping to manage the property of the grantor does not become the attorney's personal debt responsibility.

As attorney, you are responsible for paying the debts of the grantor with the grantor's own money. Generally speaking, you are not personally responsible for the grantor's debts. However, you may become responsible if you do not act with the necessary skill, prudence and diligence required. In other words, if you fall below the standard of care that is expected of an attorney, or if you commit fraud, you will be found personally liable for losses and the subsequent debts of the grantor.

As an estate trustee you have personal liability for any outstanding debts of the deceased should you make any distribution of the estate without first advertising for creditors or obtaining any necessary tax clearance certificate from the Canada Revenue Agency.

If I am an attorney for property or estate trustee, do I need to do the person's tax return?

Where the grantor is fully competent and managing their own affairs, there is no requirement that you as attorney have to prepare and file the grantor's income tax returns. However, as attorney you should at least be aware that all appropriate returns have been filed by the grantor. If there are any returns not yet filed, then you are in a good position to assist the grantor with the task of getting any outstanding returns filed.

In the case were the grantor has become incapacitated, as attorney you are responsible for the financial affairs of the grantor, and you do have an obligation to see that all tax returns are filed and taxes paid out of the grantor's assets. See Step 4 in Chapter 5 for a more in-depth discussion of this topic.

As an estate trustee, you are legally required to ensure that the deceased person's final T1 Return is filed within the prescribed time frame set by the Canada Revenue Agency. You are also responsible for any T3 Trust Income and Information returns required. For a more detailed discussion of this responsibility, see Chapter 7.

To whom am I responsible for the decisions I make while managing a person's financial affairs?

As an attorney, your primary responsibility is to the grantor of the CPOAP while that person is alive. This differs from acting as an estate trustee where you find yourself primarily responsible to the beneficiaries under the will. Ultimately, you may be answerable to a court of law should you ever be called upon to give an account of your actions as attorney or estate trustee.

For a more in-depth discussion of this topic, see the section "Who am I accountable to as an attorney?" in Chapter 2.

If I know there is another person looking after health-care issues of the grantor, how does this impact my financial management, and what kind of records of their spending do I need to request from them?

The grantor's financial resources will affect personal care decisions. Thus, the attorney for personal care, or the guardian of the person if one has been appointed by the court, or the person recognized as being the "substitute decision maker" will need to contact the attorney for property before making any significant decisions. If you are aware of an attorney for personal care or guardian or substitute decision maker and no contact has been made, you as the attorney must initiate the communication. It is important that this communication is kept timely and relevant to serve the interests of the grantor. You will need to determine your ability to work with the person involved with heath care decisions.

Any monies that you advance to the attorney for personal care should be supported by an invoice or statement from the service provider or supplier, whether received prior to payment or after the fact. A more detailed discussion of your responsibilities in this area can be found in Step 10, in Chapter 5.

Do I receive compensation for acting as a power of attorney for property or as an estate trustee?

Yes, generally speaking you may be entitled to receive compensation as an attorney. However, there may be valid reasons why you may choose not to. See "How is payment for acting as an attorney determined?" in Chapter 2 for a fuller discussion.

An estate trustee is also entitled to receive compensation. However, there may be valid reasons why they may choose not to, similar to those of an attorney discussed in Chapter 2.

Chapter Recap

In this opening chapter, we have discussed 10 important questions that one should ask before jumping into the role of attorney/estate trustee. These questions touched on a number of different aspects, namely:

1) Reporting responsibilities—to whom, how and why?

2) Financial responsibilities—do their debts ever become mine, and what about their tax return?

3) More than one attorney—what happens if there's more than one attorney for property and/or an attorney for health-care decisions?

4) Compensation expectations—should I expect to be paid?

Though some responses were brief, they directed the reader to a more in-depth discussion contained in this book. The questions along with answers should enable you to make an appropriate response to the ultimate question you are currently considering: Do I want to be an attorney at this time, for this person? The answers have probably prompted additional questions, many of which will be addressed in the next chapter. In Chapter 2 we progress from contemplating whether we want to take on this role to thinking about legal issues affecting financial record keeping that need to be understood in order to execute this responsibility with minimal chance of anything going too far amiss.

Chapter 2

Just the Basics: Fundamentals the Attorney Needs to Understand

In this chapter we will review the fundamental legal context in which the attorney operates. A basic understanding of this legal context will go a long way to helping attorneys appreciate the importance of record keeping and the fact that proper record keeping will make their task of being an attorney less a burden and more a joy.

What is a power of attorney?

A power of attorney (POA) is a legal document in which a person (the grantor) gives to another (the attorney) the authority to act on the grantor's behalf in matters related to the POA. There are many types of POAs. For example, some are restricted to specific or limited transactions, such as the transference of shares or the selling of real estate, or managing a specific bank account. Other POAs are of a more general nature. These will be discussed in more detail below.

Because the POA document gives authority to manage the affairs of the grantor, it must be read and understood by the attorney to ensure that the attorney is acting in accordance with the powers granted them by the grantor. In other words, while most POAs give a general power to manage another's affairs, there can be terms, conditions and restrictions imposed on that ability to manage. An attorney should be fully aware if any terms, conditions or restrictions exist in order to not only carry out their duties correctly, but also to decide whether the attorney wishes to act in the first place. Such restrictions can include express terms and conditions respecting banking and/or investment arrangements, or when the POA is to become active (e.g., only in the event of the grantor's physical and/or mental incapacity).

In Ontario, there are two main categories of powers of attorney, personal and property[1]. The first category of POA is known as a power of attorney for personal care (POAPC). The POAPC allows you to name a substitute decision-maker to make healthcare decisions and decisions affecting your person on your behalf when you are incapable of doing so.

---

[1]   In Ontario, the main legislation governing powers of attorney is called the *Substitute Decisions Act, 1992*, S.O. 1992, c.30. Herein after, *Substitute Decisions Act, 1992*. Copies of the Act can be obtained either from the Queen's Printer, or by accessing the Ontario Government's e-Laws' website at: http://www.e-laws.gov.on.ca/html/statutes/english/elaws_statutes_92s30_e.htm. This categorization of POAs is common across Canada.

The second category of POA is concerned with property and consists of two types.

1) General POA, which gives the attorney a general power to do all things the grantor can do with respect to property, except make a will.

2) Specific Purpose POA, which gives the attorney power to do a specific action (or actions) as identified in the POA.

Both types can contain specific terms, conditions and restrictions with respect to their operation, designed for the particular circumstances in which they will be used.

In addition, the duration of each of these two types of POAs is qualified by being either

1) continuing, meaning that the POA, whether general or specific, continues to be effective during any incapacity on the grantor's part; or

2) non-continuing, which means that the POA, whether general or specific, is not valid should the grantor become incapacitated.

The following diagram provides an overview of the two types of POAs for property:

Type of POA	General	Specific
Duration	Continuing (survives incapacity)	Continuing (survives incapacity)
	Non-continuing (does not survive incapacity)	Non-continuing (does not survive incapacity)

Although powers of attorney can appoint different people as attorney to deal with these specific issues, it is often the case that the same person, usually a family member, is appointed under both the continuing power of attorney for property (□POAP) and the power of attorney for personal care.[2] For those readers who are interested in the particulars of the □POAP in a province/territory other than Ontario, Table 1 sets out the different legislation as well as the name used in each of the provinces and territories for the □POAP.

The continuing power of attorney for property allows the attorney nominated to manage the financial and property affairs of the grantor; the power of attorney for personal care deals with health care, nutrition, shelter, clothing, hygiene or safety decisions affecting the grantor.

---

[2]   If a grantor has granted a personal care POA, it is likely that a property POA also exists. In fact, it is possible that there is only one POA document covering both types, although it is usual to have two separate documents, one dealing with property and the other with personal care matters.

Apart from the difference in subject matter of the two types of POAs, another important difference is that the POA for personal care does not become effective until the grantor is incapable of making their own decisions with respect to personal care matters, whereas generally a CPOAP is effective the moment it is signed, unless there is a restriction on when it comes into force. Such a restriction might be that the CPOAP becomes effective only in the situation of the grantor's incapacity to manage their own financial affairs due to physical and/or mental decline.

Although the actual date that the CPOAP becomes effective is usually the date on which the document is signed, the actual start date for the attorney is the date on which the attorney first starts making transactions in accordance with the terms of the CPOAP. This means that you as attorney are accountable from the date you start acting under the POA rather than the date that the grantor signed the POA document.

When a POA is given, it is important to realise that the grantor is not giving up any of their own rights to manage their property. Unless incapable of doing so, the grantor still has access to their funds and is entitled to participate in and fully control the management of their financial affairs. In such a case, the role of the attorney is to potentially provide a degree of assistance. By having a POA document in place, the grantor is enabling another to share the grantor's legal rights to manage financial affairs. The degree of assistance required will vary with the personal circumstances of the grantor and will undoubtedly change over the years as the grantor's health changes.

What are the general expectations of me as an attorney?

In a nutshell, the general expectation is that you will act in a diligent manner, with honesty and integrity and in good faith, in the best interests of the grantor and for their benefit. In law, this is expressed as being a "fiduciary". In other words, you are acting as a trustee for the grantor. More specifically, you are expected to:

1) Fully understand the powers and duties of an attorney

2) Be reasonably careful in making and carrying out decisions, always acting honestly and in good faith

3) Avoid any conflict of interest between yourself and the grantor

4) Include the grantor as much as is reasonably possible in decision making

5) Maintain open lines of communication at all times between the grantor and yourself and any supportive family members or friends as identified by the grantor

6) Make no secret profit from conducting the grantor's affairs

7) Maintain proper records of all transactions

8) Be prepared to account for your management of the grantor's affairs

Table 1: Power of Attorney Legislation Across Canada

Jurisdiction	Government Website	Legislation	Name of Document
British Columbia	www.bclaws.ca	*Power of Attorney Act Patients Property Act*	Enduring Power of Attorney
Alberta	www.qp.gov.ab.ca	*Powers of Attorney Act*	Enduring Power of Attorney
Saskatchewan	www.gov.sk.ca	*Power of Attorney Act*	Enduring Power of Attorney
Manitoba	www.gov.mb.ca	*Powers of Attorney Act*	Enduring Power of Attorney
Ontario	www.e-laws.gov.on.ca	*Power of Attorney Act Substitute Decisions Act*	Continuing Power of Attorney
Quebec	www.publicationsduquebec.gouv.qc.ca	*Civil Code, R.S.Q. c. C-1991, Chap. IX, ss.2130–2135*	Mandate Given in Anticipation of Incapacity
New Brunswick	www.gnb.ca	*Property Act*	Power of Attorney
Nova Scotia	www.gov.ns.ca	*Powers of Attorney Act*	Enduring Power of Attorney
Prince Edward Island	www.gov.pe.ca	*Powers of Attorney Act*	Power of Attorney
Newfoundland and Labrador	www.hoa.gov.nl.ca	*Enduring Powers of Attorney Act*	Enduring Power of Attorney
Yukon Territory	www.gov.yk.ca	*Enduring Powers of Attorney Act*	Enduring Power of Attorney
Northwest Territory	www.gov.nt.ca	*Power of Attorney Act*	Power of Attorney
Nunavut	www.nunavutcourtofjustice.ca	*Powers of Attorney Act*	Power of Attorney

Always remember that all decisions you make must always be in the best interest of the grantor, consistent with any received instructions from the grantor, given the existing set of circumstances you find the grantor in. Obviously everyone's circumstances are different, and therefore what works for one person may not necessarily be appropriate for another. Thus, it may be the case that the attorney has to consider not only the grantor but also the grantor's dependents (if any) and beneficiaries. However, no matter what the circumstances, care should always be taken to ensure that the grantor's interests and wishes are given priority so that reasonable expenditures may be made to support and care for the grantor.

Why care about accurate financial record keeping?

Most of us are busy with the daily process we call living. When confronted with the opportunity to assist someone with their financial affairs, our hearts want to say "Yes", yet our brains often say "No". Our hearts and brains engage in a somewhat lively debate, the brain finally relenting while at the same time anticipating the shortcuts available and concluding that it will not be that much work. The amount of work will of course depend on the amount of financial activity of the grantor and the level of assistance being asked. Regardless of the level of your involvement, there are a number of reasons to consistently carry out this task diligently and as accurately as possible.

For the benefit of the grantor:

1) **To ensure timely and accurate financial information is always available**: If the grantor becomes incapacitated, and personal-care decisions have to be made quickly, knowing the state of the grantor's financial position will be essential both in making decisions in the present and in planning for the future.

2) **To create an accurate evidentiary record**: If events become acrimonious with other potential interested parties, providing an evidentiary record of your management will be required and may reduce the possibility of litigation. In addition, having a complete record will make filing tax returns easier as well as making the management of the grantor's affairs a relatively easy matter.

3) **To preserve the estate**: Safeguard the assets and liabilities that you are managing.

For the benefit of the attorney:

4) **To safeguard your own reputation**: You do not want any accusations of malfeasance or mismanagement that might result in a tainting of your professional and/or personal reputation. Also, deficient record keeping may result in the attorney being held personally responsible for debts of the person whose affairs are being managed

5) **To save time and money**: If a formalized set of accounts are required to be presented to the court, both legal and accounting fees will be significantly reduced if well-maintained financial records are available.

6) **For the sake of doing it right**: Because you have agreed to take on this task, there is no reason not to carry it out to the best of your ability, for no other reason than a job worth doing is worth doing well.

Who am I accountable to as an attorney?

In a situation where the grantor is still in a position to actively participate in the managing of their affairs, the attorney is accountable only to this person.

In a situation where the grantor becomes unable to govern their own affairs, i.e., becomes incapacitated, you will be responsible for ensuring the person who is the attorney for personal care is aware of the financial circumstances of the grantor in order to assist in determining the level of care that can be afforded. To this end, you will be accountable to this person to provide complete and accurate information.

It may be that there are no family members or other individuals who can take on the role of attorney for personal care. In this instance, the courts will appoint a guardian. An attorney for property will be responsible for ensuring all financial information is made available so that the best level of care can be provided for the grantor.

> **A Word to the Wise!**
>
> When communicating information, be sure to keep it simple and relevant to the question asked. Avoid legal/financial terms because the people you are dealing with may not be familiar with such terminology.

When the grantor becomes incapacitated, supportive family members and friends of the grantor may enter the picture and start asking questions. In Ontario, there is a requirement that in such cases the attorney for property will consult with "supportive family members and friends" as well as persons who are providing care to the incapacitated grantor.[3] The content of that "consultation" is a matter of discretion on the part of the attorney, but such discretion must be informed by considerations as to the best interests of the grantor. Thus, in order to properly manage the affairs of the grantor, and if it is consistent with the best interests of the grantor, it may be necessary and prudent to provide relevant information to address any legitimate concerns that supportive family members and friends may have. Common sense will assist you in deciding what and how much information should be disclosed. If in doubt, the safest action will be to seek legal advice to determine how much and exactly what information may be disclosed.

> **A Word to the Wise!**
>
> If in doubt about what information and/or to whom it is okay to disclose, consult a lawyer. It may cost you and/or the grantor a little bit now, but it might just save you a whole lot of money down the road.
>
> **$**
>
> Pay a little now . . .
>
> **$ $ $**
>
> . . . Or pay a lot down the road.

---

3   *Substitute Decisions Act, 1992*, S.O. 1992, c.30, s. 32(5).

You also need to be aware that failure to enter into a satisfying dialogue with relatives may lead them to seek a court order requiring you to account for your stewardship.

In fact, in addition to relatives who may assume they have a right to information, in Ontario under s.42 of the *Substitutions Decisions Act, 1992* (Appendix IV), the following individuals/entities can ask an attorney to account for their stewardship:

1) an attorney—either yourself or if there are other attorneys named in the CPOAP;

2) the grantor;

3) the grantor's or incapable person's guardian of the person or attorney for personal care;

4) a dependant of the grantor or incapable person;

5) the Public Guardian and Trustee;

6) the Children's Lawyer;

7) a judgment creditor of the grantor or incapable person; or

8) any other person, with leave of the court.

How do I formally account for my stewardship?

The legal term for providing an account for the stewardship of property is called "passing of accounts". It means that a set of accounts in a prescribed form must be presented to the court for its review and judgment on the completeness and competency of the management of the property. Once informed that a formal set of accounts are required to be presented to the court, it is time to call on a lawyer and accountant who can either prepare the accounts in the prescribed form or assist you to do so. In Ontario, the requirements for the set of accounts are set out in Ontario Regulation 100/96 for attorneys (Appendix III) and in Rule 74.17 of the Ontario *Rules of Civil Procedure* for estate trustees (Appendix V).

Nevertheless, it is hoped that by following the recommendations and suggestions in this book, you can avoid the situation arising where you have to formally account. This is not to say that queries from entitled persons will never arise. However, presenting to the enquiring party an organized and up-to-date set of records will hopefully address any questions they might have about your management of the grantor's financial affairs.

While such questions will differ in each situation they could include: questions about dispositions of specific property items, the nature of investments and income received from them and questions regarding amounts spent (or not spent) on specific items. In addition, the way in which each query is dealt with will differ depending on the personalities of the people involved, the level of participation of the grantor, the sum of the money being managed and any number of other variables. The general recommendation is that the attorney focus on whom they are legally responsible to and proceed to satisfy those obligations. As a last resort, persistent harassing from other parties (family or otherwise) can always be dealt with through the legal process.

Where do I keep all the paper/documentation related to the record keeping?

Ah, yes—the paperwork! Keeping the paperwork—such as receipts, bank statements, tax records etc.—organized and together might be the most daunting task of this whole exercise. While some might be inclined to throw everything into a shoe box with the hope that no awkward questions will ever be asked, it is strongly recommended that the shoe box method not be used. Exactly what method is used will depend, in part, on the complexity and volume of activity involved. Below are some suggestions on the types of filing system that have proven successful. One type of tracking and filing system may seem most suitable at the beginning, but there is nothing to prevent you from changing your methodology as time passes. It is quite common that as you develop a more complete understanding of the grantor's affairs, adjustments to the organization and filing of the paperwork become necessary.

When there are a limited number of assets and liabilities being looked after, a standard accordion file folder with 8-12 pockets will be adequate to store the documentation as it accumulates. As far as required bookkeeping records, it may be adequate to make a notation beside items on each bank statement as to what the disbursement or receipt relates to, putting a number against each item to indicate what pocket in the accordion file the supporting documentation can be found.

For more substantial assets and liabilities, it is recommended that a banker's box be used to store all the documentation. Be sure to label envelopes or file folders appropriately so that source documentation is easy to find. This preparation will enable you to quickly and effortlessly respond to any questions that might arise from the grantor or other entitled persons.

For the task of keeping track of the receipts and disbursements, it may be prudent to use *Excel* or other spreadsheet software package if you have the skill.

Depending on the complexity and number of assets and liabilities being managed, an accounting package such as *Quickbooks Simple Start Plus* might be worth considering. If two or more attorneys are acting jointly, using an online bookkeeping program that would allow all attorneys to have access to the same information might be an option to consider. Each attorney would enter the data pertaining to the assets and liabilities that they are managing. If you decide to go this route, ensure appropriate security can be enacted so that each of you is able to edit only your respective original entries and not delete them.

A Word to the Wise!

If you use a software program to keep records, remember the Golden Rule: It's not a question of *if* you lose data, but *when*. Therefore, you must back up your files regularly to ensure a safe archive is available. Backup should occur after every major session in which the records have been modified/updated. Each time a backup is done, you can overwrite the previous one because you only need a copy of the most up-to-date record of the transactions. The backup disk/CD should be stored separately from your computer.

It is also important to remember that no matter what system you use, you must have source documents to support the activity going through all bank and investment accounts.

13

Regardless of what method of storage and recording is used, you must at all times make sure that the grantor's financial affairs are kept separate and distinct from your own. This will avoid confusion as well as any suggestion of wrongdoing on your part.

Finally, whichever method of storing the documentation you use, the following items need to have a clearly identified section (i.e., pocket/envelope/file folder):

1) Original CPOAP or reference to where original CPOAP document is and a copy of CPOAP document.

2) Copy of grantor's will, if one exists, and the location of the original.

3) Inventory of grantor's estate at the time you start acting under the CPOAP.

4) List of assets and liabilities for which you as the attorney are responsible.

5) Each asset and liability will have its own section.

6) General correspondence received and sent pertaining to management of the assets and liabilities. This might include requests for information from legitimate persons or the grantor themselves.

7) Correspondence received specific to an asset or liability should be filed with any activity statements received. For example, the general bank account from which day-to-day transactions are reflected (receipt of CPP and/or OAS income; monthly expenses such as credit card or rent) will have its own pocket, and all documentation supporting the activity can be attached to each monthly bank statement.

If the most appropriate place to file something is not obvious, photocopy it and file it in all the places that seem relevant. Alternatively, file it in one location and make a note about its existence in the other location(s).

Finally, whatever filing system is adopted, be sure to file documentation in a timely manner. Most appropriately, it will be once a month when you sit down to review the bank and/or investment activity, ensuring you have all the relevant back up information. (For more detail on this review process, see Step 9 in Chapter 5.)

When is the job as an attorney over?

There are a number of circumstances that terminate your role as attorney. The most common is when the grantor of the CPOAP dies, because all powers vested in the CPOAP also terminate with the death of the grantor. At the date of death, all financial and property matters are the responsibility of the estate trustee. This general rule is modified to include actions made in good faith without the knowledge of the CPOAP being terminated or becoming invalid.[4]

In Ontario, apart from the death of the grantor, there are other circumstances that terminate the role of the attorney.

---

[4]   *Substitute Decisions Act, 1992*, s.13.

> ➤ When the attorney dies, becomes incapable of managing property or resigns.

> ➤ When the court appoints a guardian of property for the grantor under s. 22 of the *Substitute Decisions Act, 1992*.

> ➤ When the grantor executes a new continuing power of attorney, unless the grantor provides that there shall be multiple continuing powers of attorney.

> ➤ When the power of attorney is revoked.

In each case, there will be a need to account for the management of the grantor's affairs in order to ensure that you, the retiring attorney, have acted properly and to prepare properly for the next step in the management of the grantor's affairs.

When the job is over, what am I required to do?

If you are also the estate trustee, the maintenance of the estate's financial records is expected to continue in the same fashion as adhered to when you were the attorney.

If the attorney is not the same person as the estate trustee under the will, the attorney will be contacted by the estate trustee. The attorney will be requested, and is required, to pass along all the records associated with the CPOAP activities. In the event there is no will and an estate administrator has been appointed, the attorney will be required to pass along all records to the estate administrator.

In either case, it will be important to have maintained complete records in order to ensure that communication with either the beneficiaries or the estate trustee is able to happen efficiently and satisfactorily. Having conducted your duties as an attorney with even a small amount of discipline will have big payoffs at this stage of wrapping up the grantor's affairs.

In cases other than the death of the grantor, when your job as attorney is over, you will want to be able to present a complete and accurate set of financial records to those who will be taking over the role. In the event that you are being replaced because of your own death or incapacity, it is even more important that accurate records have been kept for your own estate trustee or attorney/guardian to pass along.

When the records are passed to a new party, whether it is the estate trustee or a new attorney, it is possible that a formal accounting will be requested—if not by them, then perhaps yourself.[5] The more organized and complete your record keeping is, the easier it will be to conclude this final formal step of your stewardship.

How long do I have to keep the financial records once my job is done?

Unlike tax records, which must be kept for a set period of time (six years), the retention of accounts and records relating to attorneys acting under a CPOAP is event-based. In other

---

[5] The reason you yourself might seek to have your accounts passed by the court is to give you closure and finality in the management of the grantor's affairs and preventing any subsequent questions about your stewardship.

words, the destruction and disposition of those records is dependent upon certain events happening rather than on the mere passage of time. This is illustrated in the case of Ontario, where accounts and records are to be kept until the attorney ceases to have authority *and* one of the following occurs:

➤ a release of liability from a person who has the authority to give the release is obtained;

➤ you deliver the accounts and records to your successor attorney or person appointed to look after the incapable grantor;

➤ on the death of the incapable grantor, and you have delivered the accounts and records to the deceased's personal representative;

➤ you are discharged by the court on a passing of accounts under the *Substitute Decisions Act, 1992,* and no appeal of that discharge has been taken, or if an appeal has been taken, it is finally disposed of and you are discharged on the appeal; or

➤ a court order has been obtained directing you to destroy or otherwise dispose of the accounts and records.

As stated above, these are the circumstances particular to Ontario, contained in regulations made under the *Substitute Decisions Act, 1992.* While these particular rules are straightforward and understandable, the reader is advised to confirm with their own lawyer—who will be familiar with the legislation in their jurisdiction as it relates to record retention—before destroying any documentation that relates to the grantor's affairs.

You should note that any of these circumstances described above does not relieve you of the obligation to keep sufficient and proper records to support the income tax returns filed while you were acting as attorney. The Canada Revenue Agency's rules with respect to keeping records exist in addition to the requirements under the *Substitute Decisions Act, 1992* or similar legislation.

How is payment for acting as an attorney determined?

In Ontario, in the absence of specific fees detailed in the CPOAP document, s. 40 of the *Substitute Decisions Act, 1992* permits an attorney under a continuing power of attorney for property to take compensation according to the prescribed fee scale. The prescribed fee scale is set out in Ontario Regulation 26/95 (Appendix II).

Currently, compensation consists of the total of three components:

a) 3% on capital and income receipts, plus

b) 3% on capital and income disbursements, plus

c) 3/5 of 1% on the annual average value of the assets (this final component being referred to as the care and management fee).

Compensation under the *Substitute Decisions Act, 1992* can be taken monthly, quarterly or annually. If compensation greater than the prescribed fee scale is sought, then the consent in writing must be obtained from the public guardian and trustee and from the incapable person's guardian or attorney under a power of attorney for personal care. In cases where the public guardian and trustee is the guardian or attorney for property, compensation greater than the prescribed fee scale can only be received with court approval.

Whereas an attorney is entitled to request compensation greater than the prescribed fee, the grantor, when arranging the CPOAP document, could indicate an amount in excess of the prescribed fee that the attorney is to receive. This would enable the attorney to avoid the aggravating and lengthy process of making an application to the relevant court.

Remember, just because there is a prescribed fee for compensation or an expressed fee contained in the CPOAP, it does not mean that the attorney has to accept the compensation. It is also important for the attorney to be aware that any compensation received is to be included in the attorney's tax return as earned income in the year received, and therefore it is liable to income tax at the attorney's marginal tax rate. Depending on the personal tax situation of the attorney, it may not be in their best interest to take the compensation. This is particularly the case in a situation where you are a beneficiary of the estate under the will of the grantor, and as such you will receive your bequest without tax consequences to yourself. Thus, it might make more sense to keep the money in the grantor's bank/investment account, earning interest, rather than taking it now.

In addition, attorneys should be aware that should they receive compensation, they will be held to a higher standard of care. Generally speaking, if you do not receive compensation, the standard of care to which you are held is one in which you exercise the degree of care, diligence and skill that a person of "ordinary prudence" would exercise in the conduct of his or her own affairs. If on the other hand, you do receive compensation, then you will be held to a higher "professional" standard—using the care, diligence and skill of a person in the business of managing the property of others.[6]

Be sure to confirm by reading the CPOAP whether there is any provision for payment of any kind. If the CPOAP document does not set out the amount or formula for calculating the fee to be paid, then the formula contained in government regulations will govern the amount paid, if any. The attorney can confirm the current rates in their particular jurisdiction by consulting the lawyer who drew up the CPOAP, or another lawyer practicing estates and trusts law, or by checking the relevant legislation governing such matters. If no reference is made to compensation, you may want to consider having a conversation with the grantor about the time and effort you will be spending on their behalf while acting as their attorney to determine whether a nominal amount might be appropriate. When discussing this, it is important to remember that any reasonable expenses incurred on behalf of the grantor while acting as attorney will be covered by the grantor, e.g., the costs associated with tax return preparations. Expenses, however, are not the same as compensation which seeks to pay you for your time and effort in managing the grantor's financial affairs.

In this regard, it should be noted that the prescribed rates of compensation are specifically for work you do as an attorney, e.g., going to the bank, reviewing bank activity, speaking with the investment advisor, regular updates with the grantor regarding specific financial transactions and keeping the financial records up to date. Compensation is not paid, nor should it be expected, for such activities as doing grocery shopping, having coffee with the grantor

---

6   See, for example, *Substitute Decisions Act, 1992*, ss. 32 (7) and (8).

once a week or going to the library on behalf of the grantor. Though you might do these personal tasks, presumably you do so because of your personal relationship with the grantor and not because of the legal relationship that now exists because of the formal CPOAP.

Chapter Recap

This chapter has provided substantial discussion and information on the fundamentals an attorney needs to be aware of and understand. The ten questions and answers have been designed to provide an understanding of the level of stewardship required when looking after someone else's property affairs, and the why behind these expectations. In summary, the attorney should understand the following:

1) The law provides a framework against which your record keeping will be measured.

2) The law is designed to safeguard both the grantor and the attorney by providing a framework of accountability.

3) The law necessitates the attorney approaching their role in a responsible and methodical manner.

The information contained in this chapter provides the basic legal context for people as they begin the record-keeping tasks associated with managing someone else's property. You are probably anxious to get into the actual record keeping now. However, before we outline those record-keeping procedures, it is important to have a basic understanding of the legal regulations that govern financial record keeping. It is always a good idea to know the formal rules before you advance too deeply into a new process. With this in mind, the next chapter will present an overview of the legal regulations governing financial record keeping, including a brief discussion of operating within these regulations in a transparent manner while maintaining the privacy of the grantor.

Chapter 3

The Legal Rules of Financial Record Keeping

In this chapter we will provide a brief overview of what records the law actually expects to be kept as well as the confidentiality of those records. Each province and territory has its own legislation, setting out requirements for accounts and record maintenance in estate matters, whether of the living or the dead. The substance of these requirements is remarkably similar among jurisdictions. For the purposes of the present discussion, Ontario's requirements will serve as an example. For those living in Ontario, the legal requirements for accounts and record maintenance for attorneys and guardians of property (those appointed by the court) are set out in s. 32(6) of the *Substitute Decisions Act, 1992*, and more specifically in Ontario Regulation 100/96 (Appendix III). For estate trustees, their requirements are found in Rule 74.17 of the *Rules of Civil Procedure* (Appendix V).

Section 2 of Ontario Regulation 100/96 identifies the type of information required. Basically, the regulation requires that all the property—assets, liabilities, income and expenses—of the grantor's estate be accounted for in nine lists. The following are the lists that need to be kept:

1) Assets: a list of assets, including real estate, money, securities, investments, cars and other personal property, as of the date of the first transaction by the attorney;

2) Asset Management: an ongoing list of assets acquired and disposed of on behalf of the grantor, including the date and reasons for the acquisition or disposal and identifying the source of the acquisition and the person to whom it was disposed;

3) Income Received: an ongoing list of all money received on behalf of the grantor, including date, amount, source of payment, reason for payment and the bank account into which it was deposited;

4) Expenses: an ongoing list of all money paid out on behalf of the grantor, including date, amount, reason for payment and to whom it was paid;

5) Investment: an ongoing list of all investments made on the grantor's behalf, including information regarding the amount, date, interest rate and type of investment purchased or redeemed;

6) Liabilities: a list of the grantor's liabilities as of the date of the first transaction by the attorney;

7) Liabilities Incurred/Discharged: an ongoing list of liabilities incurred and discharged, including date, nature and reason for liability being incurred or discharged;

8) Attorney Compensation: an ongoing list of all compensation taken by the attorney, including amount, date and method of calculation; and

9) Care and Management Fee: a list of assets and their value used in calculating the care and management fee.

If compensation is not taken, then there are seven lists that must be kept. However, in presenting any accounts, you would want to prepare two schedules confirming that you took neither compensation nor a care and management fee. Do not despair at seeing a list of nine items. These nine items can be condensed into three categories:

1) Money in

2) Money out

3) Fixed assets

As will be explained below, all the activity comprising money in and money out is most likely to be found in a minimal number of bank and investment accounts and represents the physical movement of money as bills are paid, investments are renewed and income is received. The fixed assets under your care are such items as the house, car or cottage of the grantor. Items that in themselves are not reflected as cash movements in or out, until such time as they are sold, need to be reflected in opening statements of assets as an acknowledgment of their existence and an awareness that monetary activity might flow as a result of holding these assets. For example, if a house is still owned, there will be expenses expected to flow through the bank statement with respect to property taxes and general maintenance to ensure the value of the house is maintained. A major component of your time spent on maintaining adequate financial records to meet these legal standards will be the identification of amounts coming into and going out of accounts and ensuring supporting documentation exists to substantiate the legitimacy of the item as belonging to the grantor's estate.

You are required to maintain these accounts from the time of your first transaction on behalf of the grantor. In other words, so long as the grantor is mentally competent, you are not required to keep these accounts because the granter is still capable of managing their own affairs. It is only when the grantor becomes incapable, or if you have reasonable grounds to believe so and you act for them, that a formal account/record-keeping regime is mandatory.[1] However, as will be explored in the next chapter, there may very well be good reasons to keep some records of your activities on behalf of the competent grantor, even though it is not statutorily required to do so.

---

[1]   *Substitute Decision Act, 1992*, ss. 32(6) and 38(1).

As one reads through the items listed above, it might appear at first glance to be a daunting task to have so much with which to be concerned. However, be assured that the most onerous part of this process is to ensure that all the relevant information (date, amount, reasons, persons involved) relating to assets and their management, income and expenses has been gathered. The monthly activity of the average person is not going to be an enormous task to manage if done regularly and accurately. Using the steps outlined in Chapter 5 will assist the attorney in gathering all the information and developing an effective and efficient discipline for managing the record keeping required to keep the accounts up to date.

When all is said and done, the lists required by Ontario Regulation 100/96 are nothing more than an itemization of activity relating to a person's assets and liabilities. Most of this activity is recorded in the grantor's bank and/or investment statement(s). Thus, once the extent of the assets and liabilities are known, the legal obligation of record keeping basically boils down to three requirements, albeit important ones:

1) Benchmarking assets and liabilities from the time you first start to act as attorney;

2) Ensuring all items on the bank/investment statement(s) are identified in terms of income, expenses, assets and liabilities; and

3) Having invoices/bills/statements/confirmations to support the activities contained in the second requirement.

It should be remembered that there may be some activity for which there will be no supporting documentation, e.g., receipt or voucher, as in the case of the monthly Old Age Security (OAS) received from the Government of Canada as a direct deposit. No one will expect the attorney to have supporting documentation for something of this nature. What is expected, however, is that the nature of the activity for which there is no supporting documentation be identified in terms of date, amount, source, reason etc. Other examples of supporting documentation are: cheque stubs, notations in the bank book (some banks will identify OAS and CPP payments with those letters; other banks use DEP only, indicating a deposit without identifying the source or nature of the deposit) and credit card statements. In other cases, perhaps there should have been some official documentation, but it has been lost. In such cases, make a note of what you believe the documentation to be and why and what you did to try and obtain the missing information. Let this note form the basis of the documentation. Although all activity needs to be identified, your own common sense will tell you whether you have made enough of an effort to determine and obtain a source document.

> *Regardless of the jurisdiction you and the grantor live in, the most important thing to remember is that you must keep the financial affairs of the grantor separate and independent from your own personal financial arrangements. This means separate bank and investment accounts for the grantor that provide a complete and accurate record of **ALL** transactions.*

Privacy Issues

Ensuring privacy and respecting confidentiality can be one of the trickiest areas to navigate. As an attorney, you have a fiduciary duty, i.e., you owe a duty of loyalty—to the grantor, which includes a duty of confidentiality. In other words, as long as the grantor is capable of managing their own affairs, you are under an obligation to keep the grantor's affairs to which you are privy in confidence, unless the grantor indicates differently. If others have questions about the grantor's financial affairs, their recourse is to ask the grantor, not you, for information. Thus, all transactions and activity covered by the CPOAP document as well as the existence of the document is subject to privacy laws, including the general expectation of privacy that we all have about our own personal affairs, financial or otherwise. Obviously, once someone starts to act as an attorney that becomes a matter of public record to the extent that other people are now aware of the attorney's existence. However, up to that point, it is up to the grantor to decide who needs to know that the CPOAP exists, who the attorney is under the CPOAP and also when they and others might need to know this information. In an ideal world, the grantor has already asked you to be their attorney for property—no need for surprises after the fact, as well as telling, at a minimum, close family members that they have made the appropriate arrangements.

When accepting the responsibilities of acting as an attorney, it is important that you take steps to clarify with the grantor (or the grantor's lawyer) if there are any particular instructions/wishes of the grantor in this area with respect to privacy and transparency in the management of the grantor's financial affairs. As an attorney, you are acting as an agent of the grantor, and as noted above, this includes the obligation of confidentiality. In other words, if the grantor has not told others just how much money they have invested, it is not up to you to reveal that information. In fact, revealing such information could be construed as a breach of trust and be detrimental to your relationship with the grantor. Should you be questioned by anyone about the existence of a CPOAP and/or your role, you should simply request that they direct their question to the grantor.

In the case where the grantor becomes incapacitated, however, the duty of confidentiality is shifted somewhat to take into account the obligation to consult with relevant individuals involved in the grantor's life. In Ontario, this obligation is captured in s. 32(5) of the *Substitution Decisions Act 1992*, which provides that the attorney will consult "from time to time" with "supportive family members and friends" who are in regular contact with the incapable grantor, as well as persons who are giving personal care to the grantor. This duty to consult is in addition to the duty to make decisions "consistent with decisions concerning the [incapable] person's personal care that are made by the person who has authority to make those decisions"[2] and to encourage the incapable grantor "to participate to the best of their abilities" in decisions about their property.[3] In each of these cases, the law does not provide checklists of the content of the consultation required, other than to require that the consultation be governed by the best interests of the incapable grantor. Thus, while circumstances and prudence may dictate how much information is shared in the consultation process, its sharing must always be in the best interests of the grantor, including considerations of their personal comfort and well-being.

---

[2]   Ibid., s. 32(1.2).

[3]   Ibid., s. 32(3).

In addition to the *Substitution Decisions Act, 1992*, s. 4 of Ontario Regulation 100/96 made pursuant to the Act imposes a duty of confidentiality on records as well as an obligation to disclose those records to either specific individuals or in certain circumstances.

Privacy versus Transparency

In addition to the expectations of privacy, anyone who has taken on the task of being an attorney must also be aware of the fine line that exists between privacy and transparency—that is, upholding the right of privacy attached to the activities governed by the CPOAP document and the relationship between the grantor and the attorney. At the same time there must be some level of transparency with respect to conducting those activities. In this context, transparency means being an open book, not keeping any secrets and not hiding anything from the grantor or from those who have a legitimate interest in the grantor's affairs.

As attorney, you need to be concerned with transparency in the case of questions being asked by a member of the family of an incapacitated grantor who has been told about the CPOAP document. This is why it is important to document, as best as possible, conversations with these family members that pertain to the grantor's financial affairs, particularly if the grantor is not present when any of these conversations take place. Your documentation will serve as a reminder to you when sitting down with the grantor at the next review session (see Step 10 in Chapter 5). This is particularly the case where consideration is being given to lending large amounts of cash or property (e.g., car) to anyone, or potentially questionable investment purchases are being suggested while the grantor is still actively involved in managing their own affairs.

For example, Jean (the grantor) has a sizeable amount of money tied up in investments. She wants to continue having some say in how these investments are managed. At the same time, she wants to lend a considerable amount of money to her niece, Portia, to attend university in the autumn. The attorney meets with Jean and her lawyer and minutes the meeting as follows:

> Met with Jean and her lawyer, July 5, 2000, at 10:00 a.m. and went over any special instructions. The only requirement is that Jean really wants to maintain as much control over the decision making on her investments as possible; she wants to be consulted before any changes are made to her investment portfolio. In addition, she wants to lend $10,000.00 to niece Portia for university; lawyer to draw up promissory note and give copy to me for file.

These minutes would then be filed in a folder or sleeve marked, "Notes from Meetings." In addition, you should also be recording the wishes of the grantor with respect to future assistance of her niece in the event of Jean's incapacity.

Chapter Recap

Three legal topics of importance were covered in this chapter:

1) The activities related to looking after someone's property were identified and categorized into nine types, further simplified into three categories: money in, money

out and fixed assets. As well as being able to label each item, one must be sure to retain any documentation that supports this activity.

2) The grantor's right to privacy and the fiduciary relationship that exists between the grantor and attorney.

3) While maintaining the right to privacy of the grantor, be aware that the attorney must conduct their management and record keeping with some degree of transparency, especially where the grantor is incapacitated. This will strengthen the relationship between the grantor and attorney, as well as increase the level of acceptance displayed by other interested parties. This can only help in the future should the grantor's health and their ability to take part in their affairs declines, and you find yourself making more decisions independently of the grantor.

With an understanding of the legal context in place regarding what records must be kept and when those records must be kept, along with an awareness of the importance of privacy and transparency, the reader must now make a determination with respect to how involved they are required to be with the grantor's affairs. If the grantor is still actively participating in their financial affairs, the next chapter will be of particular interest because it discusses the minimum standard of record keeping that should be adopted as well as reasons for doing so. Even if the attorney is in the position of managing the affairs of an incapacitated grantor, they may find the next chapter useful in helping them understand what kind of records may have been kept by someone assisting the grantor.

Chapter 4

Record Keeping and the Capable Grantor

As we all know, life is very seldom "either/or"; it is usually "both/and," and this holds true for being someone's attorney under a CPOAP. In other words, it is entirely possible that your first experience acting for the grantor will be in a situation where the grantor is still fully capable of managing their own affairs. For example, snow bird parents may be out of the country when GICs come due; as attorney, you can ensure that the GICs are renewed without difficulty. Perhaps the grantor is in the hospital at a time when investments are coming due and, while mentally capable, is unable to get to the bank to renew the investments. You, acting as attorney and on their instructions, can go to their financial institution to renew the investments. In both examples, the grantor is mentally capable of managing their affairs and has made decisions about what to do with the investments. The attorney's job is to ensure that those decisions are carried out. Similarly, just because an aged grantor may be residing in a retirement/nursing home does not necessarily mean that the grantor is not mentally capable of managing their own affairs. However, they may need some assistance in doing so, and this will require you as their attorney to supply the necessary level of assistance. This chapter will address the minimum standard of record keeping that should be adopted as well as reasons for doing so.

While there can be unfortunate instantaneous capacity-altering events, such as strokes or serious accidents, most often one finds that one is acting for an incapacitated grantor only after watching them decline in health over a number of months or years and at some point during their decline one finds oneself becoming (more) involved in their financial affairs. Moreover, because people are living longer, there is an increasing occurrence of Alzheimer's and other impairments of mental faculties that can often occur over a period of months, and the likelihood that the attorney will be working with the grantor increases while the grantor still retains sufficient capacity to look after their own affairs. The ability to look after our own affairs with no or minimal assistance is an important aspect of our dignity as persons and should be respected by the attorney.

When to start?

Although strict legal requirements for starting to keep formal records (i.e., in the format required by law) can be a specific event, such as "the first transaction for the incapable grantor" as defined in Ontario's Regulation 100/96 "Accounts and Records of Attorneys and Guardians," it should be noted that that is not the only event. Indeed, notwithstanding the language of Regulation 100/96, courts in Ontario have held that attorneys must also account for their activities even when assisting a capable grantor. Other jurisdictions are more open-ended and simply require that records from the time you first start acting *be available* should you be required to account for your activities as attorney. Thus depending upon where you live in Canada, the legal beginnings of formal record keeping may vary. However, where the grantor is incapacitated, formal records will always be required.

Quite apart from the formal legal requirements of when to begin record keeping, it is important to bear in mind that the law only provides a minimum standard to which one is held accountable. In other words, just because the law may be vague or open-ended does not mean that you as attorney should not be proactive in record-keeping arrangements to protect both you and the grantor. This is especially true when you consider the fact that one is more likely than not to be acting as attorney within a continuum of capacity in changing circumstances. That is, you begin your role as attorney with a fully competent grantor, assisting minimally if at all, and you progress over time to providing total assistance to an incapable grantor. The following table illustrates that continuum and suggests the type of record keeping required and the appropriate steps (as presented in Chapter 5) to follow.

Table 2—Record-Keeping Requirements from Fully Competent Grantor to Court Review[1]

Circumstances of Grantor	Fully Competent Grantor	Physically Incapable but Mentally Competent	Incapable Grantor	Court Review
Type of Record	At least attorney activity records[1]	At least attorney activity records	Formal, as required by law	Formal, as required by law
Record-Keeping Steps	1, 5, 10	1 – 10	1–10	1–10

Why keep accounting records before you have to?

"If the law doesn't require that I keep records, why should I go to the time and trouble before I am legally required to do so"

Such a question is certainly not out of place given the time demands that most of us already face. The time required to act as someone's attorney, even where the grantor is fully capable of managing their own affairs, is going to add one more demand. Every circumstance is going to vary with respect to how much time is required, but there are nevertheless a

---

[1] See "What kind of records do I need to maintain" later in this chapter for a description of what these records should include.

number of fundamental reasons why starting to keep records sooner rather than later is a good idea. The following, in no particular order, are some of those reasons.

1) Working with the grantor while the grantor is fully capable will allow you to better understand the grantor's concerns, obligations, financial abilities and limitations. By becoming familiar with such things sooner rather than later, the attorney will better be able to appreciate what constitutes the best interests of the grantor should the grantor become incapacitated at some subsequent point.

> ### A Word To The Wise!
> Working with the grantor will require more than just record keeping skills. The attorney will also have to remember that they are sharing in very private matters, and that tact and sensitivity to the grantor's privacy is just as important as being able to keep records of transactions and banking activity.

2) Becoming familiar with the grantor's financial and estate circumstances may be the best practical reason why you want to start to keep a record—this will save you time and trouble in the long run when it does become necessary to keep records.

3) Keeping a record to protect yourself against later accusations of mismanagement as the record will provide evidence of the nature and extent of your involvement from the outset of assisting the grantor with their affairs.

4) Keeping a rudimentary record and becoming familiar with the grantor's affairs allows you to work with the grantor and to help protect them from fraud, elder abuse or mistakes made by others with whom the grantor is dealing, i.e., banks, investment brokers, etc.

5) Keeping records will also allow you to detect unusual spending habits or other transactions that may be indicative of capacity issues that require you to, among other things, start to maintain more formal and detailed records of the grantor's estate and your management of it.

What kind of records do I need to maintain?

Having been convinced of the practical and common sense reasons for keeping at least basic records of your activities on behalf of the grantor while the grantor is still fully competent, the next question is, "What kind of records?"

Again, the answer will very much depend upon the type of circumstances in which you find yourself. At this stage, prior to express and exact legal requirements, there is no "one size fits all" approach. Nevertheless, the following are some general guidelines that should assist you in determining the kinds of records that might be appropriate.

1) At the very least, you should keep a simple diary of all transactions with which you are involved, identifying date, nature of transaction, amount and reason for your

actions.[2] This diary can be supplemented with written instructions from the grantor should the nature of the transaction warrant a more formalized notation (e.g., large cash transaction or payment).

2) Keep a note of all regular/preauthorized activities, such as utility payments. This will help in highlighting any unusual or unexpected withdrawal activity that may occur and prompt a timely question.

3) Schedule a monthly recap session with the grantor to review bank activity statements to ensure accuracy of those records. Monthly sessions are suggested because banks usually require discrepancies to be reported within 30 days. These recap sessions need not be long or involved, but they will ensure that you and the grantor are both fully aware of not only the grantor's current financial circumstances, but also your role in assisting the grantor with their affairs.

4) Review Chapter 5 to determine which steps are of the most value to you now, even though the grantor is fully capable and your role may be minimal. For example, knowing where the keys are to the safety deposit box and where the box is located is certainly something that the attorney should know regardless of whether they have reason to access it in the early stages of their role.

5) Use Chapter 6 to prepare an informal inventory and ascertain whether any items may have a potential for becoming contentious issues later on (e.g., inheritance expectations among different beneficiaries). Ensuring information or confirming particulars now about any property (whether financial in nature or physical, such as the grantor's house or cottage) that you may be expected to make decisions about later, while the grantor is still fully capable, will make your job as attorney much easier as time progresses and you take on more of the management responsibilities.

At the end of the day, assisting the competent grantor with their affairs will largely be at the discretion of the grantor—who may very well need no assistance whatsoever. Moreover, whatever assistance may be required will depend on individual circumstances. No matter what level of involvement, working with the competent grantor allows the attorney the opportunity to become not only familiar with the grantor's affairs, but also to start to practice record-keeping habits. These habits will prove invaluable once the attorney is left with no other alternative but to take on greater responsibility should the grantor's health deteriorate.

Chapter Recap

In this chapter we have discussed the practical aspects of keeping records while assisting the fully capable grantor with their affairs. In particular, we have:

---

[2] For example, a day planner diary can be purchased from all office supply stores and at bookstores. It should be used only to record activity and discussions involving the grantor's affairs.

1) Recognized that the law provides only a mandatory minimum, which does not prevent the attorney from being proactive with respect to record keeping.

2) Provided some practical reasons for why it is better to start keeping records sooner rather then later when you are required to do so.

3) Suggested the nature of the records which ought to be kept.

4) Advised a review of the 10 steps found in Chapter 5 and in particular the benefit of preparing an informal inventory (Chapter 6) to ensure a complete understanding and awareness of the grantor's property.

5) Remembered that in assisting the capable grantor, one has to be mindful of both their privacy and independence to ensure that assistance does not become hindrance.

In the next chapter we turn our attention to the practical steps involved in keeping financial records. Specifically we will identify 10 *practical* steps with straightforward instructions on how to successfully complete each step. Following these 10 steps will allow the attorney to manage and maintain the necessary records with a minimum amount of stress and a maximum amount of confidence.

Chapter 5

Ten Steps to Carefree Record Keeping

Finally, the real reason why you purchased this book—the steps to follow to make sure you stay out of trouble! This chapter will provide the critical steps required to assist you to manage someone else's financial affairs appropriately. Regardless of the degree to which you are assisting someone with their financial affairs, this chapter is a must read. Although some aspects may not apply right now because your involvement is limited, reading through this chapter will alert you to potential issues down the road. Having this knowledge now and working with the grantor while the grantor is capable will smooth the road later when the deteriorating health of the grantor necessitates greater involvement by you.

This chapter identifies all the steps in a logical, progressive order that will enable the attorney to approach the tasks associated with financial record keeping with efficiency and a minimum of stress. A flow chart has been provided in Appendix I to provide an easy-to-follow road map for the attorney. While it is not necessary to completely finish each step before progressing to the next, it is certainly recommended that you initially consider each step in sequence. These steps have been listed in a specific order for a reason—they are cumulative. In other words, the steps required later in the process are dependent on having the information gathered in the earlier steps. For example, there is little reason to consider cash management decisions (Step 8) if you do not yet know the number of bank accounts that exist (Step 2).

There is nothing inherently difficult about these tasks. It is recognized that some of the tasks may take a little perseverance only because their outcome is dependent on someone else. For example, financial institutions can at times operate under the slogan, "Our way or no way." However, following the advice set out in Step 5 will minimize the difficulties that might arise when dealing with a financial or other large institution.

Steps 1-5 are administrative in nature, consisting of the need to gather information and inform various third parties of your new legal status with respect to the grantor's property-related affairs. Steps 6-9 identify actions required with respect to financial decisions and documentation of the financial activity of the grantor. Step 10 concludes with the final administrative task of communicating with the grantor and/or their attorney for personal care, substitute decision maker, supportive family members or friends on a regular basis.

The 10 steps are:

Step 1—Obtaining the CPOAP Document and Will
Step 2—Preparing an Inventory and Gathering the Information
Step 3—Safety Deposit Box(es)

Step 4—Past Tax Returns
Step 5—Informing the Businesses
Step 6—Bank Account Amalgamations
Step 7—Arrangements Outside the Activity of the Bank Statement
Step 8—Cash Management Decisions
Step 9—Keeping Track of Cash In/Cash Out
Step 10—Review of Activity with the Grantor and/or Grantor's Representative

At the end of this chapter is a checklist to assist your progress through these steps. In addition, answering the three key questions presented at the end of each step will help to ensure that you have gathered the most essential information.

Step 1—Obtaining the CPOAP Document and Will

Obtain the original of the CPOAP document, or know where the original is being held. The original needs to be in your possession once you start fully acting as attorney, and it should form part of your file. Never give up possession of the original. If a bank or other institution wants a copy of the CPOAP, have a notarized[1] copy made and give that copy to the institution. Be sure to make a note of where you have given copies of the CPOAP because should you ever resign, it will be necessary to convey that resignation to those who have copies (see Step 5).

As soon as you are informed that you are the attorney under a CPOAP, make time to read through the document. Make sure you understand all that is being asked of you, both in terms of time commitment and potential difficulties—especially in cases were there are other family members who might question your appointment as attorney. Depending upon the size and nature of the grantor's estate, you may need to consult a lawyer or accountant who specializes in this type of work. Ensure you have a complete understanding of the responsibilities, as well as limitations or restrictions on your authority, before accepting and acting.

In addition to the original CPOAP, particularly in the case of acting for an incapacitated grantor, you will also want to ascertain the existence of the grantor's will and ensure that it is being kept in a safe place, either with the lawyer who drafted it or in a safety deposit box to which you have sole access. You must review the contents of the will and make a note of any specific bequests, because they could become an issue as you manage the incapable grantor's affairs. For example, in Ontario, s. 35.1 of the *Substitute Decisions Act, 1992* expressly provides restrictions on, and rules governing, the disposition of specific property if named in the will as a gift.

You will want to have at least three notarized copies of the CPOAP document on hand to start with. Three copies will be sufficient to ensure you access to any of the grantor's property (e.g., bank accounts, home) should you need immediate confirmation of your

---

[1] A notarized copy is a photocopy of an original document that has been certified by a notary public to be a true and accurate copy of the original document. The lawyer who prepared the original CPOAP document may be able to assist you in obtaining notarized copies; because not all lawyers are notaries, you may be directed elsewhere. There will probably be a fee for this, and it should be the responsibility of the grantor to cover such costs.

authority once you start acting as attorney. File them in the appropriate section of your filing system (discussed in Chapter 2).

Completing Step 2 will identify additional businesses that may require a notarized copy of the CPOAP document. It is suggested that you wait until you have confirmed with these businesses that they require a notarized copy (see Step 5) before obtaining the copies. The reason for this is simply to avoid having more paperwork to keep track of than absolutely necessary, as well as avoiding unnecessary costs of notarizing documents. You may find that a business is satisfied with reviewing the CPOAP and making a note that it was reviewed and a copy taken.

After contact is made with the initial list of businesses identified in Step 2 and they have been provided with copies of the CPOAP, you will still want to have three copies of the CPOAP on hand. This will avoid any panic should one be needed at short notice. Also remember that you are required to keep a copy of the CPOAP as part of the record of accounts as defined in Ontario Regulation 100/96, s. 2(2).

Finally, be sure to record the name and contact details of the lawyer who prepared the CPOAP document and file this information with the notarized copies of the CPOAP document. Should you have any questions about your duties and obligations down the road, or questions about the grantor's affairs, this person is a good choice as the first person to contact.

Essential Questions

1) Has the original CPOAP document and a copy of the will been obtained and reviewed?

2) Have three notarized copies been obtained and filed?

3) Have the contact details of the lawyer who prepared the CPOAP been recorded and filed?

Step 2—Making an Inventory and Gathering the Information

You will need to ascertain the particulars of the grantor's financial activities and financial position pertinent to your involvement as outlined in the CPOAP document. Though you might not be acting for the grantor right away, you should sit down with the grantor to familiarize yourself with their financial position and arrangements. The grantor should tell you in general terms what their financial arrangements are, and most important, the location of this information in the event you need to find it. Do not forget to ask about the existence of any safety deposit boxes and location of the keys.

When you start to act as the grantor's attorney, you will need to become more matter-of-fact and practical about the information required. This means, among other things, making an inventory of assets and liabilities and determining the

---

A Word to the Wise!

If it is not possible to get the information directly from the grantor, keep an eye on the grantor's mail. Bank and investment statements often arrive on a regular basis—even if only every six months. You can compare these account numbers to information already obtained and fill in any that are missing from your original listing.

physical location and existing treatment of those assets and liabilities. Do not forget safety deposit boxes and their contents, which can include money, stock certificates and jewellery. More information about safety deposit boxes can be found in Step 3. Also, do not forget to find out whether the grantor is supporting any dependents, such as a former wife or children for example, and if so, the nature of that support. These dependents may have to be considered as you manage the grantor's affairs.

If the CPOAP document is a general one, use the checklist in Table 3 to determine what assets and liabilities exist for the grantor. For any item you place a tick beside, refer to Chapter 6, "Preparing an Inventory," for an explanation of what kind of documentation should exist and suggestions on where it might be found if the grantor has lost originals. You will also find suggested questions to ask that may be pertinent in different situations to jog the memory of either the grantor or family members.

Table 3—Assets (A) and Liabilities (L) of a Person

Item	Type (A) Asset (L) Liability	Yes	No	Held Jointly
Annuity	(A)			
Bank Accounts	(A)			
Business and/or Partnership Agreements	(A and/or L)			
Contents of House, Condo and/or Cottage	(A)			
Credit Cards	(L)			
Dependants	(L)			
Insurance Policies				
Business/Partnership	(A)			
Car	(A)			
Condo	(A)			
Cottage	(A)			
Critical Illness	(A)			
Disability	(A)			
Health	(A)			
House	(A)			
Life	(A)			
Pet	(A)			
Investments				
Bonds	(A)			
GIC/Term Deposits	(A)			
Limited Partnerships	(A)			
Mineral Titles and Leases	(A)			
Mortgage-Backed Securities	(A)			
Mutual Funds/Income Trusts	(A)			

Item	Type (A) Asset (L) Liability	Yes	No	Held Jointly
Real Estate	(A)			
Shares—Public Company	(A)			
Line of Credit	(L)			
Loan Guarantees	(L)			
Loans Payable	(L)			
Loans Receivable	(A)			
Maintenance under a Court Order	(A and/or L)			
Miscellaneous Amounts	(A and/or L)			
Mortgage Payable	(L)			
Pensions				
Foreign	(A)			
Government	(A)			
Private	(A)			
Survivor	(A)			
Real Property				
Condo	(A)			
Cottage	(A)			
Farm	(A)			
House	(A)			
Undeveloped Land	(A)			
RRSP/RRIF	(A)			
Shares—Private Company	(A)			
Tax-Free Savings Account (TFSA)	(A)			
Will	N/A			

However, if the CPOAP is specific with respect to identifying those assets and liabilities that are to be the responsibility of the attorney, the list from the CPOAP will establish the inventory. Although the assets and liabilities have been identified, referring to Chapter 6 will ensure all the necessary information pertaining to each one is collected.

For each asset and liability that you have responsibility for, you will have to determine the value as at the date you start acting as attorney. You will also want to have basic identification details for each item. In Chapter 6, the specific details required for each type of asset and liability can be found following the discussion of each. Once you have collected the detailed information, use the worksheet provided in Appendix VII to create a summary listing for quick referral. Because a picture is worth a thousand words, a sample worksheet has also been completed to show you what yours may look like after you have completed Step 2.

If you identify an asset or liability that you do not know how to handle, consult with a lawyer or accountant who specializes in estate matters. Under no circumstances should it be ignored. It is often an item that is ignored that becomes an obstacle down the road.

Essential Questions:

1) If it is a general CPOAP, has Table 3 been completed?

2) Have any assets or liabilities been identified with which you are not sure what to do?

3) Have you contacted a lawyer or accountant for advice with respect to those items identified in question two?

Step 3—Safety Deposit Box(es)

You will have already ascertained the whereabouts of any safety deposit boxes (SDB) in Step 2. Step 3 however, is concerned with issues pertaining to the SDB beyond its mere location. The bank and/or trust company will require proof of your authority to access the SDB. Be sure to have the original and notarized copy of the CPOAP document with you when you first go to the bank/trust company, and be prepared to leave the notarized copy of the CPOAP document for their records.

Complete an inventory of each box. The types of things one might find in a SDB are: stocks, bonds, title to home, original will, cash and small valuables like jewellery.

If more than one SDB exists, consider amalgamating contents into one box with one complete single inventory (see Template 1 below), showing the original source of each item. However, before doing so be sure to read the will, if there is one, to make sure that there are no specific instructions pertaining to the contents of any SDBs.

You might also consider using the SDB to store other important documents that you gather even if not originally found in a SDB. If the grantor does not have a SDB, you should consider renting one at the branch where the main bank account is held. Annual rental fees are still quite reasonable, and the amount is a tax-deductible expense for the grantor. This would be a particularly sensible action if the grantor is still living at home, and there are a number of different people coming and going (family and non-family), or if the grantor is preparing to move from their home. Placing documents such as their will or stock certificates and house deed and items such as jewellery into a SDB would be an excellent location to ensure their safe keeping during the chaos that any move generates. Knowing that important papers and valuable jewellery (monetary and sentimental) have been placed out of harm's way will relieve one aspect of stress for the grantor, their family and ultimately you who will need to know the location of such items to fulfill your attorney role properly. If you decide not to rent a SDB, you should make a note of why you decided one was not needed at the present time—there might be very good reasons. However, you should review this decision periodically (at least annually) because circumstances might change that make it more of a necessity rather than an option.

A Word to the Wise!

Once you know where the safety deposit boxes are, it is just as important to know where the keys are kept for each box. The financial institution can provide copies. However, they will probably charge a key replacement fee.

Template 1—Safety Deposit Box Locations and Inventory List (Appendix VIII)

Location(s)

Bank:
Address:

Contact Person:
Phone Number:
E-mail:

Bank:
Address:

Contact Person:
Phone Number
E-mail:

Bank:
Address:

Contact Person:
Phone Number
E-mail:

Inventory of SDB
Location of SDB:

Item	Original Location of Item

Essential Questions:

1) Have the number of SDBs been determined?

2) If more than one, have contents been amalgamated and an inventory list prepared?

3) If no SDB exists, has it been decided to obtain one? If no, why?

Step 4—Past Tax Returns

In Canada, by law we are required to retain tax returns and supporting documentation[2] for a period of six years after the date on the Notice of Assessment for any given year. For example, for a T1 (General Tax Return) filed for the year ending December 31, 2006, where the Notice of Assessment received is dated May 16, 2007, supporting documentation should be kept until May 16, 2013.

If the most recent return is available, the name of the person or firm that has prepared the return should be found on the last page of the T1 jacket.[3] If it has not been, you might be able to ascertain this information by asking either the grantor or a family member. If they were satisfied with this person's work, you might consider using them again for future tax return work. This person may also have historical knowledge of the grantor's tax affairs and thus could provide invaluable assistance when completing the inventory listing as well as with the preparation of future tax returns.

A Word to the Wise!

When locating contact details of the accountant, be sure to record:

Name of Firm:
Name of Accountant:
Address:
Phone Number:
E-mail:
Will Use for Future Returns? Yes___ No___

If the previous tax return cannot be found, and the grantor (and family members) cannot remember who prepared the last return, look at cancelled cheques or cheque stubs for the previous year of the grantor to see if an accountant or tax preparation service was paid. To begin, concentrate your search on the months March to May because this is the most likely time period that the tax return would have been prepared.

In the absence of a copy of the T1, you should look for the Notice of Assessment issued by the Canada Revenue Agency (CRA) for the previous tax year. This document will at least give you an overview of the grantor's total income and tax liabilities.

In most instances, not having a copy of the previous year's tax return is not going to present any overwhelming problems. Having it, however, will make life easier for two reasons.

1) It will make the preparation of this year's return easier because you have a previous document to refer to (if you are going to prepare the return yourself).

---

[2] For tax purposes, supporting documentation usually consists of T-slips issued from financial institutions and brokerage houses, the most common being T3s, T4As and T5s. In addition to the T-slips, receipts supporting medical expenditures, donations and education are the most common for people over the age of 50.

[3] The word "jacket" is commonly used by accountants when referring to the four or five pages of the T1 that contain the personal information of the taxpayer and summarizes the income earned, tax credits and final taxes payable/refund due. Whether the jacket is four pages or five will depend on what tax package (e.g., Quicktax or Ufile) has been used to produce the return and what year.

2) Knowing what T3s, T4s and T5s were received last year will help you to determine whether you have received all the slips for this year.

Obtaining a number of past tax returns will also help in determining the completeness of the list made in Step 2. By comparing sources of income reported, you will have a good idea of the income-generating assets of the grantor's estate. This is particularly important in cases where, for whatever reasons, you have not had the opportunity to sit down with the grantor and obtain this information directly.

Locating the most recent tax return will also assist you in determining whether you have identified all the investments. The attached T3, T4 and T5 slips will identify companies that have issued dividends, interest or other benefits during the previous year. Your worksheet compiled in Step 2 will probably contain all these companies. If it does not, there might be a legitimate reason why the grantor is no longer associated with the company, but the following question should be asked: Does the grantor still have money/stocks invested with this company? It may be that the shares or securities were sold/redeemed earlier in the current year, prior to you taking over as attorney. If so, you need to establish this as a fact.

Many CPOAP documents contain a clause that specifically states that the attorney is a "'legal representative', for all purposes of the Income Tax Act (Canada), with respect to any dealings with the Government of Canada or any institution controlled by the Government of Canada." If the CPOAP document you are working under does not contain this type of clause, you should consider filing a T1013E—Individual Consent Form with the CRA. This form, signed by the grantor, authorizes the CRA to release and discuss all tax return information with you. If you are not comfortable with dealing with the CRA, then ensure that whoever prepares the grantor's annual tax return is identified as being authorized on this form T1013E. (A copy can be downloaded from the CRA's website at www.cra-arc.gc.ca/E/pbg/tf/t1013/.)

While not legally obliged to ensure a tax return is filed for the grantor who is capable of looking after their own affairs, from a practical perspective, the attorney is well-placed to assist in making sure that this happens. In the case of the incapacitated grantor, your obligation to look after the grantor's finances does include the duty to ensure that all tax returns are submitted on time and that all tax liabilities are paid. If you are not comfortable with dealing with tax matters, then you should have a licensed accountant who specializes in tax matters prepare the annual tax returns.

A Word to the Wise!

Here are five key tips when dealing with the Tax Man (aka Canada Revenue Agency, aka CRA):

1) Make sure the T1013E is in place or that the CPOAP specifically designates you as "legal representative".
2) Have the Grantor's Social Insurance Number at hand.
3) Have the most recent annual tax assessment that would have been received after the filing of the most recent tax return.
4) If possible, have a copy of the most recent tax return that was filed with the CRA.
5) Remember that the person on the other end of the phone is a person too and as long as the T1013E is in place or a copy of the CPOAP has been filed with the CRA, will want to help you as much as they can.

In the interests of having the tax returns prepared correctly, the first time, the attorney may want to avoid do-it-yourself tax packages or franchise tax services.

Professional preparation of the tax return does not have to be costly. The Ontario Institute of Chartered Accountants offers a free tax clinic open to the public across Ontario from mid-February until the end of March. It is geared predominantly towards low-income earners. To qualify for this free tax return assistance, total annual household income must be below $22,500 with dependents, or below $15,000 without dependents.[4] Also, individuals with rental income and/or business income do not qualify for the Free CA Tax Clinics program, regardless of the amount of annual income.

These Free CA Tax Clinics operate in cooperation with a variety of agencies, including food banks, charities, hospitals, senior centres and homes, community centres, social service agencies and libraries. The Institute of Chartered Accountants of Ontario offers additional support to these agencies by providing them with an honorarium based on the number of tax returns prepared at their location. These funds help the agencies carry out their valuable work. See www.icao.on.ca/public/apps/TaxClinics/ to locate a tax clinic operating in your area should you reside in Ontario.

For those readers from other provinces, refer to the reference section at the back of this book for a complete list of provincial Institutes and contact information. Although not all provincial Institutes offer free tax clinics, they will most certainly be able to assist you in locating a qualified tax accountant in your area.

Essential Questions

1) Is a copy of the most recent tax return filed the CRA available?

2) Has contact details of the preparer of the most recent tax return prepared been ascertained?

3) Has appropriate notification been made to the CRA—either a copy of the CPOAP or Form T1013?

Step 5—Informing the Businesses

It is important that the attorney make contact with persons identified in Step 2 in a timely manner. The first two objectives are to:

1) make them aware that you are now acting under the CPOAP document; and

2) confirm the requirements for adding you, the attorney, as a signatory and authorized person to the relevant account(s).

In some cases, the business will need to see the original CPOAP document. They may also require a notarized copy for their files and therefore the attorney may need to have on

---

4   These thresholds are effective for the 2010 tax year and are subject to change in subsequent years.

hand a number of notarized copies. This is a good time for you as the attorney to establish the relationship with these various businesses. As discussed above, under no circumstances should the attorney give the original CPOAP document to anyone. A notarized copy, yes; the original document, no. Be sure to note to whom and when you gave a notarized copy of the CPOAP.

Use Template 2 provided below to record all businesses contacted and whether a copy of the CPOAP was left with them.

The attorney may encounter a business that will not accept the CPOAP document prepared by a lawyer, but will insist on having their own form completed and signed by relevant parties. A properly executed CPOAP document that meets the legal requirements as to form and execution is binding (i.e., sufficient) in all respects and for all purposes for which it was signed. Although many banks do have their own forms, a properly executed general CPOAP document is valid for all banking purposes and supersedes the form that the banking institution may have created in-house for their own uses. Encountering insistence for internal documents is probably an indication that you are not speaking with the appropriate person at the bank. Be sure that you are dealing with a person knowledgeable enough to assist you. This should minimize problems. If problems persist, a last resort is to have your lawyer contact the branch manager on your behalf.

Proof of identity and a sample signature will certainly be required by any banking institution in order for the attorney to be able to write cheques and authorize any investment transactions. Be sure to confirm with the bank what it considers proof of identity so that you have the correct items with you when you visit.

The attorney may decide to visit the business in person, prior to any telephone introductions. If this is done, be sure that once there, you are speaking with the correct person. Remember that at some companies (especially banks) turnover and transfers can be significant. The attorney may need to be patient as they attempt to find the most appropriate person that can assist them. Remember, always start at the top with the bank branch manager and then go from there.

This is probably going to be the most time-consuming task. Once this step is complete, congratulate yourself on your perseverance and take a deep breath—the most tedious task is behind you.

Template 2—List of People/Companies to Contact (Appendix VIII)

Company	Person	Date Contact Made	Date CPOAP Copy Delivered	Other Notes

Essential Questions

1) Have all businesses identified in Step 2 been contacted?

2) Are there any businesses that require their own copy of the CPOAP document?

3) Has the "List of People/Companies to Contact" (Template 2) been completed?

Step 6—Bank Account Amalgamations

It is not unusual for a person to have more than one bank account. However, once the management of an individual's financial affairs is shared, numerous accounts may only add confusion and increase the burden of accurately recording the activity in the accounts. Thus, there are two decisions to be considered.

1) If there are numerous bank accounts and/or investments in the grantor's name only, consider amalgamating some or all. Though there might have been very good reasons at one time supporting the existence of multiple accounts, the attorney (in consultation with the grantor, if feasible) needs to decide whether those reasons are still valid. If not, then determine which accounts are the most appropriate ones to be closed and balances transferred. Background information about multiple accounts should have been acquired in your initial discussions with the grantor. If this information was not obtained, there is no time like the present to fill in any missing information. In addition, the attorney will also want to check the grantor's will, if there is one, to see if there are any specific instructions relating to the disposition of bank accounts.

2) Whether accounts are amalgamated or not, you and the grantor need to decide if it is necessary to roll the active accounts into one or more trust account(s), particularly where the grantor's capacity is or will be an issue.

The advantages to doing this are:

a) protection for the attorney, because it provides a more formal framework in which disbursements and receipts are being transacted;

b) protection of the grantor, because it prevents the grantor from being taken advantage of in situations of diminished capacity;

c) simplification for handover of accounts to the executor at the time of the grantor's death; and

d) it makes it clear that you are acting as a trustee—that is, on behalf of the grantor, and not yourself.

Under no circumstances should the grantor's financial assets be mixed or amalgamated with the attorney's personal accounts.

Although it is important to review all accounts to ascertain whether changes are necessary, there are two types of bank or investment accounts that, if they exist, will in all likelihood retain their current status.

1) Joint accounts—that is, accounts held with another person, other than the attorney.

2) Account(s) that exist because of a partnership agreement.

If either of these accounts exist, it will be important to ascertain the exact nature of such accounts. The existence of joint accounts may be a result of estate planning and has likely been done to minimize probate tax liabilities. This is usually a good thing, although it must be remembered that the grantor has an interest in the money contained in such accounts and may require access to it.

In the case of an account that exists because of a partnership agreement, you will need a copy of this document. You will also, in all likelihood, have to contact one of the other partners to confirm the status of any joint accounts before being able to make a decision about the continuance of the account(s). As the language and terms used in partnership agreements are not familiar to most of us, if such an agreement exists, it may be appropriate to obtain professional advice on how this account should be treated.

Essential Questions

1) Based on your knowledge of the grantor's affairs, have all bank and investment accounts been identified?

2) Have amalgamations of accounts been discussed with the grantor, agreed and documented?

3) Has a trust account arrangement been discussed with the grantor, and has necessary action been agreed upon and documented?

Step 7—Arrangements Outside the Activity of the Bank Statements

You will need to ensure that all current financial arrangements outside the activity of the bank statements are documented and understood by the relevant parties. For example, an independent adult (relative or friend) might be residing in the principal residence of the grantor although the grantor is in a long-term care facility, such as a nursing home. In such a situation it will be important to have it plainly understood who is responsible for the upkeep of the property and the monthly expenses, including telephone, cable, gas and hydro utilities, house insurance and property taxes. You should be aware of any automatic withdrawals from the grantor's bank account that may be covering these monthly expenses. Arrangements such as those described above should be documented and initialled by the grantor, if able, as proof that the granter is aware of these arrangements and in agreement with them. The record should also be signed by the person who is receiving the benefit of these arrangements. This will hopefully avoid any misunderstandings later. If the existence or management of these arrangements ever becomes an issue, you will have the necessary documentation with the relevant signatures to support your position.

Another property item that needs to be attended to could be the grantor's car. For example, the grantor may have moved into a care facility but has "lent" the car to a relative or friend. If this is the case, the specific arrangements must be ascertained and recorded. The arrangements might be that the grantor will continue to pay for the maintenance and annual registration on the car, but the person who is using it is responsible for obtaining insurance and paying for all the gas. If the grantor becomes incapable, you may be required to bring such arrangements to a conclusion by taking possession of the vehicle. Whatever the circumstances and whatever your decision, be sure to adequately document both.

Template 3 below should be completed for each activity identified. Once completed, place the records in the working file in the section titled "Special Arrangements" and, if related to continued financial commitment of the grantor, the relevant bank statement that incurs the automatic withdrawals related to the arrangement.

Template 3—Appendix VIII

Does an arrangement outside the bank statements exist?

Identify the person(s) benefiting from the arrangement (e.g., Charlie, the grantor's nephew) and whether they are "dependent" upon the grantor.

If so, describe the general nature of arrangement (e.g., remaining in the grantor's home, although the grantor has now moved to a nursing home).

Describe the payment obligations of each (e.g., house insurance covering house, property and contents and property taxes will be paid by the grantor, but all other expense to be paid by nephew).

What is the term of the arrangement (e.g., until nephew finishes post-secondary education or by December 31, 2010, whichever is earlier)?

Describe any conditions that, if they occur, would mean the immediate conclusion of this arrangement (e.g., if nephew drops out of post-secondary education and is unemployed for more than two months, or upon the death of the grantor).

Essential Questions

1) Do any arrangements outside the activity of the bank statement exist?

2) If so, have the specifics been documented, agreed with the grantor and signed by the grantor and other person(s) involved?

3) Are there any conditions or time restrictions as part of the arrangement, and if so, what are they?

Step 8—Cash Management Decisions

This step has two components. The first focuses on the day-to-day cash requirements of the grantor and the management of debit and/or credit cards. The second component addresses assessing the ongoing income requirements of the grantor in order to meet all current, as well as reasonably anticipated future, expenses. It is in this second component that we will discuss in some detail the mechanics of preparing a cash flow statement.

Day-to-Day Cash Requirements

There are two issues to consider with respect to daily cash requirements: first, the general question of whether safeguards have to be put on the grantor's access to their own funds; second, safeguarding the physical debit and/or credit cards.

The existence of a CPOAP document does not mean that the grantor is giving up control of, or access to, their property, especially their bank accounts. However, there may be reasons to establish an agreed maximum amount that the grantor might withdraw on a weekly or monthly basis that requires minimum substantiation in any records being kept by the attorney. Ensure that this amount has been documented and initialled by both you and the grantor as proof of the agreement. Substantiation requirements will be limited to the attorney being sure to verify during their monthly review that the particulars of this agreement are being adhered to by the grantor. Although an attorney, absent the grantor's incapacity, has no legal right to prevent the grantor from withdrawing amounts larger than the agreed amount, such activity might alert the attorney to ask pertinent questions regarding capacity issues.

Should such questions need to be asked, it will be important for the attorney to document the date, time and details of these conversations. The written report of these conversations should be filed with the relevant bank statement that prompted the enquiry. The approach taken to this conversation will differ depending on the relationship between the attorney and the grantor. Just remember: it is usually not the question that offends someone, but the way in which the question is asked.

It may be that the question never needs to be asked, either because the reason for the large withdrawal(s) becomes apparent as you and the grantor are conversing in your monthly catch-up meeting, or you are already aware that larger withdrawals were going to be happening due to certain events in the grantor's life (e.g., a relative's birthday, an upcoming marriage, or an anniversary). It is important that the attorney or grantor mark these large items with a relevant notation to describe the reason behind the withdrawal, (e.g., niece Sandra's university graduation).

Unfortunately excessive use of the credit card has become an all too common occurrence among seniors who are on their own for prolonged periods of time. The existence of 24-hour shopping channels offers enticements in the form of goods that can be acquired with the simple action of phoning in a valid credit card number. It is not uncommon for large and/ or numerous charges to start showing up on the monthly statements for items that are of questionable necessity for the grantor. This could put you in an awkward position. It is never the attorney's role to tell the grantor what they can or cannot spend their money on. However, if you note excessive spending jeopardizing the grantor's financial ability to provide for themselves in the long term, you need to have a conversation with the grantor. It is strongly recommended that you not ignore this situation should it arise.

If the grantor continues to take an active role in their financial affairs, having a debit and/ or credit card on or near their person all the time with other people about (e.g., care attendants, housekeepers etc.), this may create a setting where unauthorized and/or unreasonable expenses are incurred. Therefore, vigilant review will be required of the bank and credit card statements.

Frequent changes of the password might be considered. If there are memory problems or similar concerns, this may not be a viable option. If so, then perhaps more frequent review of the bank and credit card activity could be performed as an alternative, to diminish some of the risk in this area. You should also agree with the grantor where these cards will be kept (e.g., bedside table in wallet; bureau drawer; top right hand desk drawer in study). You will want to ensure that you check this predetermined storage place when you visit the grantor to make sure all cards are accounted for.

Determining the Ongoing Income Needs of the Grantor

How involved the attorney becomes in this particular exercise will depend largely on the level of participation the grantor has, and continues to have, in the managing of their financial affairs. Keeping in mind that you are not required to take on the role of a "certified financial planner", it is quite conceivable that your role will extend to ensuring the grantor has determined whether their income they receive each month will in fact cover their living expenses on an ongoing basis.

The attorney will likely get a fair idea of whether income received is going to continue to cover regular monthly expenses from reviewing a couple of months' worth of bank statements. This is determined by keeping an eye on the ending balance of the bank statement each month. If the balance remains approximately the same month to month, it is a reasonable conclusion that the grantor will continue to meet their living expenses into the future, assuming there is no change to their current circumstances. The importance of performing this specific review every quarter or six months cannot be overstated. A more detailed description and approach to this exercise is presented below when the cash flow statement is discussed.

A new close relationship and failing health are the two most common changes that could significantly impact the state of financial stability of the grantor. The attorney is likely to become aware of either of these occurrences as a result of the regular review sessions with the grantor (discussed in more detail in Step 10). In the case of the former, it is not proposed that the attorney take any action, but simply be aware of a potential change in spending habits of the grantor. Should the grantor begin to make significant changes to their spending habits, as a trusted friend, you will be in a good position to have a conversation with them about the impact of the increased spending on their long-term financial health.

In the case of deteriorating physical health of the grantor, this might be the time to discuss with the grantor a number of scenarios with respect to their long-term living arrangements. In order for you to have this discussion with the grantor, you need to:

a) identify the possible living arrangements with estimated costs associated with each[5]; and

---

[5]   There are a number of organizations, public and private, that offer assistance with elder care planning. Because health care is a provincial responsibility, the Reference section at the end of

b) take a prudent look at the assets of the grantor to determine whether any divesting or rearrangement of investments is required to ensure sufficient income for the expenditures that are going to be incurred.

Depending on the complexity of the assets and investments held by the grantor, the services of an investment manager or financial planner might be a prudent route. Each case will be different; the important thing to remember is that as an attorney you are not expected to be an expert in any or all fields related to financial management. It is not only acceptable for an attorney to request the assistance of relevant professionals when needed, it is expected and is part of the standard of care required of you acting prudently with care, diligence and skill, whether that be of an ordinary person managing their own affairs or that of a person whose business it is to manage the property of others. If you engage a professional to assist with the asset management of the grantor, the grantor will be responsible for the fees. However in most cases these fees are tax deductible.

Should the question of long-term living options become an issue, you as the attorney should find out, if you have not already done so, whether there is a power of attorney for personal care document and who has been appointed attorney under that document. In most cases, it is better to call in the attorney for personal care sooner rather than later, particularly in cases where the grantor is incapacitated. It can take a number of months to arrange placement in any type of senior living facility, even when the applicant is in good health, so this is an area where being proactive is absolutely necessary. It is important that the attorney for personal care knows if there is a power of attorney for property, because all of their decisions will hinge on the information that the attorney for property will be able to provide. Whether there is an attorney for personal care or a substitute decision-maker (discussed below), or whether the grantor is making their own long-term residential decisions, a close look at the financial position of the grantor will be absolutely necessary to ensure the optimum results can be achieved. This is one more reason to ensure that the month-to-month financial record keeping is kept up to date.

Should there be particular concerns about the ability of the grantor's financial resources, these should be brought to the attention of the attorney for personal care and family members and friends sooner rather than later, but only where the grantor is incapacitated or you as the attorney have reasonable grounds to believe so. If there is family, you will need to convene a family meeting to discuss the grantor's continuing welfare. If by some chance the family is not aware that a CPOAP exists, then the attorney might be more comfortable having the grantor's lawyer or another qualified third party contact the family members and facilitate at least the first meeting. It will need to be determined if family members are able to make financial or other contributions to cover any anticipated shortfall. It may be that the grantor is able to move in with a family member and not have to rely on accommodations provided by a third party.

If there are no supporters who can offer financial assistance, then there are a number of actions the attorney will have to take.

---

the book provides contact information to provincial health departments. A search of the Internet or the yellow pages using the words "elder care" will also provide a number of resources.

1) Ensure that the attorney for personal care is aware of this.

2) Determine whether the grantor is already receiving all the social assistance available, and if not, ascertain what forms are required to be completed to initiate any additional subsidy.

3) If the grantor is still residing in their home, investigate the possibility of establishing a reverse mortgage to enable the grantor to afford sufficient care within their home.

4) If there is no attorney for personal care, inquire of the grantor whether the grantor needs assistance to gather information of possible living arrangements, or whether there are any family members that might be able to assist with this task.

If the grantor is no longer able to make decisions regarding their health and living arrangements, and no power of attorney for personal care exists, then the attorney for property needs to be aware that there are legal provisions that cover the designation of a person who will take on the role of decision maker for personal care issues. In most provinces and territories of Canada, the spouse or a child (meeting certain requirements) will be designated the "substitute decision maker". However, if for whatever reasons the attorney is not comfortable with the way events are unfolding, the attorney should contact a lawyer familiar with this area of law for advice. Also, should there be no spouse or surviving children, the attorney for property needs to be aware that the tasks associated with personal care do not automatically attach to the attorney for property. In such cases, the attorney needs to contact a lawyer (preferably the same lawyer who prepared the CPOAP document, as they may have greater familiarity with the grantor's affairs) who will know how to proceed.

Predicting the Future Now: The Cash Flow Statement

As stated above, an essential aspect of helping someone to manage their day-to-day financial affairs also includes keeping an eye on the future and, from time to time, assessing the continued ability of their income to meet their living expenses. Depending on the amount of financial activity each month and the initial wealth of the grantor, this periodic assessment may never be a particularly onerous task, requiring little discipline or particular methodology. However, in situations where, for example, there are not significant investments or other income sources, and health-care costs are on the rise, it will be of particular importance that the attorney adopts a more systematic approach to this periodic assessment. How detailed the documentation needs to be that supports this review will depend on many factors such as the mix of income and expense items and to whom the document will be shown. The most likely document required in this particular case will be what accountants call a "cash flow statement." Do not be intimidated by the fact that this term is commonly used by professional accountants or business people. A cash flow statement is nothing more than a presentation of the money coming into a bank account and the money going out.

There are two approaches that can be taken to develop the cash flow, annually and monthly. The first approach is summarizing the income expected to be received during the next 12 months into the grantor's bank account and the expenses that are expected to be flowing out (Appendix X). Whether this exercise takes an hour or the better part of a morning will depend on the circumstances of the grantor. For someone living in a retirement or nursing home where many or most of their meals and living expenses are part of their monthly fee, the expense side of the cash flow statement will not take a lot of time. However, incidentals should not be ignored. For example, if the person has a generous nature and a large family and has been in the habit of recognizing birthdays, anniversaries and other special occasions such as graduations, the attorney will need to estimate a certain amount of money expected to be given as gifts. Annual donations, theatre excursions and trips to the hair salon are also items that need to be considered.

For individuals who are still living in their own home and are therefore still incurring property tax and other home ownership type expenses (hydro, oil, natural gas), the cash flow will likely take more time because there are seasonal adjustments to take into account, in addition to the number of different expenses that have to be accounted for. The requirement for seasonal adjustments introduces the need to consider adopting the second approach to a cash flow statement—that is, assessing cash needs on a month-to-month basis (Appendix XI). Preparing a month-to-month cash flow can be very time consuming, and thus it is recommended only for those who have a particular enjoyment working with numbers or who already have experience in this area. In this regard, if you are already keeping track of the grantor's finances with the aid of an accounting software package, the preparation of a cash flow statement could be only a few clicks away! This is because many software programs can generate cash flow statements (historic and future) based on the information you have recorded in the system. If you only have historical data entered (i.e., you have not recorded a budget), the system can still provide information that will help to create a cash flow forecast. You can use the historical data as a starting point and make adjustments for the coming period based on the current information you have gathered during your update sessions with the grantor (see Step 10). If the attorney concludes that such detail is required but is not able to take on the task due to either time or skill constraints, the solution is to seek out a professional accountant.

It may be that the accountant can prepare the cash flow statement initially and explain the methodology, the attorney can then continue with the revisions every quarter or whatever revision period has been set. Appendix X and XI contain cash flow templates for both approaches to assist the attorney in getting started.

Knowing that the record keeping of historic activities (income and expense) is complete and up to date will aid the attorney greatly in finishing this exercise of predicting the cash flow requirements of the grantor regardless of whether the attorney adopted the more simple (annual) approach or the more detailed (month to month) approach. This is because once a projection has been made of the grantor's cash flow requirements, the reasonableness of it will need to be considered in light of:

1) these historical results; and

2) knowledge of events that will impact the continuation of these results.

Essential Questions:

1) What debit and/or credit cards does the grantor still use, and what is the weekly/ monthly amount of cash withdrawal agreed upon for which no substantiation is required?

2) Has a safe place been determined to keep the debit/credit card(s)?

3) Has a note been made on the attorney's calendar to (at least) annually consider the necessity for the preparation of a cash flow statement?

Step 9—Keeping Track of Cash In/Cash Out

Keeping track of specific amounts of money coming in and going out of a bank account may seem like a daunting task. You may say to yourself, "I don't even balance my own cheque book; how am I going to balance Aunt May's?" Do not over-think this part of the process. This step provides basic instructions on how to approach this task. There are three main areas where financial activity is most prevalent: bank statements, investment accounts and insurance premiums.

Bank Statements

On Starting to Act as Attorney

➢ Review current activity at time of starting to act as attorney and determine the appropriateness of automatic withdrawals already established.

➢ Consider if there are any other payments that could be set up as automatic withdrawal.

➢ Cancel any automatic withdrawals that are not required.

➢ Identify regular deposits and their source (e.g., OAS, CPP).

On a Monthly Basis

➢ Reconcile all accounts. This means ensuring paper statements are received, downloading it from the Internet or ensuring the passbook is updated at the banking institution.

➢ At the very least, review and label all items with a description.

➢ Ensure all payments to third parties (e.g., telephone, credit card companies) are substantiated with hard copies of invoices/bills.

> Where an attorney for personal care is involved, ensure that all expenditures requested are supported by an invoice and/or statement from the service provider or supplier. Where an invoice or statement is not available, make a note that you requested such documentation, the date you requested it and the fact that you have been advised that there is no documentation.

> Review items on any credit card statement with the grantor to ensure all amounts are authorized.

> Ensure all receipts that were expected have been received (pension payments, OAS, CPP, interest, etc.).

> If it has been decided to use an accounting software package or similar recording tool, enter activity on a monthly basis to avoid the task becoming too overwhelming.

> **A word to the wise!**
>
> It is easier to jog people's short-term memories with successful results than long-term ones. Also, if receipts or invoices are missing, most companies can readily supply a copy when they are only going back into their records one to two months. Retrieving copies of archived records often incurs an administrative handling fee.

Investment Accounts

GICs, Term Deposits, Bonds, Interest-Earning Financial Instruments:

> Based on the information gathered in Step 2, you will need to ensure that amounts expected due to maturities or scheduled interest payments are received.

> Determine if there are bank accounts that have been specified to receive amounts upon maturity or to receive interest/dividend payments, and make any necessary changes to this information as a result of account closures decided in Step 6.

Insurance Premiums

Having completed Step 2 above, you will have a list of all insurance policies. Be sure that premium payments are being made according to the information gathered in Step 2. It is extremely important that premiums continue without interruption for any insurance policies that exist. This will ensure that when and if events take place that trigger the payout of a portion or all of the policy's face value, there will be no reduction in benefit entitlements or administrative irritations that might slow down the settlement process.

Essential Questions

1) Have automatic withdrawals been identified and cancelled if no longer required?

2) Has contact been made with the attorney for personal care (if one exists) and the requirements for documentation supporting expenditures related to personal care issues discussed?

3) Have maturity dates of investments and insurance policy anniversary dates been noted on a calendar to ensure timely action?

Step 10—Review of Activity with the Grantor and/or Grantor's Representative

This final step provides guidance on determining the frequency and agenda of review sessions with the grantor (or if the grantor is incapacitated, the attorney for personal care or guardian). There are three types of review sessions, each having a slightly different agenda.

1) **Regular**—monthly/quarterly/half-yearly; concerned with general matters, primarily dictated by the attorney's level of involvement and amount of activity to be reviewed.

2) **Annual**—concerned with year-end tax information requirements and cash flow management decisions for the coming year.

3) **Ad hoc**—concerned with specific matters that need addressing as they arise.

Each type will be discussed with a suggested agenda, although it is important for the attorney to customize their agendas to their own situations.

Regular Reviews

The frequency of these reviews will in part be determined by the level of your involvement and the amount of activity in the grantor's bank and investment accounts. However, it must be remembered that in the case of the incapacitated grantor, you have a duty to consult from time to time with not only the grantor's attorney for personal care, but also their supportive family members and friends and caregivers. As discussed in Chapter 4, the content of your discussions with others must be guided with regard to the best interests of the grantor. In addition, you also have an obligation to continue to consult with the incapacitated grantor and encourage them to participate, to the best of the grantor's ability, in your decisions about their property.

In addition to discussing health and general matters about their property affairs, the regular reviews might also involve:

1) Clarification of specific transactions that were unusual in nature and/or large enough that the attorney noticed when reviewing bank and/or investment statements.

2) A look at anticipated expenses and income for the period between the current review date and the next.

3) Confirming any changes to dependent's circumstances that will impact your responsibilities, and if changes are expected, make notes and make arrangements (if possible) to discuss financial implications with the dependent's attorney (or legal representative).

51

4) Investment maturities and renewal plans given current information known (e.g., monthly rent requirements) and new information as a result of completing this and the above items.

5) Review of a summary of cash in/cash out transactions.

6) Discussion of any changes to the level of your assistance and, if more assistance is agreed upon, confirmation that the current CPOAP document allows for this (i.e., it is a general CPOAP and not specific; if specific an updated document will be required).

7) Collecting all medical/drug receipts supporting expenditures that the grantor may have made since the last review and placing them in an envelope clearly marked "Medical and drug receipts for the year 20__" in anticipation of year-end tax preparation requirements. Such receipts that you already have due to your assisting the grantor during this period will already be in this envelope. Collecting these receipts throughout the year will significantly reduce lost slips.

For an idea of how frequently regular reviews should take place, take the situation where the attorney is making most of the investing decisions while sharing access to the grantor's bank accounts for day-to-day cash requirements—that is, both parties accessing the account(s) regularly. In this scenario, it is recommended that monthly meetings take place to review all transactions and to confirm that they are all properly identified as being authorized by either the grantor or the attorney.

If the attorney is performing a more restricted role, perhaps doing physical banking for the grantor on a periodic basis, then a quarterly or semi-annually review might be adequate.

Every situation will be different. What is important is that there is some kind of regularly scheduled review. This discipline will ensure that the record keeping is kept up to date and that any crucial information is identified as missing as soon as possible. As mentioned in Step 9, it is much easier to follow up on items that are two months old than items that are six months or older.

If there have been two or more attorneys acting jointly and severally, all records should be amalgamated into a central record no less frequently than the review period. Even if the review is carried out with each attorney individually, a consolidated picture should be available. Ensuring this is done will have three benefits when the annual review takes place.

1) Accumulating the information required for the tax return preparation will be efficient and hassle-free with limited follow-up required for missing documentation.

2) If a cash flow projection is required, information required for the first step—that of considering historical cash position—will be readily available.

3) Preparing for the annual review will require minimal time because records for most of the preceding year have already been amalgamated and the presence of supporting documentation has been confirmed.

Annual Review

Regardless of how frequent the regularly scheduled reviews take place, you will want to ensure that there is one review session when the primary purpose is twofold:

1) To ensure all the information required for the tax return preparation is available; and

2) To provide an opportunity to close out the previous year (consolidate the accounting records and supporting documentation for the past year) and update cash flow management requirements.

Depending on the amount of activity and information being reviewed at the regularly scheduled session, this annual review might be included at the one taking place during late March or early April. By this time, most of the tax slips should have been received for the previous year. Specifically, the annual review should:

1) Include a review of the contents of the envelope that contains the medical and drug receipts for the previous year to ensure all obvious receipts are there;

2) Determine if all tax slips have been received. Using a master list of bank accounts/securities/investments (Appendix VII) to help determine whether all slips have been received, place the slips into envelope marked "Tax Receipts—20__". Also, be sure to check that receipts have been received for charitable donations made; and

3) Ensure that all adjusted cost base (ACB) information and substantiation for all investments sold during the year has been received from relevant sources. (See "Investments" in Chapter 6 for a more detailed discussion.)

All T4 and T5 slips are required to be issued by February 28 for the preceding tax year, so these should all be received by mid-March. Unfortunately T3 slips often arrive well into the month of April. However, knowing specifically which ones are outstanding will help cut down any unnecessary follow-up work. Having both medical-related receipts and investment/income tax slips in their respective envelopes will mean that a significant amount of the supporting documentation required for income tax return preparation is accounted for. This will make the tax return preparation process much easier and minimize the opportunity for mistakes. If an accountant prepares the return, this level of organization on the attorney's part will also help to keep the fees reasonable. Note also that you do not have to wait until you have all the slips before providing the accountant with the above information. While you do want to avoid constant trips to the accountant with "one more" slip, it is certainly reasonable to provide 90 percent of the information as soon as possible with a note of what is missing.

This annual review also provides a good motivation to bring the past year to a close. This will include such tasks as ensuring:

> ### A Word to the Wise!
>
> Taking notes of the review sessions is an absolute necessity. As a minimum, the details should include the following:
>
> - When was the meeting held?
> - Where was the meeting held?
> - Who was there?
> - What was discussed?
> - What records were specifically reviewed?
> - What actions are required as a result of discussions?
> - Who is responsible for completing each action?
> - When is each action to be complete?

1) Any necessary consolidation of records has occurred where there has been more than one person involved with different bank and investment accounts. This will be the case when there is more than one attorney actively involved and/or the grantor is still capable and thus contributing to the activity in their accounts.

2) All outstanding items are adequately resolved, including obtaining any missing documentation, or a decision that enough effort has been made to obtain it, and a note has been made for the file explaining what was done and that no further time will be spent trying to get substantiation.

This is also the ideal time to take a look at the cash position of the grantor for the next twelve months (i.e., doing a cash flow projection as outlined in Step 8 earlier in this chapter).

Ad hoc Reviews

These reviews may take place from time to time, in addition to the regular schedule of reviews. Examples of when an ad hoc review might become necessary are:

➤ A sudden change in circumstances of either the grantor or dependent;

➤ An unplanned change in market conditions or legislation that necessitate a re-thinking of investment strategy; or

➤ It is realized that something that should have been discussed at the last review was overlooked, and it is preferable not to wait until the next session to address it.

Regardless of the type of review, the grantor may request that a third party be present. Such requests on the part of the grantor should be welcomed by the attorney because it is another indication of the attorney's willingness to be transparent.

It is quite conceivable that there are situations where the activity is so regular and minimal that the review will happen once a year, as part of the tax return preparation process. Whatever is decided, be sure that a record is made of the frequency agreed upon and the identification and contact details of any third party who the grantor has requested be present at the review sessions. You should also confirm with third parties their willingness and what notice period they need when being reminded of an upcoming review session.

No matter what type of review is held, ensure there is acknowledgement from all parties present of what was reviewed and discussed. Such acknowledgement can be initials and date on the bank and investment statements, on the written record made of the meeting or on the agenda prepared for that particular meeting. This will provide solid evidence that the reviews are being undertaken as agreed in respect of frequency, as well as issues covered.

If the grantor has become incapacitated, a regular review should take place with the guardian or the person who has POA of personal care or the statutory substitute decision-maker. This will provide the opportunity for the two of you to work together to effectively manage the affairs of the estate in the best interests of the grantor. Indeed, the attorney for property has a duty to the incapacitated grantor to manage the grantor's "property in a manner consistent with decisions concerning the person's personal care that are made by the person who has authority to make those decisions."[6] For example, an attorney for property does not decide into which care facility the grantor will be placed; that decision is one for the attorney for personal care or substitute decision-maker (unless the attorney for property is also the attorney for personal care or substitute decision-maker). However, the decision-maker will need to know what the financial resources are of the grantor in order to make this decision.

Essential Questions

1) What review frequency has been determined?

2) Has the grantor requested another person be present at these meetings, and if so, who?

3) If more than one attorney, what has been decided regarding the amalgamation of financial records prior to review with grantor?

Chapter Recap

There may appear to be a lot of details required to complete these ten steps. Just how much time and effort it will take to move through the steps will depend on three main factors:

1) The ability of the grantor to assist.

2) The size and nature of the grantor's estate—that is, how many bank and investment accounts exist, whether the grantor owned a business, whether the grantor is a partner in a partnership, etc.

3) How organized and methodical you are when recording your findings and actions as each of the 10 steps are considered.

To assist the reader in moving through these ten steps with ease, a checklist has been provided comprised of three essential questions to be asked and answered. For each step it is recommended that the remarks column be used to list any relevant contact information of someone who is assisting you to acquire a particular document (e.g., indicate whether an investment manager is assisting with information on the investment portfolio). If more space is needed, use the back side or attach a new sheet of paper to the checklist.

---

[6] *Substitute Decisions Act, 1992, s.* 32(1.2).

Many will find Step 2, "Gathering the Information and Making the Inventory," to be the most onerous step. From the number of items listed in Table 2, at first glance it might seem too big a task to start collecting the particulars on so many items. However, most people will only have a few of these items, and so the reader is encouraged not to despair. Chapter 6 offers even more assistance, presenting each item with a brief description of what supporting documentation might look like and where you might find this documentation if the grantor is unable to assist you.

Checklist for Chapter 5

Possible entries to Status: Done, Yes, No, O/S (outstanding), N/A (not applicable), See Remarks

STEP	STATUS	REMARKS
1. Obtain the CPOAP Document and Will		
a) Has the original CPOAP document and a copy of the will been obtained and reviewed?		
b) Have three notarized copies been obtained and filed?		
c) Have the contact details of the lawyer who prepared the CPOAP been recorded and filed?		
2. Gathering the Information and Making an Inventory		
a) If it is a general CPOAP, has Table 3 been completed?		
b) Have any assets or liabilities been identified with which you are not sure what to do? (Record them in Remarks column.)		
c) Have you contacted a lawyer or accountant for advice with respect to those items identified in b)?		
3. Safety Deposit Box(es) (SDB)		
a) Have the number of SDBs been determined?		
b) If more than one, have contents been amalgamated and an inventory list prepared?		

a) If no SDB exists, has it been decided to obtain one? If no, why?		
4. Past Tax Returns		
a) Is a copy of the most recent tax return filed with the CRA available?		
b) Has contact details of the preparer of the most recent tax return prepared been ascertained?		
c) IIas appropriate notification been made to the CRA—either a copy of the CPOAP or Form T1013?		
5. Informing the Businesses		
a) Have all businesses indentified in Step 2 been contacted?		
b) Are there any businesses that require their own copy of the CPOAP document? If so, list them in Remarks column.		
c) Has the "List of People/Companies to Contact" (Template 2, Appendix VIII) been completed?		
6. Bank Account Amalgamations		
a) Based on your knowledge of the grantor's affairs, have all bank and investment accounts been identified?		
b) Have amalgamations of accounts been discussed with the grantor, agreed and documented?		
c) Has a trust account arrangement been discussed with the grantor, and has necessary action been agreed upon and documented?		
7. Arrangements Outside the Activity of the Bank Statement		
a) Do any arrangements outside the activity of the bank statement exist?		
b) If so, have the specifics been documented, agreed with the grantor and signed by the grantor and other person(s) involved?		

c) Are there any conditions or time restrictions as part of the arrangement, and if so, what are they?		
8. Cash Management Decisions		
a) What debit and/or credit cards does the grantor still use, and what is the weekly/monthly amount of cash withdrawal agreed upon for which no substantiation is required?		
b) Has a safe place been determined to keep the debit/credit card(s)? (Record location in Remarks column.)		
c) Has a note been made on the attorney's calendar to annually consider the necessity for the preparation of a cash flow statement?		
9. Keeping Track of Cash In/Cash Out		
a) Have automatic withdrawals been identified and cancelled if no longer appropriate?		
b) Has contact been made with the attorney for personal care (if one exists) and the requirements for documentation supporting expenditures related to personal care issues discussed?		
c) Have maturity dates of investments and insurance policy anniversary dates been noted on a calendar to ensure timely action?		
10. Review of Activity with the Grantor and/or Grantor's Representative		
a) What review frequency has been determined? (Record in Remarks column.)		
b) Has the grantor requested another person be present at these meetings, and if so, who? (Record name, relationship to grantor and contact details in Remarks column.)		
c) If more than one attorney, what has been decided regarding the amalgamation of financial records prior to review with grantor?		

Chapter 6

Preparing the Inventory: The Foundation of Financial Record Keeping

When the grantor becomes incapacitated, or when you as attorney have *reasonable grounds*[1] to believe that this is so, a significant event has happened in your role as attorney that requires you to become fully informed of all matters touching upon the financial affairs of the grantor. In addition, you now have an obligation to keep accounts and records starting from your first transaction on behalf of the incapacitated grantor. The keeping of those accounts begins with an inventory of all the grantor's property, both assets and liabilities. This initial inventory is not only the means by which the attorney gains an overall picture of the financial circumstances of the grantor, but it also serves as the baseline from which you and others will measure your stewardship of the grantor's affairs. In those situations where the grantor is still active in the management of their property, this chapter will provide a comprehensive list of items, the existence, physical location and supporting documentation of which, should be confirmed by the grantor.

Similarly as an estate trustee, you have an obligation to ensure that a full accounting takes place. This will begin with collecting a list of all assets and liabilities existing at the date of death and determining a value as at that date. Although this chapter is written from the perspective of the grantor/attorney relationship, the estate trustee need only exchange references to "grantor" with "deceased" and likewise, references to "attorney" can be replaced with "estate trustee" and the contents of this chapter will provide the assistance necessary to ensure successful completion of the estate's inventory.

The ease at which a comprehensive list of a person's assets and liabilities is accumulated will depend in a large part on the mental health of the grantor. This is one good reason to complete this review of assets and liabilities as soon as you are aware that you have been appointed attorney, even if your role is primarily one of minor assistance. If the grantor's mental health deteriorates quickly, and you find yourself managing their affairs without their assistance, you will know exactly what you are managing without having to worry about anything coming to light long after it should have been addressed. It is quite possible that if the person has been wise and thoughtful enough to have a CPOAP document put in place, they have also prepared a will. In such a case, it is possible that the grantor has prepared

---

[1]   What constitutes "reasonable grounds" is dependent upon the factual circumstances of each case. Generally speaking, however, reasonable grounds would be based upon evidence of the grantor's behaviour that is a departure from their normal behaviour.

a list of assets to determine what money and/or property might be left for distribution to beneficiaries and/or charities.

Remember that you may be the only person other than the grantor who is aware that a CPOAP exists or that you are named as attorney. Thus, you may not have the freedom to ask family members or business partners to fill in missing information. Be sure that you have confirmed with the grantor whether it is okay for you to confer with other parties to collect this information. Depending on the situation, it may be prudent to have the grantor make a list of those individuals they wish to have excluded from any such fact finding. Alternatively, a list of persons they approve of may be the way to go.

One of the most important aspects of preparing the inventory is to remember that when collecting this information, you must be able to substantiate the values collected. For example, if the grantor indicates ownership of an RSP mutual fund account with "around $500,000 in it," you need to be able to verify the exact amount. In doing so, you will take the information provided by the grantor as the starting point and obtain the exact value by obtaining a copy of the most recent activity statement either from the grantor themselves or directly from the mutual fund company. Keep in mind that if any starting values—that is, the value of assets at the time you start to act as attorney for the incapable grantor—are ever called into question, the attorney's best answer will be to show documentation from an impartial third party. If after reasonable attempts to obtain a proper valuation of an item, e.g., a piece of artwork such as a painting, there simply does not seem to be official substantiation, be sure to document what you did to obtain documentation and, when none could be obtained, what methodology you used to arrive at your starting value.

If you are in doubt about whether to ask a question, do not doubt, always ask! Remember that probably the most important reason the grantor picked you was for your honesty and the belief that you would do a thorough job. Asking for clarification or information is simply going to provide further assurance to the grantor that they have chosen the correct person for the task.

The following list of common assets and liabilities is in alphabetical order, and each has been identified as either an asset (A), a liability (L) or both. The important thing to keep in mind as you gather this information is simply to do your best. If you suspect that there is missing information but cannot jog the grantor's memory to ascertain the particulars, make a note of this; it is possible that it will come to light when you are looking for something else. Templates have been provided after the discussion of each item, and you will also find them in Appendix IX. The template in each section provides a specific checklist for that item, highlighting the most important information you need to determine. Do not hesitate to add additional information that you think might become relevant. If unsure whether a piece of information is relevant to your specific situation or may become relevant down the line, it is better to make note of it now than find you have to go searching for it later. Also, if you find yourself using the services of a professional, whether it be an accountant, financial planner or lawyer, the more information you are able to provide them, the better they will be able to assist you.

Annuity (A)

An annuity is a contract between two parties, the purchaser (in this case, the grantor) and seller (a financial institution such as a bank or insurance company). The grantor will have made a large payment to purchase the annuity and in exchange will receive a predetermined amount on a regular basis, usually monthly. They will show up in the grantor's bank statement at the same time each month.

An annuity can be held within a registered retirement plan as well as an unregistered retirement plan (see RRSP/RRIF below for a discussion of registered and unregistered plans). There are three types of annuities: fixed term, life annuity and prescribed. If the grantor has a fixed term annuity, it will be important to know when the term expires. This information will be necessary as you review the grantor's long-term cash sources and requirements.

An annuity, if one exists, will have been purchased from any number of financial brokerage companies and financial institutions such as TD Waterhouse, Desjardins Financial Security, RBC Insurance or Scotiabank. This is not a complete list, but it gives you the idea of the types of companies with which you might be dealing.

The issuing companies will provide a T5 at the end of each calendar year. The T5 will show how much was received, what portion was interest versus a return of capital (i.e., a return of a portion of the money originally paid to purchase the annuity) and what if any taxes have been withheld and already remitted to the Canada Revenue Agency on the grantor's behalf. Thus, reviewing the most recent tax return will be a way to confirm the existence of any annuities.

Template 4—Appendix IX

Is annuity income received?

Is the annuity registered or non-registered?

What financial company is it received from?

What is the identification/account number?

Name and contact of account manager:

Is the annuity a fixed term? If so, when does the term end?

Have you made a note in your personal diary of the end date of this income stream to ensure the cash flow assessments properly reflect the cash available to the grantor?

Bank accounts (A)

Bank accounts include savings and cheque, interest-bearing and non-interest-bearing, as well as any accounts that may be held jointly with another party (either a private individual or by virtue of a partnership agreement).

A decision will be required for accounts that are held jointly when the second person is not the attorney. Any joint account held by both the grantor and someone who is not the attorney should be specifically documented and closed if no longer considered necessary in the circumstances. In most cases the preference will be to have such accounts closed. This will avoid any confusion over ownership and entitlements upon the death of the grantor.

However, as discussed earlier (Chapter 5, Step 6), there may be legitimate reasons that a joint account should stay active. If so, ensure that the reason is documented, and at least on an annual basis, make enquiries about the continued need for the account to stay active. File documentation in the sleeve labelled "Bank Account Information" in your "Accounts and Records" binder/box.

Reviewing the most recent tax return is a good place to look to confirm whether you have identified all the bank accounts. Remember that although T5s are only issued by financial institutions when more than $50 is earned on any given account, all interest income needs to be declared as earned income on a person's annual tax return. Thus it is possible that you will have more bank accounts identified than you have T5s.

The existence of foreign bank accounts should also be considered. It is not uncommon for people who travel frequently to the United States to have a bank account at a US banking institution. If the grantor has retained strong ties to the country where they were born, either by frequent visits or extensive family connections, an account held at a bank in that foreign locale could also exist. You will need to ensure that all details are known with respect to these accounts.

Template 5—Appendix IX

Account Number:
Bank/Trust Company:
Street address:
Mailing address (if different from street):
Phone number:
Fax number:
Account manager:
Direct phone line of account manager:
E-mail address:
Name of account manager's boss:
Alternative contact, if account manager unavailable:
Value at Date of commencing to act as attorney:

Business or Partnership Agreements (A and/or L)

Ascertain whether there is any business or partnership agreements still in effect. Even if there is no current activity, as a result of the agreement(s) existing, the attorney should endeavour to obtain a copy and place it in the documentation file. The attorney should also read the agreement to become familiar with any potential liability that may become due or revenue streams that might exist, either currently or expected to begin at some future point in time.

When a formal business agreement exists, it is important to determine whether it includes or refers to a Shareholders' Agreement or Buy/Sell Agreement. If there is a separate agreement, ensure you obtain a copy of this and treat it the same way as you treat the general business agreement.

If the grantor or deceased person's business affairs does not include the holding of private company shares (see Shares—Private Company), some or all of their business affairs may have been done within a legal entity known as a partnership. There are three main types of partnership in Canada: general, limited and limited liability. Briefly, they can be described as follows:

General partnership is one in which all partners manage the business and are 100 percent personally liable for its debts. That is, if expenses of the business are in excess of the money coming into the business from sales, each partner is personally responsible for ensuring all amounts owing are paid.

Limited partnership (LP) is one where some partners choose to give up their right to take part in managing the business in exchange for limiting their liability for the partnership's debts. That is, they would not be personally responsible for sharing equally in such debts.

Limited liability partnership (LLP) is one in which all partners have some degree of limited personal responsibility for debts created by the business.

Whatever type exists, there will be a document, signed by all partners, that sets out clearly what type of partnership it is along with any exceptions or limitations to each partner's right to share in the profits and losses of the business. Profits and losses include income earned and expenses incurred not only from the day to day business activities but also from any unusual, non-recurring activities. An example is if the partnership has legal action taken against it. Legal fees incurred and amounts owing if the case is lost will be expected to be shared according to the terms set out in the partnership agreement. Alternatively, any money received as a result of a legal case would be shared.

Contact information for all the persons who have signed any such agreement should be ascertained and filed with the agreement. It might also be a good idea to determine the relationship of the individuals (e.g., father/son; brothers-in-law). This might be useful information in the future if relationships start to sour, the attorney will be better able to understand the situation. The attorney should also document current addresses of the business/partnership itself and the business lawyer and accountant.

Template 6—Appendix IX

Does a business or partnership agreement exist?

Has a copy been located and either filed with the attorney or with the grantor's important papers in a secure place?

Indicate where it is filed:

Is the business/partnership still active?

If still active, address of the place of business:

Are there any potential liabilities that need to be planned for when determining the grantor's cash requirements? If so, describe and estimate amount if possible:

Are there any potential windfalls that should be considered when determining the grantor's cash requirements? If so, describe and estimate amount if possible:

Who are the other parties that signed the agreement? Provide contact details for each person:

What are the relationships between the parties who signed the agreement?

Name and contact information of the business/partnership's lawyer:

Name and contact information of the business/partnership's accountant:

Contents of Grantor's House, Condo and/or Cottage (A)

The contents of the grantor's house, condo and/or cottage need to be inventoried to determine if there is anything of noteworthy value. Examples of items that might have monetary value are antiques, paintings and other artwork (prints and sculptures), jewellery and collections such as stamps or coins. The nature of the contents is most often called "personal property" to distinguish it from "real property" (i.e., real estate). These items will be comprised of both items specifically identified in the grantor's will as well as items that need to be recorded as a matter of taking a complete inventory.

Reading the will or discussing specific plans with the grantor regarding the disbursement of their worldly goods will give you a good starting point in determining what needs to go on this list. Although discussing this with the grantor might seem a little ghoulish, be assured that as they get older, most people generally feel better about their future (as limited as it may be) when they know their possessions are going to the "right" person.

Depending on the health and memory of the grantor (and remembering if there are any family members the grantor has told you not to talk to), you may have to ask family members for assistance to determine whether your list is complete. The earlier in the process you do this, the better it will be should something not be there that a family member is expecting to be. The more time that has passed, the greater the suspicion might be that you are responsible for the item not being present.

Assigning values to items such as these might be tedious and difficult. In some cases, the grantor may remember the cost. In the case of original artwork, some grantors may even have the receipt tucked away somewhere among their important papers. Some examples of content items and possible sources to investigate for valuation purposes are provided below.

➢ Collections of memorabilia, such as comic books, vinyl LPs, vintage lace: Specific shops that deal in that item or related items

➢ Stamp or coin collection: A specialist such as well-known stamp or coin collector

➢ Art work: Auction house, galleries and art shops

➤ Antiques: Auction house, antique shops

➤ Jewellery: Auction house, antique shops, long-established jewellery shops

➤ Automobiles: Dealerships; Kelley Blue Book

➤ Boats: Marina, boat seller

If there are items for which you simply cannot come up with a reasonable estimate, document what attempts you make and either make an estimate based on what you do know or simply state that you decline to assign a value. It may be that the item has no commercial value but rather has sentimental value and is intended to be given to a particular beneficiary of the grantor's will. A review of the grantor's will can provide this information and should be made part of your documentation.

Template 7—Appendix IX

Use the chart below to list the contents of the grantor's residences:

Item Description	Location	Estimated Value	Beneficiary (if applicable)

Credit cards (L)

You will need to determine what stores and/or financial institutions have issued credit cards to the grantor. You and the grantor may want to consider reducing the number of active cards to one. It is most likely easiest to have it issued by the same financial institution where the active current account is.

An important question to ask and have answered is, "Who has access to the credit cards?" If the grantor is still in their own home with various people coming in to assist them, it will be important that the grantor and attorney are clear about the use of the cards and the need for a regular and timely review of transactions. (See Step 8 in Chapter 5 for a more detailed discussion.)

Template 8—Appendix IX

Have all credit cards been listed on the summary sheet found in Appendix VII?

Does anyone other than you and the grantor have access to these cards?

If so, who and for what purpose?

What system has been agreed upon for keeping track of receipts that support purchases charged to the cards?

Dependants (L)

Ensure that if there are any dependents on either side of the grantor's age, you inquire about the financial resources of these individuals: What pensions or other sources of revenue do they have? What are their monthly living costs? With the rising proportion of Canada's population living past their 80s, it is not inconceivable that you may be asked to assist someone in their 60s with their financial affairs and yet they still have a 90-year old parent living. And on the other side, people with various forms of disabilities are living longer lives also. Thus a 60-year-old parent may very well have a 40-year-old dependent child. Due to your relationship with the grantor, you will most likely be aware of a dependent, although perhaps not the financial implications. A review of bank statements will help to fill this potential knowledge gap. However be sure to ask the question outright. It may be that currently, the elderly parent or young dependent need no financial assistance, but down the road they will. You need to be aware of this now.

If an elderly parent exists, is there a CPOAP in place, and if so, who is the attorney? It may be sensible to ascertain the person's name and whether both grantors are willing to have you discuss their respective financial affairs openly with the objective of ensuring both their futures are adequately planned for.

Another possible situation is that the grantor is an attorney of either an elderly parent or other person. If this is the case, you will want to discuss with both parties (your grantor and their grantor), and perhaps their lawyers as well, what alternative arrangements have been made for substituting another attorney for the elderly parent.

Template 9—Appendix IX

List any dependents of the grantor, include their relationship to the grantor (e.g., child, parent, aunt):

Describe the extent of the dependence (e.g., daughter with Down's Syndrome, lives in group home during week but comes home on the weekends and holidays; father is in nursing home):

Is there a CPOAP document in place for any of the dependents?

Has contact been made with the attorney identified in such document?

Record the contact details of the attorney:

Is the grantor acting as attorney for another party?

If so, record name and contact information:

Has contact been made with that person and/or their lawyer to discuss alternative arrangements?

Insurance policies (A)

Most common insurance policies are for such items as business/partnership, car, condo, cottage, critical illness, disability, health, house, life and pets. In dealing with insurance you will need to follow three basic steps.

1) Ascertain what insurance policies currently exist.

2) Determine whether they are still required.

3) Ensure premiums are kept current for those policies determined to continue.

You should make a note on your own personal calendar of the renewal and premium payment dates. This will help jog your memory at specific times during the year to make sure policies remain in effect with no disruption of benefits.

Template 10—Appendix IX

Business/Partnership Insurance

Insurance Broker:
Insurance Company:
Policy Number:
Period of Coverage
Premium Due: $ (monthly, quarterly or annually)

Car Insurance

Insurance Broker:
Insurance Company:

Policy Number:
Period of Coverage:
Premium Due: $ (monthly, quarterly or annually)

Condo Insurance

Insurance Broker:
Insurance Company:
Policy Number:
Period of Coverage:
Premium Due: $ (monthly, quarterly or annually)

Cottage Insurance

Insurance Broker:
Insurance Company:
Policy Number:
Period of Coverage:
Premium Due: $ (monthly, quarterly or annually)

Critical Illness Insurance (Private or Group)

Insurance Broker:
Insurance Company:
Policy Number:
Period of Coverage:
Premium Due: $ (monthly, quarterly or annually0
Benefits Provided:

Disability Insurance (Private or Group)

Insurance Broker:
Insurance Company:
Policy Number:
Period of Coverage:
Premium Due: $ (monthly, quarterly or annually)
Benefits Provided:

Health Insurance

Insurance Broker:
Insurance Company:
Policy Number:
Period of Coverage:
Premium Due: $ (monthly, quarterly, or annually)
Benefits Provided:

House Insurance

Insurance Broker:
Insurance Company:
Policy Number:
Period of Coverage:
Premium Due: $ (monthly, quarterly or annually)

Life Insurance

Insurance Broker:
Insurance Company:
Policy Number:
Period of Coverage:
Premium Due: $ (monthly, quarterly or annually)
Beneficiaries and Contact Information:

Pet Insurance

Insurance Broker:
Insurance Company:
Policy Number:
Period of Coverage:
Premium Due: $ (monthly, quarterly or annually)

Investments (A)

GICs, Term Deposits, Bonds and Other Types

For the typical Canadian resident, the most common investments are bond, GICs, term deposits, mutual funds/income trusts and shares. Less common are limited partnerships, mineral titles and leases, mortgage-backed securities and real estate. Often these investments are made to provide a nest egg for one's retirement. Investments held for this reason are commonly referred to as retirement savings plan and can be registered or non-registered. (See the section on RRSP/RRIF for a more detailed discussion.) There are two ways in which investments can be handled.

1) Self-managed fund

2) Managed fund

Self-Managed Fund

The self-managed fund is when the grantor manages one or more of these investments. They do their homework regarding the various investing options, decide what to invest in and proceed to organize the purchase, sale or reinvestment themselves. If this is the case with your grantor's current investments, you need to determine how they receive the income. There are three different ways in which income earned from these investments will show up in the grantor's financial activity. Table 3 presents a summary of ten common types of investments and indicates how income earned (interest or dividends) is likely to be received by the grantor. This table will help to provide the attorney with assistance in knowing whether they have accounted for all the investment income.

Table 4—Investment Types and How Income Will Be Received

Description	Income Received by Cheque	Income Received by Direct Deposit	Income Rolled into Value of Investment
Bonds	Possibly	Possibly	Possibly
GICs	Possibly	Possibly	Possibly
Income Trusts	Possibly	Possibly	Possibly
Limited Partnership	Possibly	Possibly	Possibly
Mineral Titles and Leases	Possibly	Possibly	No
Mortgage-Backed Securities	Possibly	Possibly	Not likely
Mutual Funds	Not likely	Not likely	Most likely
Real Estate	Possibly	Possibly	No
Shares—Public	Possibly	Possibly	Possibly, if dividend issued is in the form of shares, not cash
Term Deposits	Possibly	Possibly	Possibly

□or e□ample, if you know that the grantor has money invested in a □□□, you need to determine whether the interest is being paid by che□ue or direct deposit (and if so into which bank account), or whether the interest is being rolled over on each anniversary and reinvested. □ncome earned on an investment in shares will be in the form of dividends□if cash, it will be received either by che□ue or direct deposit into a bank account. Thus if you know the person owns shares in □□□ □ompany, and they have not received a che□ue or bank deposit in a while, you will need to find out whether a dividend was issued. □ee the section □□hares□ □ublic□below for more guidance on finding out information on known or suspected shareholdings.

Managed Fund

□ managed fund is when a person (the grantor) works together with a professional brokerage house, such as T□ □aterhouse, □es□ardin □inancial □ecurity, □□□ □nvestments, □□□□ □ood □undy, □□□, □chieva □inancial, □utlook or □ anulife □nvestments. The individual still makes decisions about the overall investment strategy but relies heavily on the e□pertise of the account manager and the support staff at the brokerage house. The grantor's account manager should be able to provide a complete list of investments held and all the information with respect to these investments.

Regardless of whether the investments are registered or non-registered, self-managed or managed through a brokerage house, you will need to ascertain relevant information for each investment held. The precise information required is identified below after a brief description of each type. Once you obtain all the detailed information, you can create a summary list using Appendix VII.

Bonds

Bonds can be issued from a number of different sources. The most common are:

Government of Canada
Federal Crown Corporation
Provincial
Provincial Crown Corporations
Corporate (e.g., utility companies)

When determining whether the grantor may have bonds but has forgotten, looking at their last tax return should assist you. While bonds may be for a 5—or 10-year term, interest is often paid semi-annually or annually, and if so, the issuing body will also issue a T5 slip each calendar year.

Reference sites for information on some bonds are:

Canada Savings Bonds: www.csb.gc.ca
British Columbia: www.fin.gov.bc.ca/PT/dmb/bcSavingsBonds.shtml
Alberta: www.capitalbonds.alberta.ca/index.html
Saskatchewan: www.finance.gov.sk.ca/ssb/
Manitoba: www.gov.mb.ca/finance/treasury/builderbonds.html
Ontario Savings Bonds: www.ontariosavingsbonds.com
Quebec: www.epq.gouv.qc.ca/english/principal.jsp
Prince Edward Island: www.peienergysavings.pe.ca/peienergy.php?page=faq
Northwest Territories: www.nt.gov.au/ntt/tcorp/bonds.shtml

For provincial bonds, if there is no specific website devoted to bonds, the best place to start is with the specific provincial or territory website. The home page will have a link to "Ministries and Crown Corporations," or similar wording. If you are limited in your Internet skills, you will be able to find a contact phone number to call for clarification or instructions on how to locate any missing documentation with respect to bonds held by the grantor.

Template 11—Appendix IX

Part of registered or non-registered plan?

Self-managed or brokerage house?

If brokerage house, which one?

Name and contact of brokerage house account manager:

Institution/Municipality/Company:

Maturity date:

Are interest payments:

a) Received by cheque quarterly/semi annually/annually/upon maturity

b) Direct deposit (frequency, to what account—current account or brokerage cash account)

c) Rolled into investment

Current instructions on file:

GICs, Term Deposits

GICs and term deposits are similar to each other. The main difference is that GICs are usually obtained when the investor is investing for longer periods of time, and interest is received at periodic intervals during the life of the investment. Often with term deposits, the interest is paid only upon maturity.

You will want to inquire as to any current instructions already on file and make a note of these. For example, there may already be instructions to roll over the GIC along with any interest paid on each anniversary date of the item coming due. These instructions may have to be altered in light of decisions made about existing bank accounts and whether any are to be closed. You will also want to consider these automatic rollovers in light of cash requirements anticipated by the grantor as a result of your own cash flow exercise and/or recent review session with the grantor.

Template 11—Appendix IX

Part of registered or non-registered plan?

Self-managed or brokerage house?

If brokerage house, which one?

Name and contact of brokerage house account manager:

Institution/Municipality/Company:

Maturity date:

Are interest payments:

a) Received by cheque quarterly/semi annually/annually/upon maturity

b) Direct deposit (frequency, to what account—current account or brokerage cash account)

c) Rolled into investment

Current instructions on file:

Limited Partnerships

A person might invest in a business venture by becoming a "limited partner" in a partnership. Such an arrangement might exist when the grantor or deceased person has contributed or agreed to contribute a certain sum of money to a particular business project. Their liability, should the business venture not be successful, is limited to the amount the grantor contributed. There should be a formal document substantiating the amount of the investment and terms dealing with such items as payment dates of further contributions (if any), payback of amounts contributed, share of business net profits, how amounts will be paid to the investor, events that would terminate the agreement and what is to happen in the event that the agreement is terminated.

Although it is anticipated that the grantor or deceased person entered into this partnership with the expectation of making money, depending on how speculative the nature of the business venture is, this type of investment could prove to provide no income stream.

If such an investment has been made, it is important that the contract/investment document is read carefully to determine what the worst-case scenario is with respect to receiving any return on this investment as well as having the original invested amounts returned. This type of information will need to be incorporated into the cash flow statements and taken into consideration when determining the value of someone's assets.

Template 11—Appendix IX

Part of registered or non-registered plan?

Self-managed or brokerage house?

If brokerage house, which one?

Name and contact of brokerage house account manager:

Operating name of partnership:

Main contact name at business:

Phone number of main contact:

E-mail address of main contact:

Initial investment amount:

Further amounts to be contributed:

Form of revenue stream: percentage of net income, dividend, other:

Date(s) return of contributions or income expected to be received:

Mineral Titles and Leases

If the mine is producing income from its activities, this type of investment represents a right of the holder to receive a share of this income. Given the speculative nature of this type of investment, it is not uncommon for it to be a number of years from date of purchase before any income is received.

It is important to remember that when valuing this investment, consideration will have to be given to how long it has been held and, in that time, how much income has been received. If no income has been received, then it is questionable whether this investment has any value at this time. In such a case, a nominal value of $1.00 would be assigned to it. Determining the fair market value (FMV) in cases where income has historically been received regularly will require the assistance of a professional who specializes in valuing this type of investment, because there are a number of factors that could be considered important. For example, one would need to inquire about:

> ➢ whether production at the mine is expected to continue at its given rate or is scheduled for shutdown due to dwindling reserves;

> ➢ what specific mineral is being mined and what is the price on the world market; and

> ➢ whether there has been any active trading of these paper investments during the last 12 months.

While all this information is available to the public, a professional will be able to ascertain this type of information easily and assist you in determining a FMV that is realistic and based on reasonable assumptions after considering relevant facts.

Template 11—Appendix IX

Part of registered or non-registered plan?

Self-managed or brokerage house?

If brokerage house, which one?

Name and contact of brokerage house account manager:

Name of mining project:

Location of project:

Date purchased:

Amount invested:

Date of last income receipt:

Amount received:

Mortgage-Backed Securities

This type of investment is not as common as the others discussed. If an individual has made such an investment, there is usually a significant amount of money involved because it basically involves the investor providing a third party with the funds in which to purchase a piece of real estate (commercial or residential). The existence of such an investment will usually be evidenced by large monthly payments appearing in a bank or investment account. Alternatively, the grantor may hold shares in a pool of mortgages, covering a number of properties. Again, the existence of such an investment will be evidenced by monthly payments. In both cases, there should be available annual statements denoting interest and mortgage principal received. Also, as there are different tax implications for interest versus the return of capital, it is important that a tax receipt is received to assist with the preparation of the grantor's tax return.

Template 11—Appendix IX

Part of registered or non-registered plan?

Self-managed or brokerage house?

If brokerage house, which one?

Name and contact of brokerage house account manager:

Name/identity of property:

If shares held in a pool, name of fund:

Maturity date (if applicable):

Are principal and interest payments:

- a) Received by cheque

- b) Direct deposit

c) Other arrangement (if so, describe)

Current instructions on file:

Mutual Funds/Income Trusts

Mutual funds and income trusts are often held within a person's registered retirement savings plan (RRSP) or registered retirement investment fund (RRIF) portfolio, but not always. They are common investment vehicles used when a long-term investment strategy is favoured. For investments held outside of a registered plan, earnings in the form of dividends, interest, return of capital and increase in per unit value will be summarized each year when the fund or trust issues a T5. Because these earnings from mutual funds and income trusts will not usually show up in the activity of a bank statement or a cash investment account, having last year's tax return will be particularly valuable in helping you identify if such investments exist. The earnings from these investments often stay within the mutual fund. Thus you will have to ensure that you determine exactly what the arrangement is so you can verify that what is happening is what is supposed to be happening. For example, when dividends are earned in a particular fund, is this money being used to purchase more units in the fund, or is the money supposed to be transferred to a cash account for the owner (the grantor) to use? Also as the grantor ages, regular evaluation will be necessary as to the desirability of these investment vehicles given their long-term perspective. That is, as a person ages, investment advisors often encourage moving away from this type of investment to one that is more focused on short-term stability and accessibility.

When a person purchases units in a mutual fund and/or income trust outside of an RRSP or RRIF, the following should be noted.

1) All income received (dividends, interest, proceeds from any sales) will be required to be reported on the annual tax return, whether that be the grantor's T1 General Income Tax and Benefit Return or the estate's T3 Trust Income and Information Return.

2) Management fees paid to the brokerage house or fund where units are held are, in most cases, tax deductible, so the attorney will want to determine whether any such fees are paid,

3) Sales, new purchases and any amounts received as a return of capital of funds already invested will need to be noted and recorded because this affects the adjusted cost base (ACB). It is important that an accurate ACB can be determined so that any capital gains or losses arising when units are sold can be properly calculated when preparing relevant tax returns. The attorney or estate trustee will want to ensure that such gains and losses are calculated properly to avoid possible penalties and interest should the Canada Revenue Agency determine errors have been made.

The annual mutual fund and income trust activity statements will provide all this information. Thus *it is vitally important that the attorney/estate trustee obtain these statements for each fund and income trust, if not since the original units were purchased, then certainly from the date they start to act as attorney/estate trustee.*

You will need the following information for each fund and income trust for which the grantor owns units.

Template 11—Appendix IX

Part of registered or non-registered plan?

Self-managed or brokerage house?

If brokerage house, which one?

Name and contact of brokerage house account manager:

Name of fund:

Number of units purchased:

Initial investment amount:

Activity Statement available?

Real Estate

Income streams from investment properties may not be obvious at first, depending on what the particulars of the investment and terms of income splitting are. Two main types of investments in real estate are:

1) Ownership of a rental property

2) Equity interest with share of the net income

The first scenario is the situation where the grantor has purchased a property and is collecting rent from one or more tenants. They may or may not have a management company handling the day to day affairs of the property. If the grantor is managing this investment, there will be a signed lease with each tenant. If a management company is involved, there will be a signed contract with the management company stipulating duties and fee for services. As acting attorney you should review and be aware of the details of either arrangement—that is review leases or the management company contract.

The second, an equity interest, is where the grantor owns shares in an investment corporation or partnership that owns and operates one or more properties. This kind of investment may stay hidden for years if there are no loans associated with the purchase of the investment and it was intended as a long term investment, only to be realized upon sale of the assets in the corporation (or partnership) or upon the investor's death. There should be some document setting out such information along with the share certificate. If you know of a share interest but no information exists, there are two routes of enquiry you can take. The first is to contact the property management company to inquire who the contact is at the company who owns the property. To identify who the property manager is, you can either phone a tenant of the building because every tenant will have a name and contact information, or you can visit the building. The company's name and contact phone number is often listed on the directory in the lobby of the building. This contact person may not know who the shareholders are but can direct you to the company's lawyer, who will be able to provide the information you need. This lawyer should request a copy of the CPOAP document before releasing any information to you.

The second route that will yield information about the company is making an inquiry with the Ontario Corporations Search Services at www.oncorp.com. You do not need a lot of information to start with in order to initiate a search that can eventually reveal among other things: the existence of the company, its legal name, the address for legal service, its active/inactive status and the Officers, Directors or Registrant. Although it will not tell you who the shareholders are, it will at least provide you with a starting place to contact the company's Officers, who will be able to confirm shareholder status. However, queries made through this website require a fee paid by credit card prior to the search being initiated. Thus, it is recommended that should such information be required, attempts using the first approach are exhausted before referring to the website.

Template 11—Appendix IX

Rental property owned?

Address of property:

Owner-managed or management company?

Name/address/contact information of management company (if applicable):

Number of tenants:

Location of books and records (leases, financial statements, mortgage information):

Has equity interest?

Address of property:

Name of corporation/partnership holding title to property:

Contact details:

Shares—Public Company

People can own shares of any company whose shares are publically traded on any number of stock exchanges around the world. Though the most common stocks held by a person living in Canada will be those sold on a Canadian or US stock exchange, do not rule out the possibility that foreign shares might be held if Canada is not the grantor's country of birth. If the grantor has immigrated to Canada sometime in their adult life, do not assume that the grantor would have divested themselves of all their investments upon immigration. Be sure your inquiries made to the grantor are specific—that is, ask about shares held in companies worldwide.

If all you know is that shares are held of a particular company because you are aware of dividend cheques being received, but you do not know how many shares are held or what adjustments to the cost base have occurred, do not despair. You can contact the company directly as their share registry records may be able to provide all the information required. Alternatively, you may find out that the grantor has set up an account with either Computershare (www.computershare.com) or CIBC Mellon (www.cibcmellon.com), two prominent asset management companies. These companies offer, a number of investment-management related services, including the ability for an individual to register their shareholdings and manage their investments collectively through the companies' websites. Because one main function of these companies is that of a share registry, they may also be able to assist you in determining the exact shareholding of the grantor once you provide relevant documentation (i.e., a copy of the CPOAP document) even if the grantor has not set up a specific investment management account with them.

If you have share certificates but do not observe any income being received from the companies who have issued the certificates, a quick search on any of the investment/finance websites such as www.bloomberg.com, ca.finance.yahoo.com or finance.sympatico.msn.ca will provide information on what, if any, dividends have been issued in the recent past. You can also obtain company contact information from links provided and contact the company directly.

It is not always the case that companies issue dividends continuously year after year, but it is common. After all, it is one reason people choose to invest in the company. Thus, having the most recent tax return could assist the attorney to ensure they have a complete list of these financial instruments. If dividends have been paid during the year, the issuing company will generate a T5, disclosing the amount of dividends received and other information required to prepare the tax return. If shares were disposed of during the year, the trader or dealer in securities will issue a T5008. This slip will contain necessary information to enable the proper reporting of any capital gains or losses resulting from shares sold during the year.

Template 11—Appendix IX

Part of registered or non-registered plan?

Self-managed or brokerage house?

If brokerage house, which one?

Name and contact of brokerage house account manager:

Name of company:

Country of incorporation:

Number of shares held:

Original cost (if available):

History of changes to adjusted cost base (ACB) if available (attach separate sheet):

Current ACB:

Are dividend payments:

    a) Cash and paid by cheque quarterly/semi annually/annually, only periodically

    b) Cash and direct deposit (frequency, to what account—current account or brokerage cash account)

    c) Shares, increasing the number of shares held by shareholder.

Line of Credit (L)

A line of credit (LOC) is a prearranged authorization from a financial institution that allows a person (or business) to borrow up to a predetermined amount as and when required. Unless the LOC is being utilized, and thus interest and payback activity is evident on a bank statement, it might not be obvious that one exists. Whether the LOC is being utilized or not, it is important that its existence be noted and any assets assigned as security be identified. Often when a LOC exists, the financial institution requires assets to be "assigned" as security. This means that should the LOC not be paid back, the financial institution has the right to take possession of those assets assigned in order to satisfy the amounts outstanding.

Although a LOC can be a good thing to have for immediate access to short-term cash requirements—for example, to meet an unexpected expense shortly before a GIC maturity—it should never be relied upon as a long-term cash source.

In addition to the specific details identified below, you will also want to determine by discussion with the grantor what their historical use of this facility is—that is, does the grantor rely on it to any extent, and what kinds of expense activities tend to be funded from this source? You will want to incorporate this information into your cash flow assessments.

Template 12—Appendix IX

Financial institution:

Limit:

Interest rate:

Amount outstanding and date:

Terms (minimum payment amount and frequency):

Unsecured or secured:

If secured, what property/assets have been assigned?

Loan Guarantees (L)

Loan guarantees exist where the grantor has co-signed a loan with someone else (an individual or company) guaranteeing that should the principal loan holder fail in making any payments, the grantor will make up any shortfall.

Should such guarantees exist, it would be prudent for the attorney to find out as much as possible about the outstanding debt. Ideally, the grantor will have a copy of the loan document. Attempts should be made to ascertain the financial health (as best possible) of the individual or company who is the principal on the loan and regularly reassess the probability that financial assistance might need to be extended to meet the terms of the debt.

The attorney needs to read the entire loan document in order to fully appreciate risks associated with the guarantee as well as the responsibilities and obligations of the guarantor. Determine whether there are any "out" clauses that describe events that would allow the guarantor to be released from their contractual obligation.

Template 13—Appendix IX

End of the loan period:

Amount guaranteed (this may not necessarily be the full amount of the loan):

Name and address of the debtor:

Grantor's relationship to the debtor:

Nature of debt:

Are there any other guarantors, and how does their existence affect the possible financial obligations of the grantor?

Any events that would release the grantor from this agreement:

Loans Payable (L)

It is likely that any loans outstanding of the grantor will be highlighted when reviewing the banking activity. However, there may be loans outstanding that involve only an annual or semi-annual payment of interest and lump-sum payment made on the anniversary of the loan or upon maturity.

A loan payable may also be evidenced by a promissory note. A promissory note is a written promise to pay back a set amount of money at a certain point in time or when the issuer (the person who lent the money) demands it. Of course, until such time as the money becomes due or the issuer asks for their money, the existence of such a debt would not show up in the bank statement activity. Therefore it is important to ask the question whether any loans payable exist and whether they are legally supported by promissory notes.

If a promissory note does exist, be sure to notice whether there is a maturity date on it. There may not be. The attorney should try to ascertain whether there is any intention by the lender to forgive this debt. If this cannot be determined with certainty, the attorney will need to assume that the money is to be paid back in full, including any interest indicated in the loan document, and make provision for it as a payment in the cash flow statements. If the attorney hears that the loan is forgiven, written confirmation should be asked for and filed with the CPOAP document.

If the grantor has been heavily involved in business ventures or is part of a partnership agreement, be sure to ascertain whether any of these loans involved signing a personal guarantee by the grantor. If so, then debts (existing or potential) of the business venture/partnership need to be considered and made part of the schedule of payments that need to be made or potential liabilities that need to be provided for.

Template 14—Appendix IX

Who has lent money to the grantor/deceased?

Does a promissory note exist?

Term of the loan (If a promissory note, it can be for a specified fixed length of time or payable "on demand" whenever the lender demands repayment of the amount loaned to the borrower.):

Amount of the loan:

Interest rate:

Interest payment dates:

Any terms regarding the right to pre-pay the loan before the due date:

What happens if the borrower misses a payment or fails to pay when payment is demanded?

Does a personal guarantee exist as part of the loan document?

Are there any assets that have been put up as collateral for any loan payables that exist? If so, list them:

Loans Receivable (A)

This may be an awkward subject, discovering potential reasons for feuds and distrust among assumed beneficiaries. However, information about any money that has been lent to a third party—related or not, beneficiary or not—is absolutely necessary for the attorney to know. These loans may or may not be supported by a formal agreement and/or promissory note. Knowing about these arrangements is important for three key reasons.

1) To enable the adequacy of the grantor's cash resources to be assessed with greater accuracy.

2) To assist the attorney when reviewing the bank activity, to determine whether all expected money has been received.

3) To protect the attorney should queries arise regarding the size of the grantor's investment portfolio and/or cash reserves.

Wishing to assist a friend or relative to purchase a major asset such as a house or car is probably the most common reason the grantor would lend money. In the case of lending money to enable a friend/relative to purchase a house, it is important to know if, in addition to the money lent, any of the grantor's assets have been used as security for any further amounts borrowed from other parties (i.e., the bank). This of course can be a dangerous situation and should be discouraged, if at all possible.

If a promissory note does exist, be sure to check whether there is a maturity date on it. There may not be, but in either case, it is important to find out from the grantor (1) what the grantor's intentions are with respect to this money owed and (2) what the status of the note is. With respect to the first point, if it is the grantor's intent to forgive the loan, either now or in the future, you need to know this and document such an intention by the grantor, keeping it in the file. Alternatively, it is not uncommon for people to include instructions in their will regarding the forgiveness of any outstanding loans. Again, you should know if the grantor has done this, because it will help to determine what steps you may need to take to properly manage the status of the debt as discussed below.

With respect to the status of the note, it is important to ascertain the terms of the note and whether payment of either interest, principal or both have been or is being made in accordance with the terms. The reason you need to understand the terms of the note is to be able to protect the grantor's interest in recovering the money should the debtor not pay back or otherwise honour the note. Generally speaking, a promissory note with a fixed maturity date means that should the note not be paid back, the person to whom the money is owed (i.e., the grantor), or you as the attorney, has a limitation period[2] of two years from the maturity date of the note to start legal proceedings against the defaulting debtor. Where the note has no fixed date of maturity, the limitation period of two years runs from the date of the note's creation—that is, when the money is lent, not when its payment is demanded. This state of affairs can be made less risky for the grantor by an annual acknowledgement by the debtor of the debt, which has the effect of providing a new start date for the running of the

---

[2] A "limitation period" is a fixed period of time within which a court action can be started. This tends to be a very complex area of the law, varying from jurisdiction to jurisdiction. The discussion herein is based upon Ontario's *Limitation Act, 2002*, S.O. 2002, c. 24, Sched. B. The reader should consult knowledgeable legal counsel in the applicable jurisdiction for relevant limitation period information.

limitation period. If you find yourself faced with such a receivable, whether a promissory note exists or not, consult appropriate legal counsel to ensure the recoverability and security of the obligation. The original note as well as any instructions from the grantor should be filed with the will with a copy included as part of the attorney's documentation. In addition, you will also want to highlight any anniversary dates in your own calendar to ensure that you do not miss those dates.

If there are no loans receivable outstanding, the attorney should make a note of this, the date and with whom they discussed these questions with, either the grantor or someone else (in the case where the grantor is unable to answer).

Template 15—Appendix IX

Has any money been lent to business colleagues, friends or, more likely, family members?

If so, who?

Has the money been lent for a specific purpose? Describe:

If so, has either the sections Business or Partnership Agreements or Investments—Limited Partnerships been reviewed, and relevant information collected and documented?

Is there an expectation that interest should be paid?

If interest is to be received, what is the frequency?

When is the amount expected to be paid back?

Is it expected to be paid back or taken out of the person's share of the estate upon the grantor's death?

Does a formal promissory note exist, and where is it filed (e.g., in the grantor's SDB)?

Is there any property of the grantor's that has been provided as security?

If yes, what property, and what are the specific details?

Maintenance under a Court Order (A and/or L)

If the grantor is divorced or separated, the attorney will need to ensure that there are no maintenance payments due to, or being received from, a third party. If payments are being made, they will need to be maintained and reflected in any cash flow projections. Alternatively, if receipts are expected, the attorney will want to incorporate these into the grantor's cash flow document.

The best case scenario is that the attorney is able to read the agreement, noting the information listed below in Template 16.

If a copy of the agreement is available for the attorney, it should be filed with the power of attorney and the will. If the grantor does not wish to share the agreement with the attorney, then attempts should be made to confirm with the grantor that the agreement is filed with the grantor's important papers in their safety deposit box or other safe location.

Receiving Maintenance

If the grantor has been receiving amounts, and the payments stop, this may indicate the death of the ex-spouse, and the grantor may have a claim on the estate of the deceased. At the very least, should there be an end to receiving such amounts, the attorney will want to make enquiries to determine the reason.

If you are acting as the estate trustee of someone, who when alive was receiving amounts under a maintenance agreement, you will need to ascertain whether such receipts were to continue even after the death of the grantor. If so, you will want to ensure they do in fact continue. You will need to contact either the ex-spouse or their legal representative to inform them of the death. At that time, you can confirm that no further receipts are expected or that further payments should be made to the estate of the deceased person.

Paying Maintenance

If the grantor has been paying maintenance to an ex-spouse, and the grantor is notified or becomes aware of that person's death, the attorney will need to determine if any further payments are required.

If you are acting as the estate trustee of someone who, when alive, was paying amounts under a maintenance agreement, you will need to ensure you know what the arrangements were to be upon death of the person paying the maintenance. It could be that upon the death of the payer, payments were to continue (from the estate) until the death of the ex-spouse. Or perhaps provision has been made in the will of the deceased for the ex-spouse to receive a final lump sum from the estate. You will need to contact either the ex-spouse or the legal representative to inform them of the death. At that time, you can confirm with them what form future payments will take—whether they will continue as before or whether they will be advised of a final payment once the estate is closer to being finalized.

Template 16—Appendix IX

Does a maintenance agreement exist?

Are payments being made or being received?

Amount and frequency of payment:

Interest penalties should payments not be paid/received on time:

Recourse by the receiver should payments not be received within a reasonable period of due date:

Duration of payments:

Events, if any, that will result in payments no longer being made/received:

Are payments required to be paid to or from the estate when one party dies?

Name of ex-spouse and contact details (either personal or legal representative):

Name and contact details of grantor's lawyer who represented them:

Miscellaneous Amounts (A and/or L)

Inquire about any other sources of money that might be coming. For example, is the grantor expecting a share of an estate of an aging relative or a long-time friend? Obviously there is nothing to do about this right now, but if you are aware that there is potential of a gift, financial or otherwise, you will want to make sure you are aware of the geographical location of the person from whom the gift is to be received and also their current state of health. This might seem ghoulish, but part of your job as an attorney is to look out for the grantor. Even if the grantor is very active in their own affairs when you begin, as time passes, this may not always be the case, and so the more information you can obtain at the beginning, the better job you will do with limited stress when access to information may become more of a challenge.

On the other side, are there any amounts that might be owing to a third party, although no formal legal contract of repayment exists? These payments need to be incorporated into the cash flow document. Also, if the arrangements are informal and no payback schedule exists, you may want to contact the person to whom the amounts are owed and make a more formal arrangement, or have the person write a letter to the grantor specifically releasing them from the expectation of having to pay it back. This will avoid surprises down the road from this third party's estate trustee.

Template 17—Appendix IX

Describe the general nature of any miscellaneous amounts not recorded elsewhere, including the name and contact details of the other party and their relationship to grantor:

What is the anticipated frequency and/or date when payment is expected to be received or made?

What is the approximate amount of money to be received or paid out each time?

Does a formal agreement exist, and if so, where is it filed?

Are there any circumstances that would cancel the expectation to pay back any money owed or to receive any money due? If so, describe:

Are there any verbal agreements that should be formalized into a written agreement? If so, describe:

Mortgage Payable (L)

Mortgage payments will be obvious from your review of bank statements. However, if your first review of the bank statements does not highlight the existence of any, the attorney will need to ask the grantor whether any mortgages still exist on any properties. House, condo and cottage are the three assets that could have a mortgage still being paid off.

If the mortgage is a fixed rate mortgage, where the interest rate is fixed for the term of the loan, be sure to obtain an amortization schedule for the mortgage. The bank to which the payments are being made will be able to provide this if you cannot find such a schedule with the grantor's important papers. This schedule will show, on a monthly basis, what portion of the payment is interest versus principal. This information is important if the property is a rental property or becomes a rental property, because the interest is deductible against any rents received. Most important, in every case, this schedule will cover several months (if not the entire mortgage term) and thus will provide the correct valuation of the mortgage at the time you begin your attorney role. You will want to make a note to obtain a statement of mortgage at least once a year (usually as of December 31) to ensure consistency between the details showing on the statement of mortgage and the amortization schedule. If the two statements differ, you will have to make inquiries at the bank. The statement of mortgage will set out the terms of the loan, when it comes due for renewal, balance outstanding, total payments made since the last statement date and total interest charges.

If the mortgage is a variable rate mortgage, an amortization schedule cannot be prepared because the interest portion of each payment is based on the prevailing interest rate during that month. However, a statement of mortgage should be obtained on or near the date that you begin your role and no less often than on the anniversary of the mortgage term itself or as of December 31 each year. If the property is a rental property or becomes a rental property, the interest disclosed on this statement will be an important piece of information for the tax return preparation. If income is being earned on this property or has been earned at some point during ownership, the reader is encouraged to refer to the section on Real Property that identifies additional information that may be required along with the reasons why the information is important.

The statement of mortgage will also indicate whether the property taxes are being paid to the mortgage funder, who then remits the appropriate amount to the relevant municipality on the specific due dates. If this is not the case, you will want to ensure payments of property tax are being made. These amounts can be quite significant, and the attorney will want to ensure they are included in any cash flow projections.

Template 18—Appendix IX

Is there still a mortgage on the house, condo or cottage?

Address of each property covered by the mortgage:

What financial institution holds the mortgage?

Contact details of loan manager:

What bank account are payments being made from?

What are the immediate plans for this/these properties? That is, are they to be sold in the short-term or held?

Are properties held jointly? If so, with whom?

Is the mortgage fixed rate or variable rate?

Has an amortization schedule been obtained?

Have you obtained a statement of mortgage dated on or near the date of you beginning your attorney role?

Have you made a note in your personal diary in February to obtain a statement of mortgage as of December 31 each year if one has not yet been received?

Are property taxes being paid to the mortgage funder?

If not, have these amounts been recorded in the cash flow statement?

Is the property with the mortgage used to produce income?

If so, has the section on Real Property been referred to?

Pensions—Private, Government, Survivor Benefits, Foreign (A)

A private pension is a monthly amount received from a former employer. If the grantor worked in the paid workforce, it is possible that the grantor has a company pension.

If the grantor's spouse was receiving a company pension and has already died, there is the likelihood that a survivor's pension is being received from this same company.

Government pensions are such things as the Old Age Security (OAS), Canada Pension Plan (CPP), survivor's benefit, disability pension or a veteran's pension.

Canada's population is aging. A large number have emigrated from Europe, including the United Kingdom. Many of these people will continue to receive their birth country's pension benefits, regardless of being residents of Canada. Be aware that the foreign jurisdiction may require a notarized/sworn declaration on a particular form, confirming that the person is still alive. There are some jurisdictions that require this document as frequently as every quarter. As an attorney, you must ensure this requirement continues to be satisfied.

A review of the grantor's bank statements will certainly highlight regular amounts being received. The attorney will want to ensure that any paperwork that exists with respect to these pensions is filed in the main file of documentation. When the grantor dies, it will be easy to notify the relevant pension providers of the person's death and avoid the need to return funds received in error (i.e., after the death of the grantor).

Some type of T4 or T4A will also be received by the grantor for Canadian pensions; a review of the most recent tax return will prove to be a valuable source of confirmation that all pensions have been identified.

Template 19—Appendix IX

Is pension income received?

List the companies and/or governments that pension income is received from:

Are any of these from foreign countries?

If so, describe requirements of the specific pension funds for the pensioner to confirm their entitlement:

Have you made a note in your personal diary to ensure any deadlines with respect to the requirements noted above are met?

Real Property—Condo, Cottage, Farm, House, Undeveloped Land (A)

Although "real property" assets may appear to be fairly self explanatory, it is important to ensure that deeds or ownership papers are located and filed together in the appropriate envelope in the file folder/banker's box. You may also decide the safest place for such documents is the grantor's safety deposit box. If this is the case, make a note with your paperwork that this is where you have placed the deed(s).

A safety deposit box is a common place for any of these ownership papers, however should the grantor not have a safety deposit box, you will need to determine where they do file their important papers. The papers may be in the grantor's home in the linen closet, the back of the kitchen cupboard or with one of their children for safe keeping.

The attorney specifically needs to be aware of whether any of these are owned jointly, because there are ramifications should it become necessary to sell one or more of such assets. That is, if the final proceeds have to be shared with one or more people, the amount being deposited to the grantor will be less. This is important to know if the attorney is including the expected proceeds into the cash flow statement to project the grantor's financial position over the next few months. There are also tax consequences, which are explained next.

Also, if the grantor owns more than one residence in which the grantor personally lives in during the year (even for short stays), there are tax consequences to be considered when determining when and if to sell one of these properties, specifically the favourable tax treatment granted to a "principal residence." If the grantor owns and uses personally a house, condo and/or cottage, the principal residence rule will have major implications on selling decisions. The rule, put simply, is that the Canada Revenue Agency does not require a taxpayer to pay tax on the capital gain realized on the sale of a principal residence. Any property can qualify to be a principal residence as long as it was lived in at some point each year. The catch is that as of 1982, each family can only designate one property for the principal residence. Thus, while the grantor may still be married when disposing of a property, the grantor (or their attorney) have to decide with the grantor's spouse (or spouse's attorney) which residence they will declare as their principal residence because each of them cannot claim a property for this tax-free status, even if the property is in both their names. For this reason it is most important that a history of the properties is written down.

Determining original values for these items of property may not be absolutely necessary when you first start acting as an attorney for a capable grantor. Should the grantor become incapacitated, however, you will need to ascertain these values. Indeed, should there come a time when you are required to sell any real property as part of managing the grantor's financial affairs while the grantor is still alive, this information will become necessary for a couple of reasons.

1) Knowing the original price will help to determine whether the current market price indicates it is a good time to sell. If not being forced to sell due to the cash flow requirements of the grantor, you may want to hold on to such property as long as other considerations (such as insurance premiums) do not make it uneconomical.

2) In the case where a house, condo and/or cottage are owned, because only one can be designated as principal residence and thus enjoy tax-free status upon sale, this information will be required when preparing the tax return for the year in which the non-principal residence is sold.

In addition, you should also review the grantor's will to determine whether specific arrangements have been made for the disposition of real estate, e.g., cottage or foreign real estate holdings. If the grantor is incapable, the attorney is obliged to make inquiries as to whether the person had a will, and if so, what its provisions are with respect to such properties.

If any real property is located outside of Canada, the attorney needs to be aware that there could be tax implications beyond those of the Canada Revenue Agency. If a foreign property is owned, the attorney should determine what the financial implications of selling this property are. These implications may influence the decision of when to sell this asset. It is recommended that the attorney obtain advice from an accountant or lawyer who specializes in foreign transactions.

The attorney also needs to know whether these properties are income producing as this will have tax implications when the property is sold. You will need to ensure the person preparing the tax return has all the relevant information.

Template 20—Appendix IX

Type of property:

Address:

Original purchase price:

Cost of renovations/maintenance, if any (e.g., new roof):

Date of purchase:

Is there a mortgage outstanding?

Who is the lending institution/party?

What are the plans for the property?

Is it held jointly, if yes, with whom:

Is it being used as security against any lines of credit, loan facilities or investments? If so, specify:

If property is located outside Canada, has appropriate advice been obtained from a relevant professional? If so, provide contact information of professional:

Has information obtained from the professional been filed with CPOAP and incorporated into the asset management plan?

Is it used or has it been used at any time since it was purchased, to produce income? If so, list specific time periods when it was used to produce income:

Describe any instructions in the will with respect to this property:

RRSP/RRIF (A)

RRSP stands for registered retirement savings plan. If the Grantor has been engaged in the paid workforce for any part of their life, then it is quite possible that they have a RRSP to which they have been or are contributing. If the person is retired, then it is quite likely that they may be withdrawing funds from their RRSP to cover living expenses. It is important for the attorney to know how frequently funds are to be received and in what format, direct deposit or cheque.

RRIF stands for registered retirement investment fund. By the end of the calendar year in which a person reaches the age of 71, any value in the RRSP must be withdrawn. The options are:

1) Cashing it in and investing it elsewhere;

2) Converting the amount into a RRIF; or

3) Purchasing an annuity.

If options 2 and/or 3 are initiated, there will be no immediate tax consequences. If the amount is converted to cash and withdrawn, there will be tax withheld. How much tax is withheld is determined by the financial institution or fund manager at the time the money is withdrawn, and it is dependent on just how much is withdrawn. For residents in Canada other than Quebec, the rates are as follows:

$0-5,000	10%
$5,001-15,000	20%
Over $15,000	30%

For Quebec residents, the rates are:

$0-5,000	5%
$5,001-15,000	10%
Over $15,000	15%

Just to be clear, the entire amount withdrawn during the year is taxable unless it is converted into a RRIF or is purchasing an annuity by someone reaching the age of 71. The total amount withdrawn will be recorded on the grantor's T1 as income received, with the appropriate tax payable calculated. The amounts of tax withheld when the RRSP was collapsed will be set off against the amount of taxes calculated as owing. If it turns out to be more than the tax payable calculated, once all sources of income have been considered and tax credits are applied, the grantor will be entitled to a tax refund. If it turns out to be insufficient, the grantor will be required to pay the shortfall.

If funds are being withdrawn from a RRSP, the financial institution where the money is being held will issue a T4(RSP). If the funds have already been converted into a RRIF and money is being withdrawn from the RRIF, then the grantor will receive a T4(RIF) from the relevant financial institution. Both these T4 slips will show the amount of funds withdrawn during the year and taxes already paid on the amounts withdrawn.

It might be worthwhile to clarify that an RSP (retirement savings plan) may or may not be registered. Although most of us might be more familiar with a registered RSP (i.e., RRSP), non-registered RSPs also exist. The principal difference between the two is that when a retirement savings plan is registered, favourable tax treatment of amounts invested in such plans is available. That is, the amount invested can be claimed on an individual's T1 tax return as a deduction from taxable income in the year it is invested, and the income earned is not taxed until it is withdrawn. Contributions made to a non-registered plan are made with "after-tax dollars" (i.e., these amounts do not reduce one's taxable income at any point in time). People who manage to make maximum contributions to their RRSP during their working life may have been keen to save even more for their retirement. If this is the case, then a person could have both registered and non-registered savings plans.

Whether a person's retirement savings plan is registered or non-registered is an important distinction to be clear about due to the different tax treatment by the CRA of income earned and the ramifications when reviewing the cash flow situation of the grantor. With a registered plan, the earnings accumulate year to year, tax-free until the individual withdraws amounts from the plan. As amounts are withdrawn, the fund manager will withhold tax and remit this tax to the CRA on the individual's behalf. A T4(RSP) or T4(RIF) will be received from each fund that issued payments to the grantor during the year showing amounts withdrawn and tax withheld. In the case of a non-registered retirement savings plan, all income and capital gains earned by the investment need to be reported in the year earned. T3 and T5 slips will be received from the relevant financial institutions (bank or brokerage house) each year showing what kind of income has been earned on these investments (e.g., interest, capital gains or a return on capital). Because the earnings are taxed in the year they are earned, when amounts are withdrawn from a non-registered plan, tax is paid only on capital gains realized from comparing the adjusted cost base against the amount of money received for the portion of the investment that has been cashed in (i.e., the proceeds of disposition).

The most common type of investment to be held within an RRSP is mutual funds. However, other kinds of investments can also be registered such as GICs, term deposits and bonds.

If the grantor has a RRSP or RRIF, as with investments held outside of a registered plan (discussed above in Investments), they could be managing this solely on their own, deciding what mutual funds to purchase units in or if other investment options are preferable (such as a GIC earning guaranteed income). If a GIC or other similar investment has been purchased, the attorney will want to know when it matures, because at that point a decision will be required of how to reinvest it. Alternatively, the grantor could have an account with a brokerage house, using the expertise of an account manager.

It is important also to be aware that when a person dies and there exists no spouse (or common-law partner) or dependent child, the fair market value of the property (e.g., the units purchased in various funds) held in the RRSP/RRIF at the time of death is reported on the person's final T1 as income earned in the year of death. It should also be noted that from the date of death, these plans are no longer considered registered. As such, income earned during the year, post-death, will need to be reported on the first T3 Return and each subsequent T3 until the funds are dealt with in accordance with the instructions in the will. The attorney and estate trustee, if not the same person, will need to communicate to confirm which one will advise the fund manager of the death, so that the plans can be de-registered.

Template 21—Appendix IX

Does an RRSP or RRIF exist?

Self-managed or brokerage house:

If brokerage house, which one:

Name and contact of brokerage house account manager:

Name of fund(s):

Number of units purchased:

Initial investment amount: $

Activity statement available:

Are there other investments held within the RRSP (e.g., GIC)?

Types:

Amount invested:

Financial institution purchased from:

Interest being earned:

Maturity date:

Shares—Private Company (A)

Shares of private companies are not available to the public and are therefore generally not regarded as an investment; that is, they are not traded on any stock exchange. The most common situations are family businesses, initially with shares issued only to the husband and wife, and as their family grows, shares are issued to the children. Another common situation is businesses that have been formed by a small number of people, each holding shares as a representation of their portion of ownership of the business.

Shares of a private company that are held by an individual are different from shares held in a publicly traded company in a number of ways. The most significant difference is perhaps the ease in which you or the grantor will determine the value of any shares held. Although one can refer to any number of sources for share values of publicly traded shares, there are no similar resources for valuing private company shares. It is most likely that you will need to engage the services of a professional certified business valuator to ascertain a proper valuation. There is no active market on which these shares are traded, so there is no immediate requirement to obtain a valuation because you would not include these shares in any investment strategy. However, the death of the grantor will trigger the need for a valuation. Absent the grantor's death, the two most likely reasons that would require a valuation would be if the grantor became involved in a divorce situation, or the business in which the shares are held becomes part of a sale or merger agreement.

If shares are held in a private company, the attorney needs to know that these shares exist along with some general information about the business and whether the grantor is a Director of the business. Being a Director also means that the grantor has legal obligations outside of any business agreement that exists should the company find itself being sued or in breach of any legislation. For example, miscalculating payroll deductions or undercharging GST/HST. The attorney also needs to confirm with the grantor from time to time that there have been no changes to the general nature of the business, because this could affect potential liabilities down the line. Often when shares in businesses are distributed among family members or people active in the management of the company, there is a shareholder agreement. It will be important for the attorney to read this agreement and make notes of any contingent liabilities—that is, amounts that might become owing down the road, should certain events happen as set out in the agreement.

When discussing the business with the grantor and while obtaining information about the level of involvement the grantor currently has, the attorney will want to ask about the existence of any shareholder loans. This is where the shareholder has either made a loan to the company or the company has made a loan to the shareholder. If such a financial arrangement exists, it should be evident when looking at the annual financial statements of the company. Thus, in situations where the grantor is incapacitated and unable to provide this information to the attorney, obtaining a copy of the most recent financial statements will be important. There should be a note to the financial statements that describes the terms of any shareholder loan, such as what interest rate is being charged (if any) and when it is expected to be paid back.

Knowing in general terms what the business does, how active it is, whether any shareholder loans exist and what the general state of the company's balance sheet is will provide the attorney with important facts. These facts, along with the information contained in the shareholder agreement, should be considered when determining possible cash outflows and inflows, which in turn will affect the grantor's financial health.

Template 22—Appendix IX

Are shares held in a private company?

Name of company:

Briefly describe the business activities:

Is it still active?

Have most recent financial statements been obtained and filed with CPOAP?

Does a Shareholder Agreement exist?

If so, has a copy been obtained and filed with the CPOAP?

Who holds the other shares?

From reading the Shareholder Agreement and discussions with grantor and/or other shareholders, record any financial obligations or windfalls that need to be included in the cash flow statement:

Does a shareholder loan exist?

Is it a loan to or from the company?

What are the terms of repayment? Are there any conditions, if present, that would result in the loan being forgiven?

Tax-Free Savings Account (TFSA) (A)

In late 2008, effective January 1, 2009, the Government of Canada introduced into legislation a savings vehicle available to all Canadian residents 18 years and over called a Tax-Free Savings Account (TFSA). Each individual is allowed to invest $5,000 per year into this account. Contributions to a TFSA are not deductible for income tax purposes, but investment income (including capital gains) earned in a TFSA will not be taxed, even when withdrawn.

If the grantor has a TFSA, a slip will be received at the end of each year from the financial institution that holds the account confirming the amount invested and the interest earned. If the grantor has yet to open such an account, the attorney should encourage the grantor to do so. If the grantor is incapacitated, the attorney should consider undertaking the opening of such an account in the grantor's name. Although the maximum amount that can be invested annually is $5,000, there is no minimum amount. Thus, if the grantor has limited financial means, even small amounts deposited over time will increase, and the interest being earned is all tax-free. When choosing what financial institution to open the account with, one will want to check out any fees associated with the maintenance of the account. If only small amounts are going to be invested and interest rates are low, the interest income may not be sufficient to cover the bank fees.

The TFSA is not limited to being a bank account that earns interest. Once a TFSA is opened, an individual can invest in a number of different interest-earning vehicles such as a term deposit, mutual fund, GIC or publically traded shares and hold it within this account. If a GIC or term deposit has been purchased, the maturity date will be important to know so that appropriate action can be taken when it matures.

In addition to the favourable tax treatment of income earned, there are a number of other aspects that make a TFSA attractive.

1) Unused TFSA contribution room can be carried forward to future years.

2) Funds can be withdrawn from the TFSA at any time for any purpose.

3) The amount withdrawn can be put back in the TFSA at a later date without reducing contribution room.

4) Neither income earned in a TFSA nor withdrawals will affect the grantor's eligibility for federal income-tested benefits and credits, such as the Guaranteed Income Supplement and the Canada Child Tax Benefit.

5) Contributions to a spouse's TFSA will be allowed, and TFSA assets can be transferred to a spouse upon death.

The differences between an RRSP or RRIF and the TFSA are as follows.

1) Contributions to an RRSP are deductible in the year made and reduce one's income for tax purposes. In contrast, amounts contributed to a TFSA are not deductible when calculating taxable income.

2) Withdrawals from an RRSP or RRIF are added to one's income in the year withdrawn and taxed at current rates. The TFSA withdrawals and growth within the account are not added to one's income—they are received tax-free.

Template 23—Appendix IX

Does the grantor have a TFSA?

If so, what is the account number and at which bank is it held?

If one exists, what are the details of the investment?

If other than a savings account, what are the maturity dates of investments?

Have these dates been recorded in your personal diary?

Have the annual investment amount been included when considering the grantor's cash flow requirements?

Has the interest being earned been included in the grantor's cash receipts when reviewing cash availability?

If a TFSA does not exist, has consideration been given to setting one up?

Will (Neither A or L)

The final piece of property you will have to account for and be aware of is the grantor's will, if one exists. As previously mentioned, the contents of the grantor's will may impact upon your ability to manage the assets of the grantor. It is essential that if a will exists, you ensure that it is kept in a safe place, preferably a safety deposit box. If no will exists, you should consider prompting the grantor (if still capable) of having one prepared.

Template 24—Appendix IX

Does the grantor have a will?

Where is it kept?

If not and the grantor is not incapacitated, have plans been made to ensure a will is made?

If one exists, upon reading, make notes about any instructions that will impact decisions made as the grantor's property is managed:

Chapter Recap

Do not let the number of items contained in this chapter discourage or intimidate you. Most people have only a few of the items described. People who have been very active as entrepreneurs may have a few more property matters that need to be unearthed and documented, but once identified, you may find that their existence really has little impact on the amount of activity that needs to be recorded each month. The three most important points to remember are:

1) Verify the existence or lack of existence of each item on the list with the grantor as early as possible in your role as attorney.

2) Ascertain the value of each item you determine exists as of a date on or near the time you are identifying its existence.

3) Document any suspicions you may have about missing information, including what has led you to suspect this.

As noted above, once identified, many of the items may have little impact on the amount of work that is required from the attorney on a day-to-day basis. However, the estate trustee will be indebted to you when, upon the death of the grantor, there is a comprehensive list of a person's assets and liabilities with only the need to update valuations. At that point, all these items will be of particular concern because they will have to be dealt with in order to wind up a person's affairs upon their death. And it is to the concerns of the estate trustee that we turn to in the next chapter, where we look at some of the main differences in responsibilities and obligations between those of an attorney and those of an estate trustee.

Chapter 7

I'm Not an Attorney, I'm an Estate Trustee

This chapter will highlight some of the more noteworthy differences between the responsibilities and obligations of an estate trustee and those of an attorney for property. The intention of this chapter is not to go through the responsibilities and obligations of an estate trustee (also known as an executor) in any great detail; there are any number of books widely available that provide excellent guidance in this area. Instead, the purpose here is to show that despite differences, there are similarities with respect to record keeping for both the attorney and the estate trustee that make the 10 Steps applicable no matter what function you find yourself fulfilling.

Briefly, an estate trustee is responsible for the entire estate of the deceased, including funeral arrangements. An attorney for property is only responsible for the property of the grantor; someone else may be responsible for decisions affecting the grantor's person. This responsibility may be shared with, or limited by, the grantor while the grantor has capacity. The focus of the estate trustee is usually the administration of the estate with a view towards winding up the estate as soon as possible, whereas the attorney's focus is on maintaining the estate for the grantor's benefit for as long as the grantor lives. In addition, as estate trustee, the legal title of the deceased's property becomes vested[1] in you with the estate's property held in trust for the benefit of the beneficiaries under the will. As an attorney for property there is no requirement that you be vested (i.e., have legal title) with the grantor's property while helping to manage their affairs, the grantor's property remains their own, over which they may make decisions while capable to do so. Another major difference between an estate trustee and the attorney for property is that an estate trustee only becomes responsible for the management of the estate's affairs from the date of death of the grantor, unless the estate trustee renounces the appointment prior to taking any action. However, the attorney is responsible from the date on which they first act as an attorney. Finally, although both the estate trustee and the attorney for property are fiduciaries, generally speaking the former owe their duty to the estate's beneficiaries, while the latter owe their primary duty to the grantor.

Despite the differences noted above, the 10 steps presented in Chapter 5 with respect to financial record keeping, along with the more detailed presentation of Step 2 dealing with specific assets and liabilities found in Chapter 6, will provide the estate trustee with valuable assistance. Of course there are a couple of distinctions at the outset that need to be clarified, but keeping those in mind, the estate trustee will have no problem proceeding in the same fashion that an attorney would when it comes to the financial record keeping for the estate.

---

[1]   "Vested" simply means that you acquire the legal rights and title to property.

First, the estate trustees' authority flows from the will or, in its absence, from court appointment. Therefore an estate trustee must have possession of the original will and codicil or codicils[2,] if any. That does not mean, however, that the estate trustee has no interest in an existing power of attorney document. Although the most important document for the estate trustee is the original will because they will need to read through it to ascertain who the beneficiaries are, a copy of the power of attorney document will identify who the attorney is/ was, indicate whether the document was specific or general and provide a starting place to begin the gathering of information about the deceased's Estate.

Second, informing the businesses still needs to be done as described in Step 5. However, the notification is obviously of a more permanent nature. If there was a CPOAP in place, then each business will need to be notified that the CPOAP is no longer in effect due to the death of the grantor and that the estate trustee is now the principal contact.

Finally, cash management decisions, as discussed in Step 8, will not be required by the estate trustee, unless there are trusts under the will to be administered for dependent beneficiaries. As the estate trustee is the only one with access to the bank and investment accounts of the deceased grantor, decisions about the timing of investment activity and legitimate payments are solely the responsibility of the estate trustee; the authority of the attorney acting under a power of attorney ends with the death of the grantor. An exception to this will be if the will has designated more than one person to function as estate trustee. In this situation the estate trustees will have to determine how they are going to work together to administer the estate and bring it to a close.

Table 5—Comparing the Main Duties of Estate Trustee and Attorney for Property

Duty	Estate Trustee/Executor	Attorney for Property
Obtain original documentation (will or CPOAP)	X	X
Make funeral arrangements and probate the will, if necessary	X	
Find and take control of assets and liabilities of the deceased	X	X
Prepare an inventory, value the assets and liabilities and keep the accounts	X	X
Deal with debts and other claims	X	X
Ensure tax returns are prepared, pay any taxes owing by the deceased and the estate, file for clearance certificate	X	X
Account to and get releases from beneficiaries	X	
Wind up the estate by distributing remaining assets to the beneficiaries as per the will	X	

The table above lists eight basic duties associated with looking after the financial affairs of the deceased by an estate trustee. The table also indicates which duties are also relevant to an attorney for property managing the affairs of a living grantor, although incapable.

---

2   A codicil is a formal document executed like a will that amends, rather than replaces, a previously executed will.

While most of these duties are relevant to both roles, there are some differences in terms of what is expected in order to legally fulfill the specific duty under each designation. Five of the basic differences are discussed below.

Control of the Assets and Liabilities

The estate trustee must identify and take control of all assets and liabilities of the estate from the date of death of the deceased. That is, they assume full responsibility for the maintenance of everything to do with the estate. However, the role of an attorney for property differs from the estate trustee in two ways. To start with, the attorney will not take control of the grantor's assets and liabilities until such time as the grantor becomes incapacitated, if ever. In most cases, the role of the attorney is to assist the grantor in managing the grantor's financial affairs. Second, the attorney may be restricted in what they are helping to maintain and thus may have no reason to know about every asset and liability of the grantor.

Further, this duty of the estate trustee also refers to the safeguarding of physical assets. For example, if the deceased still owned a car, then the estate trustee should locate the car keys and take possession of them and the car. The estate trustee might even have to go as far as having the locks on the principal residence changed if there is any likelihood of unauthorized removal of assets from the house prior to the estate trustee being ready to make distributions in accordance with the will. Also, if there were assets being used by third parties, such as a cottage, then possession of these assets may have to be taken by the estate trustee depending upon their disposition under the will. If there is a CPOAP in place, such arrangements of third-party possession should already have been documented by the attorney as set out in Step 7 in Chapter 5. In addition, one must also be aware that in terms of safeguarding investment assets, there can be different rules for both a trustee and an attorney or guardian. For example, in Ontario, trustees are governed by the *Trustee Act,* whereas the *Substitute Decisions Act, 1992*, sets out the rules for attorneys and guardians of property. The principal difference is that trustees are more restrictive in the investment strategy they can adopt.

Inventory, Assets, Liabilities and the Keeping of Accounts

Both an estate trustee and an attorney for property have the legal requirement to prepare an inventory complete with current market values of those assets. This inventory must include *both* assets and liabilities. For estate trustees, this needs to include every asset and liability of the estate. For attorneys, it needs to include those assets and liabilities that come within their authority under the CPOAP document. If it is a general CPOAP, then the inventory should include all assets and liabilities. For the estate trustee the key date is the date of death; for the attorney it is the date they commenced acting as an attorney for the incapable grantor. The estate trustee needs this listing in order to prepare documentation to file for probate,[3] if necessary. The inventory will also become part of the required documentation needed to wind

---

[3]   Probate is the procedure by which a will is recognized by the court as the valid and last will of the deceased person who made the will. It also confirms the appointment of the person named as estate trustee/executor in the will. The court gives the estate trustee/executor documents called *Letters Probate* (or in Ontario, a *Certificate of Appointment of Estate Trustee With a Will*)

up an estate even if probate is not required, because it forms the basis of information needed for the preparation of, as well as acquiring, releases from the beneficiaries of the estate prior to its distribution. The attorney, however, needs the inventory more for administrative purposes and to have the value of assets under management that marks the start of their accounting duties. Only in the worst-case scenario, where the attorney is required to present a complete set of accounts to the court, will these values become part of any litigation documentation. Although these values may not become part of court records, the attorney will still want to be as precise as possible when collecting this data because it may be required for income tax purposes. If questions arise about the attorney's stewardship, it will definitely be important to have precise asset values at the commencement of the attorney's activities to assist in an accurate assessment of their management. Not having this information readily available might trigger a more formal accounting requirement and the full litigation process, with its accompanying costs and stresses.

Where the requirements concerning the contents of the inventory differ as between estate trustee and attorney is in situations where the deceased owns shares and other investments that will have an adjusted cost base (ACB) value. The estate trustee will need this information as soon as practically possible in order that the final tax return of the deceased can be completed. However, an attorney does not need this value in order to begin record-keeping activities. If any of the investments are sold while you as an attorney are assisting to look after the affairs of the grantor, then yes, you will need to provide this information to the person who prepares the grantor's tax return. However, you will have time to obtain this information, hopefully with the help of the grantor or their investment advisor.

The estate trustee must also ensure that all bank accounts are closed into an account in the name of the estate. If the deceased had more than one account and/or dealt with more than one bank, the estate trustee will have to decide which bank to hold the estate's bank account in. At this point, there should only be one account for the estate's cash assets and it will need to be a chequing account.

One thing to keep in mind as an estate trustee is that in cases where there is no need to keep assets in trust for beneficiaries on an ongoing basis, the estate assets are modest and the estate is a straight payout, consideration should be given to have the estate bank account earning zero interest. Generally speaking, this is because in order to finalize the estate tax returns and be able to distribute the assets, there has to be no income-producing assets for which income needs to be reported in the annual T3 Return. The estate trustee will have to determine how long they anticipate it will be before the estate can be wound up. If it is likely to be more than a few months, then putting excess cash into a short-term GIC would be a consideration. The situation that an estate trustee will want to avoid is when interest earned during the year is less than the cost of having an additional T3 Return prepared.

There are provisions in the *Income Tax Act* for distributing income earned by the trust to the beneficiaries and having it taxed as income earned by the beneficiaries, but these rules are quite complex and beyond the scope of this book. For more information on these provisions, the reader is advised to contact a professional accountant who specializes in trust income tax matters.

---

as proof of the court's recognition the estate trustee's authority to deal with the estate so that third parties may deal with the estate trustee with confidence.

Debts and Other Claims

For the most part this obligation is the same whether one is an estate trustee or an attorney. However, estate trustees must determine if there is any debt outstanding that has yet to be accounted for prior to making the final distribution of the estate. They will do this by advertising for creditors prior to making the final, or in some cases interim, distribution of the estate.

The estate trustee must also take care of all debts that exist at the time of death or become known as the estate is settled, including law suits. Under a general CPOAP document, the attorney usually has the obligation to make both financial and legal decisions and would be expected to resolve law suits of the grantor if the grantor was unable to initiate the proper responses. However, if the CPOAP is specific in its nature, interference by the attorney to resolve legal claims may not be appropriate. The attorney can certainly suggest the grantor consult a professional, but the attorney cannot force them to do so. If such a situation arises where the grantor does not make any attempt to resolve the situation, then the attorney should consult a lawyer to determine the best course of action.

Tax Return Preparation

An estate trustee is legally obliged to ensure all tax returns related to the deceased and the estate are filed and all taxes are paid. There are two types of tax returns, the T1 General and the T3 Trust Income and Information Return. With respect to the T1, in most cases this will include just one return, that being for the year in which the death has occurred. However, if the person has died between January 1 and April 30, the prior year's tax return will most likely also be outstanding. T3 returns will be required for the estate until such time as the estate is finalized and all assets are distributed to the beneficiaries.

The information provided below dealing with filing deadlines and determining the year end for an estate has been sourced directly from the CRA's "T3—Trust Guide 2010" which can be accessed at www.cra-arc.gc.ca/E/pub/tg/t4013/t4013-e.html. It is important to be aware that tax rules and laws can and do change frequently, so it is a good practice to check the CRA's website for changes on a periodic basis (at least annually), or be sure, when dealing with your accountant, to inquire of any rule changes of which you should be aware.

Generally, the final T1 return is due on or before the following dates:

Period When Death Occurred	Due Date for Return
January 1 to October 31	April 30 of the following year
November 1 to December 31	Six months after the date of death

If the deceased or the deceased's spouse or common-law partner was carrying on a business in the year (unless the expenditures of the business are mainly in connection with a tax shelter), the following due dates apply:

Period When Death Occurred	Due Date for Return
January 1 to December 15	June 15 of the following year
December 16 to December 31	Six months after the date of death

An exception arises when the person dies after December 31 but prior to filing a tax return for that year just ended. In this case, the due date for filing the return and paying any balance owing is six months after the date of death. For previous year returns that are already due but were not filed by the deceased, the due dates for filing those returns as well as payment of any related taxes owing remain the same.

Someone performing the role of attorney under a general CPOAP, when the grantor is still involved with the management of financial affairs, has no such legal obligation to file tax returns. However, because they are assisting with the grantor's financial affairs, they are certainly in a good position to ensure that this is done. An exception to this would be if the CPOAP document is specific. In this case, it might include the preparation of the grantor's personal tax return as a task that the attorney is expected to oversee. If so, the attorney is legally obliged to see that tax returns are prepared and filed on time. The other situation where the attorney is legally obligated to file the grantor's income tax return is where the grantor is or has become incapacitated.

It should also be noted that all taxes owing once the returns are completed are also due by these same due dates. Failure to file a return by the due date will lead to penalties and interest charges being levied based on the taxes that should have been paid once the return is filed. In instances where no tax is owing to the government, although no penalties or interest charges will be levied, it is in the best interest of the grantor or the estate that returns are filed in a timely fashion for several reasons.

1) When the grantor is living, it is the filing of these returns that ensures the continuance of any government subsidies and/or pensions based on previous years taxable income.

2) If a refund is due, it is important to have it received by the grantor or estate as soon as reasonably possible.

3) The longer one waits to complete the tax return, the more difficult it will be to ensure no medical and donation receipts, information slips (T3s and T5s) and other supporting documentation have gone missing, and if they have, to replace them.

4) It can take an extraordinarily long time for the Canada Revenue Agency to process final returns (even relatively simple ones), and yet final distribution of estate assets cannot be completed until a clearance certificate (discussed later) has been issued. This will only be done once all tax returns and related taxes have been filed and paid.

When a person dies, there are three separate departments of the CRA that the estate trustee will communicate with in some way. First, there is the department that deals with pensions and Old Age Security. This department will need to be advised of the person's death so that any payments can be stopped. A person is entitled to receive pension and Old Age Security payments in the month of death—even if the date of payment is after their death. However, any monies received after that date will have to be returned to the Receiver General. Second, when the estate trustee files the final T1 Return for the deceased, the trustee will send it to the department that processes T1 Returns. It is a good idea to file a copy of the will with this return. The third department the estate trustee will communicate with is that which processes the T3 Trust Income and Information Returns. It is recommended that you file a copy of the will with this return also. It is this department that will assign a "Trust Number" which replaces the Social Insurance Number (SIN). Once notification is received of this number, the CRA will expect this number to be used in all correspondence instead of the person's SIN.

Generally T3 Returns are due no later than **90 days** after the trust's tax year end, and you must also pay any balance by that time to avoid penalties and interest. You might ask, "What do you mean, the trust's tax year end? Isn't this just December 31?" No, it is not. There are a number of different types of trusts, and for a complete list of types, the reader can refer to Appendix VI. Most people's estate will fall into the classification of being a testamentary trust, and thus the information contained here will be specific to that type. If you suspect you have one of the other trusts described in Appendix VI, you are advised to consult a professional accountant who specializes in trust tax filings because the tax rules are quite complex and are subject to change frequently.

The tax-year end of a testamentary trust may be, but does not have to be, December 31. The first tax period of the trust begins on the day after the person dies, and it ends at any time you select within the next 12 months. The tax rates used, and the tax year of any slips issued to the beneficiaries, are based on the tax-year end of the trust. In most cases, a December 31 (calendar) year end for a testamentary trust is the most convenient and makes little difference for the beneficiaries of the estate for several reasons.

> ➤ **Availability of Forms.** The current-year trust returns and related schedules are usually not available until the end of the calendar year. For example, a 2007 return due before the forms are available would have to be filed using a 2006 form, which might not contain current-year changes or information.

> ➤ **Easier Form Completion.** It is generally easier to complete forms and interpret rules when the tax year coincides with the calendar year.

> ➤ **Availability of Information.** Most information slips for income amounts are issued for a calendar year (for example, a T5 slip for bank interest).

> ➤ **Minimum Delay in Assessing the Return.** Changes to law generally require changing the processing procedures for the return. If the return has a tax year ending early in a calendar year, you may have to delay assessing the return until the law is passed and the new procedures are in place.

However, there may be advantages to choosing a non-calendar-year end. As the CRA's *T3 Trust Guide (T4013(E))* suggests, being able to transfer certain estate losses incurred and certain gains realized on employee security options during the first tax year of the trust to the deceased person's return for the year of death, as well as the timing of income receipts, may play an important role when you choose the trust's tax year. Again, if you suspect that these issues are a consideration for you, then consult a professional accountant before solidifying the year end of the trust. Once you establish the trust's year end, you *cannot* change it without approval of the CRA. Requests are approved only if the change is for sound business reasons. Normally, retroactive changes will not be approved.

A clearance certificate is issued by the CRA and certifies that all amounts for which the taxpayer is, or can reasonably be expected to become, liable for under the Income Tax Act have been paid (or security for payment has been accepted by the CRA). It is imperative that you receive this certificate prior to distributing all the money from the estate. If you do not apply for this certificate or make the final distribution prior to receiving the certificate, and it turns out that there are in fact unpaid taxes, as the legal representative of the estate, you will be personally responsible for paying all amounts found owing, including any penalties and interest. Form TX19, "Asking for a Clearance Certificate" (www.cra-arc.gc.ca/tx/ndvdls/lf-vnts/dth/clrnc-eng.html?=slnk), should be filed as soon as:

a) you have filed all outstanding tax and information returns; and

b) made final payments as indicated by the tax returns.

If the estate is that of a person who had an active GST registration (i.e., the person was conducting business as an unincorporated entity), it will be necessary for the estate trustee to submit an "Application for Clearance Certificate" Form GST352 (www.cra-arc.gc.ca/E/pbg/gf/gst352/gst352-08b.pdf). This will ensure there are no further obligations outstanding with respect to GST. Again, failure to obtain this clearance certificate will leave the estate trustee open to being responsible for paying any outstanding amounts that come to light if all the assets of the estate have been distributed.

Final Accounting and Releases

As an estate trustee, you will have to prepare a final accounting of the financial activities of the estate and have the beneficiaries sign off that they are satisfied with the execution of your duties on behalf of the estate. If the accounts are prepared for the beneficiaries in the absence of a court procedure, there is no prescribed (standard) format for these accounts, but they do need to be in a meaningful format so that the beneficiaries can clearly see what the estate consists of, the expenses incurred by the estate and what revenue if any was taken in. Should there be questions from the beneficiaries, and a formal accounting is required before the court, then a specific format of the accounts is required. The lawyer handling this on behalf of the estate trustee will know how to proceed in the preparation of these accounts. Formal estate accounts are prepared in the same format that is used when passing attorney accounts.

Generally speaking, as an attorney you are primarily responsible to the grantor. On the grantor's death, the attorney will have to turn over the financial records to the estate trustee. When this happens, there may be no formal accounting required. An informal review of the financial position as at the date of death and the paperwork supporting your actions (e.g., bank statements, investment certificates, memos documenting review sessions with the grantor) during the period of time you were assisting the grantor may be all that is required. Certainly if the estate trustee is the same person as the attorney, then no formal accounting is going to be required at the date of death unless the deceased's relatives start litigation, or you as the attorney wish the court to approve your accounts, which would include any compensation taken by you as attorney.

Ongoing Trust Management

Our discussion in this chapter thus far has assumed that the estate trustee is working towards winding up an estate as soon as reasonably possible, obtaining a clearance certificate and distributing the assets of the estate in accordance with the will. However, not all wills allow for a quick (relatively speaking) finalization. Some wills, for example, require that assets be held in trust for minors or for disabled persons over the age of 18. In such cases, the estate trustee will be responsible for the financial management of the trust assets until those assets can be distributed. This date will be event-based and identified in the will. For example, a will may order that a certain amount is distributed to the beneficiaries now, with the remainder to be distributed as each beneficiary reaches a certain age.

The estate trustee will be expected to continue keeping account of these assets and therefore will find Steps 8 and 9 in Chapter 5 of particular value in their ongoing administration.

Chapter Recap

This chapter highlighted several distinctions between the duties of an attorney versus those of an estate trustee. Although very similar in terms of the expectation that both roles require one to fulfill their duties to the best of their ability for the benefit of another party (the grantor in the case of the attorney and the beneficiaries in the case of the estate trustee), there are noteworthy differences. The common theme of these differences is that an estate trustee's role is usually of a short-term duration compared to an attorney's role, which can span several years. That is, the estate trustee is interested in winding up a person's affairs as soon as possible, whereas an attorney is focused on maintaining the value of an estate for the duration of the person's life in order to support that person. Here are three important things to remember:

1) As estate trustee, you are solely responsible for the management of the estate's assets and liabilities.

2) The accuracy of the valuation of assets and liabilities become even more important because these values play an important role in the calculation of final tax obligations.

3) Obtain a clearance certificate from the CRA prior to making the final distribution of the estate to the beneficiaries.

Although this chapter has highlighted differences, it is apparent that there are also many similar aspects when comparing the two roles. Perhaps the most notable is the requirement to have an evidentiary record of your efforts (i.e., supporting documentation) when administering another party's affairs—whether that party be a living person (the grantor) or a deceased person (the estate and, by extension, the beneficiaries). The same guidelines and principals pertain to successful record keeping in either case. However, as can be seen from the letters presented in the next chapter, there are a number of things that can go wrong, even by well-meaning, conscientious people, and by those less so.

Chapter 8

What to Do When Things Go Wrong!

Despite our best intentions to execute the tasks associated with looking after another person's financial affairs with diligence and awareness, we are after all, only human. Mistakes, omissions and the desire to simply be done with it all will mark most people's time as attorney. Although no one should judge you harshly for being human and making honest mistakes, what you may be called upon to justify is how you acted to correct mistakes made. This chapter will present a number of situations that describe common errors committed (or almost committed) by those looking after another person's financial affairs, along with suggestions on what to do when you realize an error or omission has been made. They are listed in no particular order. Remember these are examples only, and the answers provided should not be read as legal or accounting advice for your particular situation. The answers will give you an idea of the type of corrective action that might be expected should you find yourself in a similar situation. However, you are advised to consult with appropriate professionals who can explain to you the specific actions required to manage your exact situation. Regardless of the type of mistake described, the most crucial step to take in rectifying the error is to take action in a timely manner as soon as the mistake is realized and to accurately record the action(s) taken to rectify the mistake and what will be done differently in the future to ensure that the mistake does not reoccur.

Being Out of Pocket

Dear Let the Records Show,

I'm helping to look after my mom in a variety of ways now that she is getting older and finds it hard to get around. Mom recently went to a lawyer and signed a power of attorney that says I'm now helping her with all her banking and investing decisions. I recently did some grocery shopping for my mother and realized when I got home that I had used my debit card instead of mom's to make the purchase. While I don't mind paying for my mother's groceries, I'm on a fixed income and so every dollar counts. Should I just use my mom's debit card to buy some of my groceries next time?

Signed,
Please Don't Think Me Miserly.

Dear You Are Not Miserly,

First, no one, least of all you, should think of yourself as being miserly because you want to rectify a payment error. The rules are very clear with respect to the expectation that an attorney should not incur any expenses on behalf of the person whose affairs they are looking after, unless they choose to do so. This applies whether the attorney is related to the person or not.

When rectifying this error, you will need to keep in mind the importance of maintaining the "evidentiary record" that supports the money being withdrawn from your mother's bank account.

Our advice is to ensure that both the grocery store receipt that lists the items purchased as well as the debit card receipt is filed with the bank statement that shows the amount coming out of the bank account. This way, should there be any questions of whether the groceries were actually purchased for your mother's use, the type of items purchased will help to ensure the correct conclusion is reached.

In terms of your reimbursement, the best solution is to have your mother sign a cheque that reimburses you for these groceries with the cheque's memo line clearly marked, "Repayment for groceries." This would give some assurance that she fully realizes what has happened and is in agreement with the steps taken to resolve the error. Should your mother not be in a position to sign the cheque, then the existence of the list of groceries will become more important should you have to justify why you took the money out of her bank account. In this situation, it matters little to the evidentiary record whether a cheque is written or cash is withdrawn. The fact is the transaction will show up on your mother's bank statement as cash coming out. What is important is that you can substantiate why this amount has been withdrawn. You can do this by ensuring that when the withdrawal of money shows up on the bank statement, a note is made against the transaction, or a separate memo is placed in the file that clearly explains why this money is being withdrawn along with the original debit card and store receipts.

To ensure this situation does not happen again, it is recommended that your mother's debit card is kept well away from your other credit cards in your wallet or purse. This will make it a more conscious action to acquire the right payment card, and therefore a repeat occurrence will be less likely.

Given your question, it sounds like you are being conscientious and trying to assist your mother with her financial affairs using care and common sense. You are not being miserly; you are being prudent in trying to ensure everything is on the up and up with respect to your mother's day-to-day financial affairs.

Yours truly,
Let the Records Show

Using the Wrong Debit Card

Dear Let the Records Show,

I'm looking after my father's day-to-day financial affairs because he is in a nursing home now and is not very coherent most days. As I was reviewing the bank statements for the last couple of months and making sure I could account for all the activity, I realized I'd inadvertently used his cash card a couple of months ago to buy gas for my car. What should I do? It's only $35.63, but my sister's going to go ballistic when she sees this next month when we sit down for the 6-month review of my father's financial affairs.

Signed,
Brother with the Unreasonable Sister

> Dear You Say "Inadvertently" but Unreasonable Sister May Say Otherwise,
>
> As soon as you read this, go to the bank and make a deposit into your father's account in the exact amount of $35.63. Be sure to make a note of why the deposit is being made and attach it to the relevant bank statement. Although the amount is not large, we cannot stress the importance of an attorney keeping their money transactions strictly separate from the financial affairs of the person they are acting on behalf of.
>
> To prevent this kind of inadvertent action from happening again, it is highly recommended that your father's debit card is kept well away from your personal debit/credit cards. This will make it a more conscious action to acquire the right payment card.
>
> Also, we are sure that we do not have to point out to you the importance of doing this review every month and not every couple of months. The sooner these little mistakes are noted and corrected, the less likely they are to cause any family disturbances.
>
> Yours truly,
> Let the Records Show

Missing Important Dates

Dear Let the Records Show,

I missed the anniversary date of a GIC, and because the standing instruction with the bank was to roll it over, they did so. However, my uncle needs some of the capital amount to cover health-care costs. If I redeem the GIC early, will there be a penalty? How do I make sure I don't do this again?

Signed,
Took My Eye off the Calendar

Dear What Happened to the Other Eye?,

The situation you describe in your letter is not an uncommon one and allows us the opportunity to emphasize the importance of two recommendations made a number of times throughout our book, *Let the Records Show*, namely the importance of:

1)   Regular reviews of the cash requirements against the availability of cash to meet those requirements (i.e., the cash flow document), and

2)   Documenting maturity dates for investments (and other transactions that are time-sensitive such as insurance policy premium due dates) in a manner that will ensure they don't get "missed" resulting in a flurry of panicked decision making that could ultimately leave the grantor worse off (even slightly) financially.

Do you know exactly how much the short-fall is going to be between your uncle's anticipated health-care costs and what will be coming in from his regular income sources? It is important to sit down with your uncle and prepare an informal budget for the next few months. Do not forget to consider other investments that might be coming due during this period, as well as any non-recurring amounts such as a tax refund for the previous year's taxes paid. Determine the exact date that your uncle will need the necessary funds.

As you sort this matter out and determine how much you can reinvest, you might consider "laddering" your uncle's investments. Laddering means dividing the total amount invested to ensure varying amounts mature at staggering times throughout the year for short-term investments and at different yearly periods for medium and long-term investments. Your uncle's investment advisor (or any investment advisor if you or your uncle do not currently have one) will be able to provide you more details on this strategy and be able to work out the best arrangement knowing the specifics of your uncle's investment portfolio.

You have questioned whether there might be a penalty if you redeem the GIC early. This implies that the GIC is, in fact, redeemable. You need to confirm this by checking with the issuer of the GIC or if you have the GIC certificate, review it to confirm the details. There are primarily two categories of GICs on the market, redeemable and non-redeemable. In addition, there are a number of varying types within these two categories. For example, there are some redeemable GICs that allow redemption with no penalty, but the funds must be held for a minimum of 30 days; other GICs allow for redemption but the funds must be held for a minimum of 90 days, and the penalty consists of a lower interest rate than previously quoted for the longer term; others still can only be cashed if the money is going to be moved into an RESP (registered education savings plan) or RIF (retirement investment fund).

In a worst-case situation, you, as the attorney, could be judged to have been negligent in carrying out your duties. As a result of such negligence, you may be legally liable to your uncle for any losses or damages suffered by him as a result of any unavailability of the capital. Examples of such losses or damages could be:

1) Any reduced interest earned due to early redemption, or

2) The cost of borrowing funds on a short-term basis until the GIC can be redeemed.

The likelihood of this happening will of course depend on many factors. Your letter does not indicate the amount of money involved nor your personal circumstance with respect to other relatives or beneficiaries of the will who might decide to take you to task for this slip-up. The most important action for you to take is to act quickly following the guidance provided in our letter and ensure that no further slip-ups occur that could cast doubts on your performance as an attorney.

Although no system involving humans is fool-proof, to avoid a repeat of this situation, you will want to mark the maturity dates of investments on a personal calendar that you are already in a habit of referring to regularly. In fact, you will want to make a notation of a maturity a few days prior to the actual maturity date in order to give yourself sufficient time to review the cash flow of the grantor and make the appropriate reinvesting decision. Also remember that when sitting with the grantor during each regularly scheduled or annual review, knowing precisely what these maturity dates are will enable realistic planning.

Yours truly,
Let the Records Show

Missing Documentation Could Cause Grief

Dear Let the Records Show,

I began acting as my aunt's attorney for property two years ago when she became incapable of managing her finances. Until recently, other than collecting information required for her tax return, I had not done any formal record keeping. Realizing I need to have a better handle on my aunt's financial assets, I've begun to organize everything, and now know I am missing documentation to support some of her expenses. Is it necessary for me to go back to "Day One" and get full support for every item on the bank statements?

Signed,
Behind the Eight Ball, but Promising to Do Better

Dear Promises Mean Nothing without Action,

The answer to your question is: "Yes." You will need support for each item of financial activity. Remember, you are responsible for record keeping from the day you first act as attorney when your aunt becomes incapable of managing her affairs or you have reasonable grounds to believe that she is incapable. Neither the day your aunt may have signed the CPOAP document nor the day you find out you need to pass accounts is relevant. Moreover, having to account for your financial management may not occur for several months or years, and at that time support will be that much more difficult to obtain.

It may not be the onerous task you are anticipating. First make a list of the items for which you are missing support. You may find that the missing documentation is straightforward and only involves one or two sources such as bank statements and income tax returns. At least one attempt should be made for each item, but if a company is unable to supply you with a copy of the bill, simply make a note of what you did to try and obtain it and move on. The detail on the bank statement should be enough to identify standard monthly direct debits for such things as local utilities and cable companies.

Finding details to support cheques written may be more difficult if the cancelled cheques have not been returned with the bank statement and no record was made in the cheque book at the time the cheques were written. In such cases you will have to request a copy of the original from the bank. You may be charged for this service. Legally you could be held responsible for the fees because it was your lack of timely attention to the record keeping that has given rise to these bank fees. Another point to be considered is whether you are receiving a fee for being your aunt's attorney. If not, then the standard of due care to which you will be compared will be lower than if you are receiving a fee. Nevertheless, you need to rectify the lack of proper record keeping immediately.

Supporting details for cash amounts withdrawn using your aunt's debit card will, if any, certainly be the most difficult to find. Perhaps you have documented a weekly amount of cash that your aunt and you decided would be her allowance. This would certainly support some withdrawals. For amounts taken in excess of this agreed amount or more frequently, there could be legitimate reasons. For example, your aunt may be in the habit of giving cash gifts to friends or relatives for birthdays or other celebrations such as anniversaries, engagements or graduations. Try and determine whether this might be the case for any of these amounts and fully document them by writing down in the file the amounts involved and the reasons why these amounts were withdrawn.

Yours truly,
Let the Records Show

Finding Tax Receipts after the Fact

Dear Let the Records Show,

When I was reviewing my father's tax return for his signature, the medical expenses did not look high enough. So I went through all his paperwork again and realized I'd missed giving the accountants all the medical expense slips. What do I do?

Signed,
Must Have Been Looking with My Eyes Closed the First Time

Dear Closed Eyes,

If the tax return has not yet been finalized and time permits, give the newly found medical expense slips to the accountant and have the tax return corrected. However, if time does not permit that, it is probably best to have your father sign his tax return and mail it off. If he owes taxes, then you don't want him to be penalized for late filing. If he is getting a refund, then the sooner the tax return is filed, the sooner your father will receive his refund.

Next, phone the accountant who has prepared the return and state that you are sending in additional medical receipts. Once received, the accountant can then prepare the T1 Adjustment form. This form has to be signed by the taxpayer or legal representative before being forwarded to the Canada Revenue Agency.

Depending on the total of the receipts, it may not be worthwhile to forward them to the accountant. When you make this call, be sure to ask how much this will cost. If the firm is going to charge you $150 to prepare the T1 adjustment and the receipts only total $50, then even with the little bit of refund you get from the government, it still means your father is going to be slightly out of pocket.

Alternatively, you can visit www.cra-arc.gc.ca/tx/ndvdls/tpcs/ncm-tx/chngrtrn-eng. html?=slnk for a copy of the T1 Adjustment form and instructions on how to complete it. It's fairly straightforward; just remember that medical expenses show up on both the federal and provincial tax calculation pages, and therefore two different line references will be required.

Yours truly,
Let the Records Show

Benefiting Inappropriately

Dear Let the Records Show,

I was acting as my mother's chief caregiver, and in this role I have been living for a number of years with her in the house in which I grew up. About six months ago it became necessary to move her to a long-term care facility. I have continued to live in the house. It only occurred to me a couple of days ago that I had never changed the bank account from which the utilities, cable and property tax bills are being withdrawn. That is, these amounts were still coming out of my mother's account. As soon as I realized this, I immediately contacted the companies and removed my mother's account from their payment instructions. What do I do about the payments already paid? Do I have to pay these amounts back to my mother's account with interest? Do I have to pay it all in one lump sum? I am legally my mother's attorney for property and am doing this without being paid. Does that make a difference? My three siblings who live on the other side of the country and overseas know about the CPOAP and that I am the attorney.

Signed,
Hoping I Don't Have to Pay It Back all at Once

> Dear Pay It Back,
>
> It heartens us to read your letter and that your question is not about whether you have to pay back the money, but what the terms of this reimbursement should be. Unsupported and fraudulent withdrawals from an elderly person's bank accounts by relatives and friends appointed as attorneys is becoming one of the most common forms of elder abuse. Although most of us think of abuse as verbal or physical, taking away the means of a person to support themselves financially—while perhaps a newer kind of abuse—is no less damaging. It is of the utmost importance that the action you take to resolve this matter makes a clear statement that there was never any deliberate intent to reduce your mother's financial resources.
>
> Your letter highlights two main issues: First, the fact that you are residing in your mother's home although she no longer resides there. Second, there is the matter of how and when the money should be paid back.
>
> Looking at the matter of where you are living, from your letter it is apparent that you are still residing in your mother's principal residence. However your letter does not say whether there exists written instructions signed by your mother regarding her wishes that you should remain in the house should she cease to live there (either due to her death or movement to a health-care facility). You need to understand that even as her daughter, you may not have a right to be there at all. This situation could be interpreted by some that you are benefitting from your position as her attorney, regardless of the fact that you are her daughter. This is in clear conflict with the attorney's fiduciary obligations of always acting for the benefit and best interests of the grantor and with no personal gain. It may be that the house should be rented out

or put on the market to provide necessary funds for the long-term care of your mother. Thus, it is important that if no instructions currently exist, a document be drawn up after discussions with your mother that stipulate her wishes with respect to the house and you living there. See Chapter 5, Step 7 of our book *Let the Records Show,* where we address the need to document all arrangements outside the activity of the bank statement. Be sure that this document includes details of the arrangements such as who is to take care of the house expenses like the mortgage (if one still exists), taxes, ongoing repairs to maintain value and utilities. Given your concern that these expenses have been paid by your mother despite her not living there anymore, we are assuming the expectation is that while you remain in the house, you would take over all household expenses. Review any existing documentation that supports this claim of yours or take steps to create the documentation.

Now we turn to the matter of the money that needs to be paid back to your mother. You mentioned that your mother has been moved to a long-term care facility. You have not indicated whether this is due to deteriorating physical health or mental capacity. If it is the former, and therefore you are able to have a conversation with your mother about this, then do so. Let her know this has happened and suggest to her the most aggressive pay back arrangement you can handle. If you have the resources to make a lump-sum payment and choose not to, obviously benefitting yourself, you are not acting honestly and will be in breach of your fiduciary obligation. Document the arrangement, date the sheet of paper, have your mother sign it and be sure to file it with all the other documentation you have supporting your management of her financial affairs. Although your mother's love for you might want her to forgive these amounts, it is strongly recommended that you do not agree to this. Remember, it is very important that the records show a consistency in acting honestly, in good faith and strictly in the best interests of your mother. Be sure that the amounts showing up on the bank statement agree with the amounts documented on the payback schedule.

You also raised the issue of interest in your letter. It is advisable that an interest component is added to the amount you are reimbursing. This will further strengthen the evidence of acting in the best interest of your mother. You can determine a reasonable rate by referring to the website of any of Canada's financial institutions to obtain loan rates. This will also reduce any claim against you, requiring you to make up income lost by your mother because the money was not in her bank account earning interest when it should have been.

When paying back the amount, it is not necessary to pay it back into the account from which the money was originally taken. If you mother has a high-interest savings account, the money should be deposited into this account, assuming she does not need the cash immediately. If your mother does not have a high-interest savings account, you might consider opening one and designating this as the deposit account for these amounts.

Yours truly,
Let the Records Show

Failing to Keep the Grantor's Best Interests in Mind

Dear Let the Records Show,

I'm something of a Bay Street wiz and have been managing my father's affairs now for a number of years. My mother passed away many years ago, and over the years my father has been suffering with greater mental impairment. I'm his only child, and I've been treating his investments as eventually coming to me and have therefore been taking a long-view investment strategy. I've also been pretty slack about keeping records, figuring that I'd be getting it all anyway. Unfortunately, the market meltdown of 2008 had a pretty devastating impact, and a lot of money was lost. It also looks like my marriage is headed for a meltdown and divorce.

Signed,
Hot Stuff on Bay Street

Dear Former Hot Stuff on Bay Street,

We cannot thank you enough for your letter, because it raises a number of important issues that often escape adequate understanding.

First, while not related to financial record keeping, your presumption about being your father's heir is just that, a presumption—you might be in for a surprise. As astonishing as it might sound to you, there is a notable trend being observed when it comes to final instructions of your father's generation. An increasing number of his peers are wishing to distribute their remaining assets to grandchildren, to persons not related to them or to charitable/educational organizations that they have been associated with throughout their lives. This is especially true in cases where the testator's children are themselves successful and fully established in the world. Your father could well be among this group. Therefore, you would do well not to "count your chickens before they hatch."

Moving on to issues directly related to your obvious less-than-stellar efforts in the management of your father's financial affairs, let's look at your investment strategy. This deliberate long-term view adopted for your father's financial assets, based on your assumption of inheritance, shows a disregard (intentional or not) for the all-encompassing rule that people looking after someone else's assets must keep in mind: all decisions must be made solely for the benefit of this person (and their dependents, if any). Given your admission to being "something of a Bay Street wiz," you would appear not to be a dependent. Without knowing more particulars of your father's situation (both physical and financial), we do not wish to suggest what a more prudent strategy would look like, but as a rule, it is common knowledge on Bay Street that the older one becomes, the less long-term their investment strategy becomes.

It is important for you to realize that should this failure of yours to adopt a more prudent investment strategy for your father result in a material decline in his ability to continue to support himself, you may find yourself having to provide financial assistance. Another scenario that might play out is one where significant bills go unpaid (e.g., property taxes if he's still in his own home, or long-term care fees if he is a resident of a care facility). This may prompt the party who is not being paid to have the court initiate an inquiry into the reason for you father's inability to meet these financial obligations. At this point, you would certainly be expected to present some sort of accounting to show how your father's financial affairs have been managed.

Your letter leads us to believe that you have not read your father's will or discussed his wishes with respect to the distribution of any financial assets that may outlive him. This is a huge omission on your part and needs to be rectified as soon as possible. You need to discuss these plans with your father, if he is still mentally capable. If not, review his will to ensure that you do not inadvertently sell something of your father's estate that is earmarked in the will to go to a particular individual, such as your soon to be ex-wife or any grandchildren, or to charity/educational organizations. Also if it turns out you are not the sole beneficiary, you need to be aware that you can be personally liable to the actual beneficiary or other beneficiaries for your apparent negligent management of your father's financial affairs. This would mean you would have to make good all the monetary losses incurred by your father due to your inappropriate investment decisions.

Another reason you need to read the will is to determine whether you have been designated as the estate trustee. Certainly if you are not, then you definitely have some work ahead of you to ensure that you are able to hand over a satisfactory accounting of your father's financial affairs to the person who has been appointed as estate trustee.

Finally, let's discuss the inadequate financial record keeping that you admit to. Let's assume for the moment that you are the estate trustee (not necessarily the sole beneficiary). As of today, if you haven't already done so, get yourself more organized and adopt the process outlined in Chapter 5, Step 9 of our book *Let the Records Show*, for keeping track of cash in and cash out of the bank/investment statements. Within the next week, ensure you allocate some time for a thorough review of the 10 Steps, identifying specific actions you need to take now in order to ensure that as you move forward, there is proper and meaningful evidence of the management of your father's financial affairs. Ensure that going forward the records are meticulously kept. If your father is indeed incapacitated, you are under a legal obligation to keep financial records regardless of your status of sole beneficiary.

The prudent and legally required thing to do is to catch up to date the record keeping. Just how onerous this is for you will of course depend on how substantial your father's assets are and the volume of transactions involved since you have taken over. Just remember that the longer you wait to collect information and copies of supporting documentation, the harder it will be to get satisfactory answers.

While we here at Let the Records Show have little interest in your domestic affairs, again thank you for sharing, because it gives us an opportunity to remind you (and everyone else) that your affairs, physical and financial, are of no concern and should have no bearing on decisions you make on behalf of another person while acting as the attorney.

Please permit us one final observation—we are perplexed over the fact that although you think your father's remaining assets are "coming to you anyway," you have not made more of an effort to ensure, first and foremost, that your father retains an asset base sufficient to ensure he enjoys the quality of life in his declining years without you having to worry about supporting him. And second, purely as an extension of your sound financial management for him, you might have been guaranteeing something for yourself, maximizing the possibility that your father's estate would have some residual assets to pass onto you—which given the impending divorce, you may have been able to use in your new life.

Yours truly,
Let the Records Show

Throwing Away Records Too Soon

Dear Let the Records Show,

I was looking after my mom's affairs for a number of years, and she recently passed away. The estate is ready to wind up as soon as I receive the clearance certificate from the CRA, for which I have applied. As you can probably imagine, I've got paperwork galore and am wondering when is it okay for me to ditch all these records?

Signed,
Needing More Storage Space

Dear Storage Space Challenged,

There are two separate time frames that you need to be aware of for record retention. One is imposed by the Canada Revenue Agency (CRA). The other time frame is specified by the provincial legislation that provides the rules and regulations for accounts and record keeping by an attorney and/or guardian.

Given that you have looked after your mother's affairs for a number of years, we are going to assume that your mother was retired from the paid workforce. The CRA is only interested in the financial records that support the numbers presented in a tax return of an individual (T1) or estate (T3). For people retired from the workforce, the most common documentation supporting a tax return will be T3s, T4As, T5s and medical and donation receipts. This documentation does not usually include bank or investment statements, credit card statements, cheque stubs and other items of similar nature. However, please note that investment statements may be required to support ACB of any security disposals. This is because the CRA requires records supporting changes to the cost base of securities also kept. The CRA indicates that supporting documentation for income tax returns of individuals (this includes living as well as deceased persons) need to be kept for six years in case the tax return is selected for review. For example, for the tax return filed for December 31, 2001, you need to note the date of the Notice of Assessment issued by the CRA. All supporting documentation would need to be retained until the corresponding date in 2008. That is, if the date of the Notice of Assessment is May 15, 2002, receipts would need to be kept until May 15, 2008. The exception to this rule is when a clearance certificate has been received. Income Tax Information Circular No. IC78-10R4, issued in June 2010 and entitled "Books and Records Retention/Destruction," provides the citation from Section 5800 of the Income Tax Regulations stipulating that receiving a clearance certificate cancels any requirement to retain records. Thus, once the clearance certificate (discussed in Chapter 7 of *Let the Records Show*, "Tax Return Preparation") has been received, you are free to dispose of all records as far as the CRA a is concerned.

As an aside, if the person has been engaged in an unincorporated business up to the time of death, then all business records supporting revenues and expenses will need to be retained for the same period, six years.

However there may be reasons why you need to retain these records a little longer. For persons living in Ontario, s. 6 of Ontario Regulation 100/96 (Appendix III) indicates that retention of records as a result of being an attorney or guardian ceases once a person dies because the requirement is that these records will be delivered to the person's personal representative, the estate trustee. Since you were also your mother's estate trustee, this transfer of records was not physically required and thus continues to take up valuable storage space. Before you destroy any records related either to your time as attorney or estate trustee, be sure to obtain a release from all beneficiaries. This is a document best drawn up by your lawyer. This document, signed by each beneficiary, is a clear agreement from them that they have received everything from the estate they were entitled to receive and that they are satisfied with your work as estate trustee. Depending on the size of your mother's estate and the number of beneficiaries involved, the beneficiaries may require you to provide a final accounting and have the accounts passed before the court. Or you may decide to have the accounts formally approved by the court to provide yourself with added protection against any potential dissatisfied beneficiaries. Note that once the court has approved the accounts, you will need to wait for any appeal time limit to pass before destroying any records. There is always a period of time after the date of a court's decision during which interested parties can appeal this decision. Your lawyer will be able to tell you what the appeal time period is in the province the CPOAP document and will have been made.

Yours truly,
Let the Records Show

Making Life Easier by Having a Continuing Power of Attorney

Dear Let the Records Show,

My auntie is 85 and is starting to slow down a bit, so I've started to help her with various things like making bank deposits, helping her write cheques (I fill them out and she signs them) and going to the grocery store for her. It would be so much easier for me and her to have a joint account. Is this a good idea?

Signed,
Auntie's Little Helper

Dear Auntie's Helper,

The fact that you have asked this question leads us to surmise that your assistance is being offered out of love and a recognition of family duty rather than because your auntie has organized a continuing power of attorney for property (CPOAP) document declaring you as her attorney. Our recommendation is that she meet with a lawyer on her own and have a formal CPOAP document prepared with any specific instructions included, appointing you as her attorney. Having a CPOAP will mean that you do not need to have joint accounts because the CPOAP document will give you access to all your auntie's financial accounts (except for any she specifically excludes by listing in the CPOAP document), as well as other property decisions that may become more of an issue as she ages. Understand that because joint accounts usually carry with them the right of survivorship (i.e., whatever money is remaining in the account at the time of death of one of the account owners automatically becomes the property of the surviving account owner), it is important to keep your aunt's estate separate from your own because it may not be her intent that you inherit all the money left in this shared bank account when she dies.

Having a CPOAP document in existence will ensure peace of mind for both you and your auntie because it provides a means by which timely management of her financial affairs can continue should something unplanned happen, such as a fall that puts her in the hospital for an extended period of time. If you have a CPOAP document to rely on, you as her attorney will be able to act on her behalf with respect to such things as paying bills, managing her apartment (e.g., having her cable TV service disconnected while she's in the hospital or signing a new lease if she's not on a month-to-month arrangement) and rolling over GICs or other investments as they come due.

Yours truly,
Let the Records Show

Becoming an All Too Common Occurrence

Dear Let the Records Show:

I'm really worried about my mother's finances. About seven years ago, I started looking after her finances under a power of attorney. Mother's mental capacity had started to go down hill several years before the death of my dad, and when he died, I started to look after things because she was not capable of doing so herself. I sold her two-story house and bought a bungalow, which was put into my name to make things easier and save on probate taxes. I've also put her investments into my name as well as having her rather generous teacher's pension, CPP and Old Age Security paid straight into my bank account. About five years ago, with her continuing mental difficulties as well as physical deterioration, plus the fact that I travel a lot, I decided that it was time that she be moved into an old age home.

Five years ago, my mother had about a million dollars, but today there's only about $300,000.00. I'm worried that there will not be enough money left. My two brothers and their families, who see mother regularly, have pretty well left me to look after things. As I don't have a 9-to-5 job, I've been living off our mother's money while looking after her whenever I'm around. Although my brothers don't really seem to care what I'm doing, I'm also worried that one of my sisters-in-law might start asking questions, especially when mother dies, because her estate is left to the three of us.

What can I do to make sure mother has enough money and that there are no awkward questions when she dies?

Sincerely,
Worried about Mother

Dear Worried about Yourself:

Wow! Before getting into any details, let us agree with you: Yes, you should be worried! Does the word "embezzlement" mean anything to you? How about the term "elder abuse"? With what you have told us, your situation is more then just a litigation nightmare waiting to happen. Your letter raises a number of issues and problems, the least of which are associated with the risks posed to your mother's welfare in the event that you die before her, and the harm you may be doing to the relationship with your siblings once your mother has passed away.

As with most questions, there is a short answer and a long answer. The short answer to your questions is: Stop spending your mother's money on yourself, get a paying job and start paying back the money you have "borrowed" to finance your travels and lifestyle.

The long answer is going to cover a lot a ground. It is recommended that you sit down with a pen and piece of paper as you read this because it will outline a number of actions that you need to take immediately.

We will first highlight how your actions to date as attorney have placed you in a very risky position for litigation. Then we will recommend some basic but very important steps you need to take to reduce this risk. Given the severity of the implications of your actions, we cannot say for certain that you can be saved entirely from threats of litigation. However, it is hoped that by following our suggestions, you can limit the monetary losses you will incur as you pay your mother back the money you have inappropriately taken. But we are getting ahead of ourselves. First, let us look at all you have done wrong.

There are a number of concerns/questions that come to mind when reading that the house has been put into your name.

1) Who are you making things easier for? Putting the house in your name could be construed as nothing less than stealing from your mother—regardless of the power of attorney (POA) document. You have forgotten, or perhaps never realized, that the existence of a POA document does not give the attorney the right to take over the property of the grantor, in this case your mother. Having a POA in place is to provide a means by which one person can arrange for another to *assist* the grantor and to look after the grantor's affairs. The existence of a POA document means that there is a formal legal framework of rules and expectations within which the attorney is to work. This framework offers protection for both the grantor and attorney. One of the rules is that the attorney, when making any decision on behalf of the grantor, always acts with the best interests of the grantor as primary concern. It is difficult to understand how putting the house purchased with your mother's money into your name shows you are putting her best interests first.

2) Your letter indicates that your mother's mental health started to decline before you started looking after her affairs and that at the time you did start looking after things, "she was not capable of doing so herself." That being the case, you can expect to be held to account for your management of your mother's affairs from the time you first started acting for her, seven years ago.

3) Because you admit to not having a job, we wonder how you are paying the household expenses such as property tax, maintenance to maintain the value, hydro, cable, gas and telephone. We do not want to jump to the conclusion that all the household bills are being paid by your mother. However, if this is the case, we can only assume that there is some documentation signed by your mother, while she was capable, expressing her wish that she continue to pay for the upkeep of a property she is no long living in and to which she has no ownership. This document should be filed with her will in a safe place.

123

4) You express the desire that your mother not run out of money, yet by putting the house in your name, you have taken away a substantial asset that could be used in a financial strategy that would ensure she does not run out of money. This is particularly the case should you die *before* your mother. Given your extensive travel habits, this is not out of the question. Is your mother the sole beneficiary of your own will? Do you even have a will? In the event that your mother is your sole beneficiary, if you have looked after your own affairs with the same laid-back attitude that you have looked after your mother's affairs, it could be years before your estate is settled and your mother receives any monetary benefits.

The only thing you got right with respect to the house was that by putting it in your name, your mother's estate will save on probate taxes. However, this savings could still have been achieved by putting together a legitimate and well-thought-out estate plan.

Why would you put her investments into your name? With a formal POA identifying you as the attorney, there are no added benefits to you moving her investments into your name. The same issues arise with this decision of yours about the house. Who are you really thinking of, given your mother's mental incapacity? We doubt that she could be aware of your management decisions with respect to her money. What happens if you die before she does? In addition to these questions, there could be significant tax implications for both of you. Depending on how you treated this income on your tax return and your mother's, you could find yourself in hot water with the Canada Revenue Agency. Knowingly reporting incorrect income on a tax return is considered a criminal offence, and as such penalties can be both monetary as well as jail time.

One of the most basic rules that must be kept in mind when managing another person's affairs is that all bank transactions are kept separate. Having your mother's pensions deposited into your bank account breaks this rule. By doing this, you are clearly treating your mother's money as your money, and as such you are violating the trust of your mother. It is of the utmost importance for you to remember: "It is not my money, it is my mother's and I need to respect that reality."

We will now discuss possible actions you should take immediately in order to limit your exposure to criticism and legal action from one of your sisters-in-law, to say nothing of your brothers once they learn what has been going on.

1) Retain legal counsel who can help you navigate through the quagmire you have landed yourself in and to advise you on the actions we are about to discuss.

2) Change the ownership of the house back into your mother's name. As this is the only house you have been living in and you have not indicated you have purchased another dwelling (such as a vacation home), we are assuming there will be no capital gain implications. If, in fact, you have purchased a vacation home, you will want to discuss this with a professional tax accountant who can advise you on the different options you want to consider as you transfer the house into your mother's name.

3) Ensure that the power of attorney document gives you the right to remain in her house while she is residing elsewhere. The terms of you living there should also be described. That is, who will pay the household expenses? If the POA is silent as to these arrangements, you should start paying the expenses associated with you living in the house, including, utilities, property taxes, insurance and maintenance.

4) If you have closed all your mother's previous bank and investment accounts that were in her name only, you will have to open new ones. You will need to present yourself at the financial institution with a copy of the POA. If you did not close your mother's accounts and simply did not use them for the last several years, you will still have to present yourself at the financial institution with a copy of the POA and have them formally recognize you as an authorized person on these accounts.

5) Change the ownership of the investments. An easy way to do this is to add your mother's name to the certificates, ensuring her name is placed first. As these investments mature and you make decisions to reinvest, be sure to renew them in her name only. Remember, just because these investments are in your name does not stop your siblings from arguing that you hold these investments as a trustee for your mother's estate and not for yourself. Do not risk litigating this issue; remove your name from the investments.

6) Notify the teachers' pension provider and the CRA of your mother's bank account details so that all future payments go into her bank account.

7) Ensure that you make a complete list of your mother's assets and any money owing. This list should include the value of all items as of the day you first started to act as her attorney, seven years ago.

8) Collect all bank statements that have been used by your mother or by yourself for your mother's financial activities and identify all entries in two ways. First, identify the transaction as belonging to you or to your mother. For entries representing income and expenses of your mother, supporting documentation will be required. This will mean collecting seven years' worth of bank statements and/or passbooks. If you cannot

find all of them, you will have to apply at the relevant banks to obtain copies. You will likely be charged a fee for this, and we suggest that you do not even think about having your mother's money pay these fees.

9) You have admitted that you have not worked a day in the past seven years, so all the income entries will probably belong to your mother and, as such, should tie into the amounts of income reported on her T1 tax returns. If this is not the case, you need to contact a professional tax accountant who can advise you how best to proceed.

10) You need to total the amount of money that you have taken out of the accounts for your personal needs such as your vacations, house expenses during the time the house was in your name, clothing, food and the like. The total represents the amount you need to pay back to your mother's estate. You will need to calculate interest on this amount. The interest needs to be calculated from the date each individual amount was "borrowed." If is advised that you hire a professional accountant to assist you with this calculation.

11) Determine a payback schedule and ensure you stick to it. To the extent possible, you have a duty to have your mother participate to the best of her abilities in decisions about her property. Therefore, you should explain to her what has happened and how you are rectifying the situation.

12) You also have a duty to consult with family members who are in regular contact with your mother; this means your brothers and sisters-in-law. You should tell them what arrangements you have made with respect to your mother's affairs. In the event something happens to you, they will need this information to look after your mother.

13) Get your local paper and start looking for a job today so that you will have the means to make the payments required according to the payback schedule.

14) The law does make provision for the attorney to receive compensation for the work performed when helping someone manage their affairs. You did not mention it in your letter, but we suggest you review the POA document to see if your mother has indicated a compensation fee larger than what the law would allow. The accountant who is helping you determine the interest component and payback schedule will be able to assist you with calculating the amount of compensation that, under normal conditions, would have been due you. Although due to your obvious mismanagement of your mother's financial affairs, it is likely that you will be denied the right to any compensation should this matter ever end up in a court of law. Even without going to court, you should

give strong consideration to not taking any compensation, because you will be held to a higher, "professional" standard.

While managing the financial affairs of your mother, your actions have clearly shown a complete disregard for the responsibilities generally undertaken by an attorney resulting in a breach of trust, a conflict of interest, failure to generally discharge duties, improper payments and loss of interest. Any one of these alone would have the court deny payment of any compensation, to say nothing of being legal grounds to find you liable for the losses sustained by your mother's estate.

Your letter indicated that about five years ago, your mother had around one million dollars, but that is now down to around $300,000. Doing our own calculations, estimating your mother's nursing home costs to be an average cost of say, $30,000.00 per year, would mean that only $150,000.00 would have been spent over five years. Given that she has a "generous teacher's pension" coming in, the pension would in all likelihood have covered these living costs. Thus, the loss of $700,000.00 from the original one million of your mother's estate is going to be very difficult to account for, but account for it you must. You have a lot of work to do in order to avoid legal liability as well as any awkward questions when your mother dies, and we suggest that you do not delay in getting started.

Yours truly,
Let the Records Show

Chapter Recap

No two situations will be exactly the same, but it is hoped that the variety of situations presented in the above letters have clarified the appropriate action to take should you find yourself in similar circumstances. Many of you have probably already concluded that the fallout from many of the mistakes discussed above would have been minimal had they been corrected in a more timely basis—more reasons why it is important to be disciplined with a monthly review of the accounts you are managing. Moreover, even though some of the amounts involved may seem trifling, it is important to remember that more often than not it is the *mistake* that causes problems, not the amount. It is the lack of rectification of the mistake, or the frequency of the mistake being made, that causes others to question your abilities to properly fulfill your duties as attorney.

Three equally important observations to make from the scenarios presented are:

1) When an error or omission is discovered, it is imperative that action is taken immediately to rectify the mistake, the action taken is documented and what if any steps are required to ensure a similar error does not occur.

2) Always come clean and admit your mistake immediately or document it for discussion at your next meeting with the grantor (grantor's representative, if incapacitated, or the beneficiaries if dealing with the estate of a deceased person).

3) If you are unsure of the appropriateness of an action (e.g., destruction of records), be sure to seek out the advice of the relevant professional.

Unfortunately, even with efforts taken to correct errors and reduce the potential for future errors, there will be someone legally entitled to request a formal accounting before the court, who will do so. For those of you who find yourself in the unenviable position of having to defend your management of the grantor's or deceased's estate, the next chapter will provide an overview of the process (litigation) and your role in this long and often stressful course of action.

Chapter 9

Oops, Litigation Pending

If the eyes are the doorway to the soul, then the accounts you are required to maintain as attorney are the doorway into the management of the grantor's financial affairs. That is why the accounts and the evidentiary record they provide are so important in defending you as attorney against accusations of impropriety and wrongdoing.

This chapter, while of general interest to all, will be of particular interest to those readers who have been served with legal papers requiring them to account for their conduct as an attorney. Specifically, this chapter will identify the most common reasons why a formal accounting might be requested, steps that should be taken as soon as you receive the legal papers requesting such an accounting and what you will have to do if you have not been keeping a proper record of the financial activities you are managing.

Unfortunately, regardless of how seriously you have taken your obligations, or how much attention you give to your role as attorney, or the depth of care you take to record all the financial activities undertaken on behalf of the grantor, there may still be those who will want a formal review of your management. Of course, it is for this very reason that this book has been written, to provide guidance for an attorney to follow so that regardless of what prompts a formal review of your management, there will be no reason for you to incur sleepless nights due to concerns over record keeping.

An Estate Trustee, either served with legal papers requiring them to account for their management of a deceased person's estate or contemplating passing the estate accounts, will also find this chapter of interest. The process of court review is the same, regardless of whether the financial management being questioned is for a person still alive or a person deceased. Thus, as an estate trustee reads through this chapter, references made to the "management of the grantor's affairs always having the best interests of the grantor in mind", should be read as "management of the estate's affairs, having the best interest of the beneficiaries according to the will in mind."

As previously discussed, the requirement to produce a formal set of accounts in a prescribed format for the court to review can be initiated by any number of persons (see Chapter 2, "Who Am I Accountable to as an Attorney"). What the initiator (applicant) will do is make an application to the court to review the performance of an attorney through an examination of the attorney's accounts. A great many only hear the phrase "pass accounts" for the first time when they receive the "Notice of Application to Pass Accounts" or such similarly worded document. This is the means by which the legal process is initiated by the person who is questioning the financial management of the grantor's property affairs. It is issued by the

Registrar of the court office where the accounts are to be presented. For those of you who have followed the guidance contained in this book, receiving such a Notice of Application from the Court may still be slightly disconcerting; however you can take comfort knowing that there should be little to prevent you from providing a clear and complete evidential record of your management of the grantor's affairs. This evidential record will, at the very least, substantiate:

1) the nature and size of the grantor's estate you are managing;

2) your diligence in record keeping to ensure the best interests of the grantor are being met; and

3) any compensation taken by you for your work as attorney.

If, however, you have been remiss in your record keeping, or if some of your decisions could be construed as having someone else's interests in mind other than the grantor's, you might be in for a few restless nights. However, by the time you finish this chapter, some of your concerns may be addressed, and your stress level will be reduced as much as it can be given the circumstances.

Finding Fault

Upon receiving a Notice to Pass Accounts, your first thoughts might be, "Why me? Why are my actions as my uncle's attorney being called into question? I've done nothing wrong; this is an outrage!"

While all these thoughts may be justified, it is important to remember that judicial review of your activities is one of the risks of acting as someone's attorney. However, instead of seeing this Notice to Pass Accounts as a risk, you should welcome it as an important safeguard that protects both you and the grantor, and provides an opportunity to show the world that the grantor's trust in you was indeed well placed.

If fault is going to be found in your stewardship of the grantor's financial affairs, it will be the result of you "having left undone those things which you ought to have done or having done those things which you ought not to have done." In other words, either acts of commission (doing something you should not have) or acts of omission (failure to do something). These two types of faults predominately occur in three areas: communication/ miscommunication, record keeping and wilful conduct.

Communication/Miscommunication

A lack of communication, poor quality of communications or an apparent lack of transparency in the management of the grantor's affairs can lead to a perception by others that there exists an inadequate written record of financial activity which results, or may result, in the loss of assets or in substandard decisions being made with respect to the management of the grantor's property. Either way, this can lead to someone filing an application to pass accounts. This perception would most likely be formed in the event that the attorney is unable to answer simple questions with respect to the financial affairs of the grantor, or if the attorney's responses to legitimate queries are vague, overly complicated and/or not made in a timely manner. This suspicion may lead an interested party into assuming the worst and accusing the attorney of more specific malfeasance (i.e., misconduct) as suggested by the activities outlined below.

Record Keeping

The three most common errors in record keeping are: (1) incorrect recording of entries, (2) undercharging of accounts and (3) incomplete records.

Incorrect recording of entries can be the misallocation of information between proper accounts or the transposition of numbers (i.e., $53.49 instead of $54.39). Misallocation between accounts is usually caused by misunderstanding the nature of the item to be recorded. For example, the failure to properly record activity between capital and income can result in serious consequences. Similarly, making an error in recording receivables (what is owed to the grantor) with payables (what the grantor owes) can lead to serious difficulties in cash management and asset allocation considerations. Although seldom the specific cause of a complaint, the incorrect recording of entries can add to the lack of confidence in your ability to manage the grantor's assets. Moreover, failure to properly distinguish and record capital and income activities is a major concern if you are completing the grantor's tax return, where the classification of receipts from investment activity between income and capital can have significant implications for the amount of tax payable for the grantor. In addition, if you are claiming compensation for your work as an attorney, the proper allocation of capital and income accounts will be important because different rates are applicable to different categories of assets in arriving at your total compensation.

Undercharging of accounts, sometimes referred to as subcharging, occurs in a number of situations such as failing to include an asset or undervaluing the asset. In addition, undercharging also occurs when there is a failure to record income earned from an asset, such as an investment or pension source.

Incomplete records are just that, incomplete. By definition, incomplete records are inaccurate records and provide the occasion for misinformation to be relayed to others, which in turn can have serious consequences not only with respect to how others perceive your abilities to fulfil your duties, but in your ability to do your job. Incomplete records can occur when there are bank accounts that are not used often and are thus easily forgotten and not reflected in the overall financial activities. This commonly occurs with passbook accounts, where there are no monthly statements coming from the bank. Another example is when the financial institution changes bank account numbers but fails to notify the account holder of the change, or the notification gets lost before it can get into the hands of the attorney. Both these situations can lead to amounts not being reflected in the overall financial activity.

Wilful Conduct

Miscommunications and errors in record keeping might be the result of honest mistakes—after all, we are only human and sometimes do not understand what someone else is asking us, or sometimes numbers can get put into incorrect columns or become transposed. These mistakes can happen inadvertently. Other types of mistakes, however, result not from inadvertence but from our wilful conduct, either by what we choose to do or choose not to do. The two most common types of problematic wilful conduct are fraud and false record entries.

Fraud is both a public offence (crime) and a civil wrong (tort). At a general level, it involves either deception for personal gain or deception to cause harm to another. Obviously, this kind of suspect activity will be the occasion of much concern and will cause others to question your activities as well as your abilities.

Falsification of accounts may be found in either cases of fraud or negligence and consists of making payments that are excessive, unsubstantiated, unrealistic, illegal or not in the best interests of the grantor. Falsification of accounts can also involve the misstatement of income received or distributed within the grantor's estate.

Finally, an accusation of negligence may arise from the perceived failure by the attorney to maintain a proper standard of care and skill while performing tasks under the CPOAP and from which harm (loss) is caused. Examples of negligence might include: making risky investments that are contrary to an investment strategy agreed to with the grantor prior to their incapacity, failure to exercise due diligence before making an investment that is illegal in nature, speculative investments, failing to maintain the value of an asset (e.g., not making necessary repairs to a residence could be construed as neglect) or the failure to make payments by known due dates due to inattention.

Estate trustees are not immune from a claim of either negligence or intentional misconduct in their management of the deceased's estate by beneficiaries who may seek damages for fraud or negligence in the management of the estate. Many of the same errors in record keeping of estate accounts that occur in the CPOAP context can lead to litigation in the estate context.

As you will note, none of the issues discussed above relate to administrative tasks involved in being an attorney, such as the failure to notify a financial institution that a CPOAP document is in effect once you start acting. Not surprisingly, complaints against an attorney or an estate trustee are primarily due to questions about the management of money (cash as well as property that can be turned into cash). At times, the complaint is made with the best interests of the grantor in mind because someone is concerned for the grantor's welfare. Other times, however, the complaint is more about applicants' desire to ascertain the exact nature of the grantor's estate that they believe will be coming to them as a result of the grantor's death, and their accompanying desire to be able to preserve as much of that estate as possible for their own self ends. At this point, if you have been served with a Notice of Application, it is important to bear in mind that the pending litigation has nothing to do with you—provided you have been acting honestly and in good faith in fulfilling your duties—and is really concerned with other things beyond your control such as infighting between family members. Remember, as long as you have been discharging your duties as attorney in a reasonable and prudent manner, honestly and in good faith and you have the records to evidence that, then you should sleep the sleep of the just.

Preparing a Response

The first thing that you will need to do upon receiving the Notice of Application to Pass Accounts is to contact a lawyer who can assist you through this process. This may be your own lawyer or some other lawyer you have chosen due to their experience with estate and power of attorney matters. You probably should not retain the lawyer who drafted the CPOAP because that person may have a conflict of interest in representing you. Whatever lawyer you choose ought to provide information and assistance in a number of areas.

1) Explain exactly what the Notice to Pass Accounts is asking for, what is the best way to respond and what is the nature of the legal process involved, including opportunities to settle matters using Alternative Dispute Resolution (ADR) procedures, whether court mandated or on your own initiative.

2) Contact the applicant's lawyer to ascertain more details with respect to exactly what it is the applicant is dissatisfied about.

3) Negotiate with the Applicant's lawyer for the withdrawal of the application upon the attorney providing specific information, if the situation allows for this possibility.

4) Establish with the applicant's lawyer the ground rules for information exchange going forward, if the situation allows for this possibility.

5) Negotiate with the applicant's lawyer to request a revised date of hearing should you need more time to prepare the information for this review, or if other avenues of review are going to be followed (e.g., ADR).

6) Set up a meeting for an informal review of your record keeping by the applicant, which in turn may lead to the withdrawal of the application for formal accounts.

Receiving a Notice to Pass Accounts can create an enormous amount of stress. This is why it is important to contact a lawyer familiar with the language and procedures used in the passing of accounts who can advise you how best to proceed in the circumstances you find yourself in. As noted above, your lawyer can contact the applicant's lawyer to see if the applicant is agreeable to an informal meeting and a review of the accounting records. In such a case, it will most likely be sufficient to have supporting documentation attached to the respective bank and investment statements, identification of activity not reflected in bank or investment statements (e.g., loan of the grantor's car) along with a written record of review meetings you have had with the grantor (or grantor's representative if incapacitated) and any notes explaining unusual disbursements (in nature or amount).

It is important that you take note of the precise period for which you are being asked to account. While the date on the Notice to Pass Accounts may specify a particular date range; if you did not start to act in your capacity as attorney until a later date, bring this to your lawyer's attention as soon as possible. You certainly do not want to be called to account for a period of time when you were not responsible for the property of the grantor. This may be of particular concern in situations where the CPOAP document was created well in advance of you taking on the role of attorney, and the grantor displayed erratic behaviour while still managing their own affairs in the period just before you took over.

The Late Starter

For those of you who have come to this book late in your journey as attorney, and whose record keeping appears to be a little haphazard, let us highlight the steps contained in Chapter 5 that are going to be of the most importance to you at this stage. Although the steps contained in Chapter 5 have been presented in a logical sequence, each building on information gathered in the previous one, latecomers do not have the luxury of starting at the beginning. Also as noted in Chapter 5, Steps 1-5 are administrative in nature and thus will most likely not be the main focus of the applicant's complaint. The information trail as a result of following the guidance in Steps 6-10 is what you will need to concern yourself with in the short term. There are two approaches available to bring the record keeping up to date. The approach adopted will depend on what your lawyer has confirmed with the applicant's lawyer, i.e., has an informal review of the record keeping been agreed?

Informal Review

If you and the applicant have agreed upon an informal meeting and presentation of the records, then your approach will be to ensure that each item on each bank and investment account being queried has been labelled and that supporting documentation is attached to the statement from the financial institution. You will also be well advised to ensure that review sessions held with the grantor, if any, are substantiated. This may be nothing more than a notation in your date book (or electronic calendar) of your meeting with the grantor. Depending on the level of involvement the grantor has with their financial affairs, there might be some notation of the cash management and investment issues discussed at these meetings. If so, this documentation should be included with the financial statements and backup. It is not recommended that you start creating documentation to make yourself look good. It is what it is, and creating notes after the fact will in all likelihood make the applicants think you are hiding something, when in fact your decisions made on behalf of the Grantor have always been with their best interest in mind. Do not let your only downfall, the lack of tidy records and/or failure to respond in a timely manner to legitimate questions, be the occasion for escalating suspicions. The following checklist will be of assistance to you to prepare for this informal meeting.

1) Balances of bank or investment accounts identified in the Notice to Pass Accounts that have been transferred to other accounts will need to be disclosed and the amounts clearly shown to be received by the accounts still operating. Bank statements will provide the substantiation (Chapter 5, Step 6).

2) Documentation of any activity or agreements that are not reflected on a bank or investment statement (Chapter 5, Step 7).

3) Notation of ground rules established between yourself and grantor (or the grantor's legal representative if incapacitated) with respect to cash and credit card usage (Chapter 5, Step 8).

4) Evidence of your periodic review of the grantor's expected revenues against expenses (medium—and long-term), and any decisions as a result of this review. (Chapter5, Step 8).

5) Bank and investment statements with descriptions against each item and supporting documentation (receipts, cancelled cheques or cheque stubs; other vouchers such as supplier invoices) attached (Chapter 5, Step 9).

6) Copies of tax returns and/or assessment notices for years that you were responsible for filing (Chapter 5, Step 9).

7) Notation of meetings held with grantor (or representative, if grantor is incapacitated) and documentation of any decisions/actions that were agreed upon (Chapter 5, Step 10).

Formal Review

If your lawyer is not able to obtain an agreement to an informal meeting, then you will have to produce a formal set of accounts in the format set out by the court. Your lawyer will be able to assist you with this and may have someone on their staff who can produce the accounts; alternatively the lawyer will be able to direct you to an accountant who is familiar with this type of accounting. Be aware that this is considered somewhat specialized because the terminology used and format of the accounts are different from those normally used by accountants. Thus the fees for providing this service could be significant depending on the amount of activity in the bank statements and the number of years for which accounting is required. Essentially, you will need to provide to the accountant everything that you would have presented to the applicants had an informal meeting been agreed. The more organized and complete this paperwork is when you hand it over, the greater the possibility to minimize fees. The following checklist will assist you in gathering the required information and limit the number of follow-up questions (which increases the cost of the service) the accountant will have.

1) A copy of the CPOAP and/or will (Chapter 5, Step 1).

2) For those bank and/or investment accounts that have been closed and balances transferred, clearly mark on the statements that they have been closed and to what bank or investment account the funds were transferred (Chapter 5, Step 6).

3) Documentation of any activity or agreements that are not reflected on a bank or investment statement (Chapter 5, Step 7).

4) Notation of ground rules established between yourself and grantor (or the grantor's legal representative if incapacitated) with respect to cash and credit card usage (Chapter 5, Step 8).

5) A statement of what you have done to determine the grantor's ability to continue to financially provide for themselves, a copy of worksheets to support your conclusions and any decisions resulting from your reviews (Chapter 5, Step 8).

6) Bank and investment statements and supporting documentation (receipts, cancelled cheques or cheque stubs; other vouchers such as supplier invoices and notations against items for which you have none) attached (Chapter 5, Step 9).

7) Copies of tax returns and/or assessment notices for years that you were responsible for filing (Chapter 5, Step 9).

8) Notation of meetings held with grantor (or representative, if grantor is incapacitated) and documentation of any decisions/actions that were agreed upon (Chapter 5, Step 10).

Remember, the more relevant and accurate information you provide to your lawyer, the better likelihood of there being a favourable outcome for you. Do not withhold any information because you think it might make you look bad. Also, you should be aware that there are serious legal sanctions if you do not disclose all relevant documents. Let your legal counsel have *all* the information and have their experience work for you as they represent you.

Who Pays?

You may also be wondering who pays for the costs related to any litigation. Just as litigation can be complex and contain a question as to its outcome, so too can the issue of costs be difficult to define with any satisfactory degree of certainty. All that can be said with any certainty, however, is that the court has full discretion when it comes to directing which party will pay costs or whether the costs will be shared and, if so, in what proportion (do not assume it will be 50/50), or whether the costs will come "out of the estate". In the Canadian litigation context, the general rule with respect to the awarding of costs is that they "follow the event." In other words, the "winner" of the litigation has its costs paid for by the loser, and this general rule is applied more in estate litigation instead of the traditional "estate pays" rule. The costs awarded are associated with the legal fees and disbursements incurred because of the litigation. Just as the general rule that the successful party has their costs paid by the losing side, the rule that an attorney will have their costs reimbursed from the estate of the grantor is subject to judicial discretion. The determination of your potential liability/ success for costs is one more reason why you are well advised to seek legal counsel who will be able to properly address this issue with you, taking into account not only the unique circumstances of your case, but also the general practice of the courts in your jurisdiction with respect to the awarding of costs in estate matters.

It is also important to bear in mind that no matter what the financial costs may be, there are other costs associated with litigation that have a more intangible existence but will impact your life nonetheless. These intangible costs are associated with the mental and emotional stress as well as the time taken up in dealing with the matter, which any litigation can cause. The avoidance of these costs, as well as the financial expenses associated with litigation, ought to be a strong motivation to perform your obligations of either attorney or estate trustee in a proper and diligent matter.

Should I Have Seen This Coming?

Much of hindsight is of course 20/20. Nevertheless, you should be able to anticipate some problems when dealing with difficult interested third parties. If you've been interacting with them, you should appreciate the type of people they are and adjust your manner of consultation accordingly.

Unfortunately, maintaining a clear and evidential record may not protect you from interested parties questioning financial decisions you make as an attorney. No book can tell you what decisions to make with respect to financial management because there are many variables to consider, and each case is different. Nevertheless, the best protection an attorney can offer himself or herself is to ensure that decisions are consistent with the information provided as a result of complete and accurate record keeping, and particular attention is paid to documenting decisions that might be construed as unusual in nature or size. Further protection is created by having these unusual transactions approved by either the grantor (or a representative if the grantor is incapacitated). Evidence of this approval should be recorded by having them either initial the document supporting the transaction or your note to the file indicating your intent to proceed with such a transaction, ensuring the details of the transaction are set out.

When you agree to take on the role as someone's attorney, being taken to court is probably the last thing on your mind. However, you would do well to remember that your underlying aim during your term as attorney will be to avoid a situation where interested parties believe litigation is their only choice. For our final piece of advice in this area, we recommend that you respond as quickly and in a transparent manner as reasonably possible to any queries received. Of course, you will need to first confirm the interested parties' right to the relevant information (either by checking with the grantor or the grantor's representative, or by seeking legal counsel). Remember to ensure that the query has been answered to everyone's satisfaction. It is also recommended that you review the guidance set out in Chapter 3 concerning privacy and transparency issues.

Chapter Recap

It is hoped that this chapter has relieved some of the concerns and questions about the litigation process. Three essential points to note from this discussion follow:

1) Consult your lawyer immediately upon receiving a Notice of Application to Pass Accounts, or similar court-issued document.

2) Ensure you understand exactly what is being asked for in the Notice—what time periods and specific issues are raised.

3) Do not jump to the conclusion that you will have to go to court. There are other less onerous options to pursue, such as ADR, and even less onerous processes, such as informal meetings with the interested parties.

Although litigation does offer a legitimate route to take for people who honestly feel something is amiss and cannot get satisfactory answers from a direct approach (i.e., a dialogue with the attorney), it can be costly—not only in terms of money and time, but even more so in terms of damage done to relationships, which as we all know, are not easily repaired. Even if you have not received a Notice of Pass Accounts, we hope that you find the information in this chapter useful in giving you an understanding of what not to do as well as what to do, to prevent litigation from arising.

Chapter 10

Final Thoughts

Congratulations! Having arrived at this final chapter, you should be feeling quite pleased with yourself on two counts. First, you were perceptive enough to realize that starting out on the right foot will mean much less work in the long run and that you needed a little bit of guidance to get started. And second, you now know that with the aid of this book and good legal counsel, even if you are brought to account for your management of someone's financial affairs, the experience, while perhaps annoying, will be minimally stressful and result in a favourable outcome for both you and the grantor.

Before we leave you with the final words of encouragement and summary, let's briefly review each chapter by highlighting one or two significant points.

Chapter One highlighted the questions that should be asked before accepting the role of attorney. Although these questions are not meant to scare anyone away, they are important to consider so that a person will accept the role as attorney with full knowledge of what they are agreeing to.

Chapter Two discussed a number of questions that introduced the attorney to the legal framework in which the financial record keeping will take place. The most significant message to take away is that there are basic ground rules that need to be understood by the attorney and that the framework provides protection for both you and the grantor. Understanding these rules and using them as the framework in which you perform your role of attorney will ensure that there are no surprises down the road.

Chapter Three focused on two main points. First, the legislative requirements, long-winded as they may appear in legislation, are essentially asking that all transactions—whether they occur through a bank and/or investment account—be sequentially identified and recorded in an orderly fashion. Second, the attorney must be mindful of maintaining the privacy of the grantor as it relates to their financial affairs and at the same time ensure that documentation and processes adopted provide a transparent information trail.

Chapter Four introduced us to assisting the capable grantor, covering the limited demands on the attorney in terms of record keeping. It also addressed the question, "Why bother with any records if the grantor is still capable?"

Chapter Five established that although no system can be guaranteed as fool-proof, the 10 Steps will certainly minimize the chance that something crucial is missed and at the same time ensure that records are maintained in an organized, methodological fashion and are always up to date.

Chapter Six provided guidance for establishing the inventory of the grantor's assets and liabilities. The identification of what assets and liabilities initially exist, along with where to look for the required information, will take a lot of the frustration out of the task of gathering the required data.

Chapter Seven is of particular interest to those who are not an attorney but an estate trustee, highlighting distinctions between the two roles and alerting the estate trustee to tasks that go beyond those of the attorney in order to finalize the estate of the deceased and distribute the final assets. However, as the information required by both the attorney and the estate trustee is the same, Steps 1-6 of Chapter 5 will be equally helpful to the estate trustee, along with the more detailed presentation of Step 2 dealing with specific assets and liabilities found in Chapter 6.

Chapter Eight contained letters to the editor to educate and entertain, as well as provide examples of some of the common errors, omissions and assumptions that have caused lengthy and expensive litigation. The response provided to each letter was designed to offer a resolution to the problem created and offer advice on moving forward.

Chapter Nine provided a brief overview of what one can expect if a formal account of the management is requested—that is, if litigation becomes a reality rather than something that happens to other people. The chapter highlighted the most common reasons why a formal accounting might be requested, stressed the need to engage a lawyer for assistance and identified the specific information that is most likely to be required in order to address the concerns raised.

We will admit that there is a lot of information contained in these pages. However it is hoped that the chapters and subheadings within each chapter have been labelled appropriately enough to:

a) enable you to use this book as your primary reference as you proceed through what can seem like a mine field at times; and

b) provide a resource to refer to if particular situations arise during your term as attorney.

Maybe it all seems like too much work, and you are thinking maybe you will not worry about anything until you have to. Allow us to make one final attempt to encourage you to proceed with this responsibility diligently and with a light heart. Adhering to the following six principles, we are confident, will ensure everyone success as they make their way through the 10 Steps:

> **Always remember that it is not your money**. Put yourself in the grantor's position and think about what your expectations would be if someone was looking after *your* money. You may very well be in the grantor's position some day. We are sure that your desire will be that your attorney is treating your financial assets with your best interest as the primary motivator.

> **When working out arrangements with the grantor, keep them simple**. Privacy and safeguarding of information are important, however, there are few situations that would warrant complicated arrangements involving such things as specific banking days or inconvenient location of documentation.

> **Make time for regular review of bank and investment statements.** By this we mean no less frequently than monthly. It cannot be stressed enough that one hour spent every month looking at the previous month's activity will save six times that if the review is done as infrequently as every quarter or worse. Errors or omissions being caught and corrected on a timely basis will ensure limited opportunities for anyone to make accusations of impropriety on your part.

> **Document, document and document!** The three most important words when looking after someone else's financial affairs. Leave nothing to rely on memory—theirs or yours. Documentation does not have to be elaborate, just legible; point form is absolutely acceptable.

> **Be organized**. A neatly organized file box with properly labelled folders and accurate and complete information is more impressive than a shoe box or grocery bag full of bits of paper and bank statements still in their unopened envelopes!

> **Have a proper frame of mind**. We all know that we often make tasks more difficult than they need to be simply because of our attitude. Remember that your attitude will determine your altitude!

Following the guidance set out in this book will take you a long way in fulfilling your role as attorney with the least amount of frustration and worry. Both you and the person who has entrusted their property management and financial welfare to you can be confident that their interests will always be put first with the minimum of effort and stress for you and that, should you be called upon to prove your stewardship, the records will show that you have indeed been a good and faithful steward.

Appendices

Appendix I

The 10 Steps At A Glance

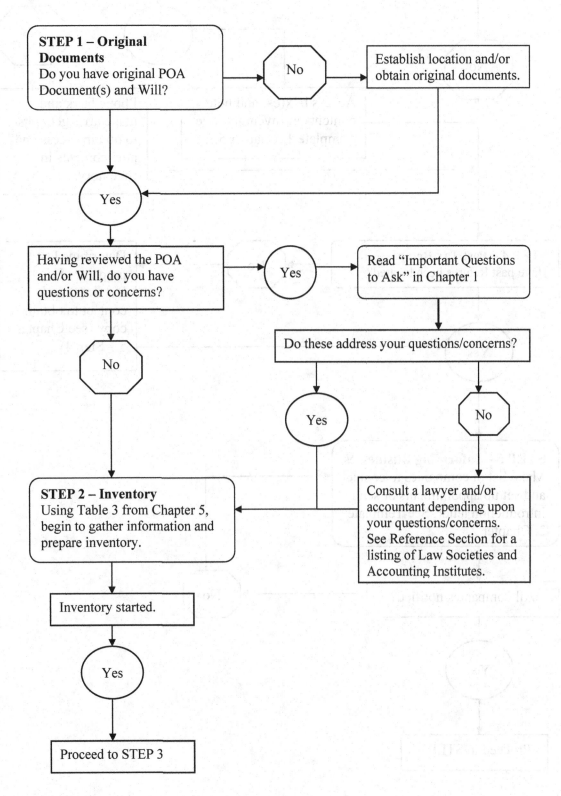

STEP 1 – Original Documents
Do you have original POA Document(s) and Will?

No → Establish location and/or obtain original documents.

Yes

Having reviewed the POA and/or Will, do you have questions or concerns?

Yes → Read "Important Questions to Ask" in Chapter 1

Do these address your questions/concerns?

Yes

No

No

STEP 2 – Inventory
Using Table 3 from Chapter 5, begin to gather information and prepare inventory.

Consult a lawyer and/or accountant depending upon your questions/concerns.
See Reference Section for a listing of Law Societies and Accounting Institutes.

Inventory started.

Yes

Proceed to STEP 3

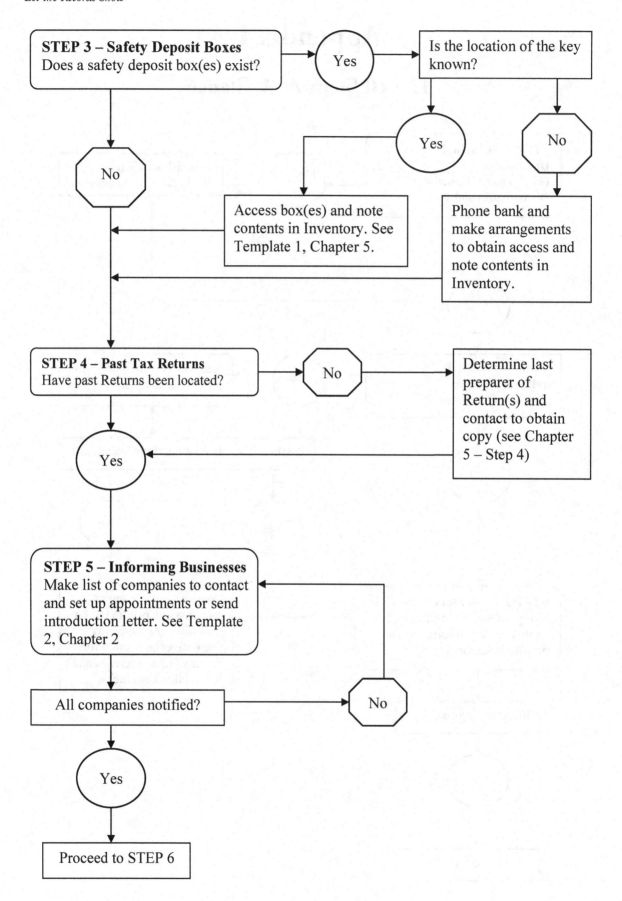

STEP 3 – Safety Deposit Boxes
Does a safety deposit box(es) exist?

Yes

Is the location of the key known?

No

Yes

No

Access box(es) and note contents in Inventory. See Template 1, Chapter 5.

Phone bank and make arrangements to obtain access and note contents in Inventory.

STEP 4 – Past Tax Returns
Have past Returns been located?

No

Determine last preparer of Return(s) and contact to obtain copy (see Chapter 5 – Step 4)

Yes

STEP 5 – Informing Businesses
Make list of companies to contact and set up appointments or send introduction letter. See Template 2, Chapter 2

All companies notified?

No

Yes

Proceed to STEP 6

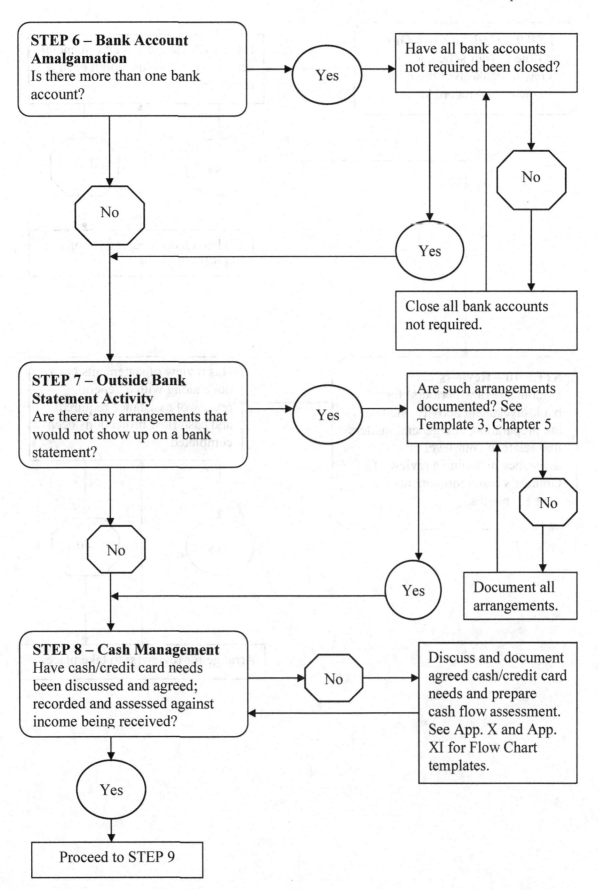

STEP 6 – Bank Account Amalgamation
Is there more than one bank account?

Yes → Have all bank accounts not required been closed?

No

Yes

No

Yes → Close all bank accounts not required.

STEP 7 – Outside Bank Statement Activity
Are there any arrangements that would not show up on a bank statement?

Yes → Are such arrangements documented? See Template 3, Chapter 5

No

No

Yes → Document all arrangements.

STEP 8 – Cash Management
Have cash/credit card needs been discussed and agreed; recorded and assessed against income being received?

No → Discuss and document agreed cash/credit card needs and prepare cash flow assessment. See App. X and App. XI for Flow Chart templates.

Yes

Proceed to STEP 9

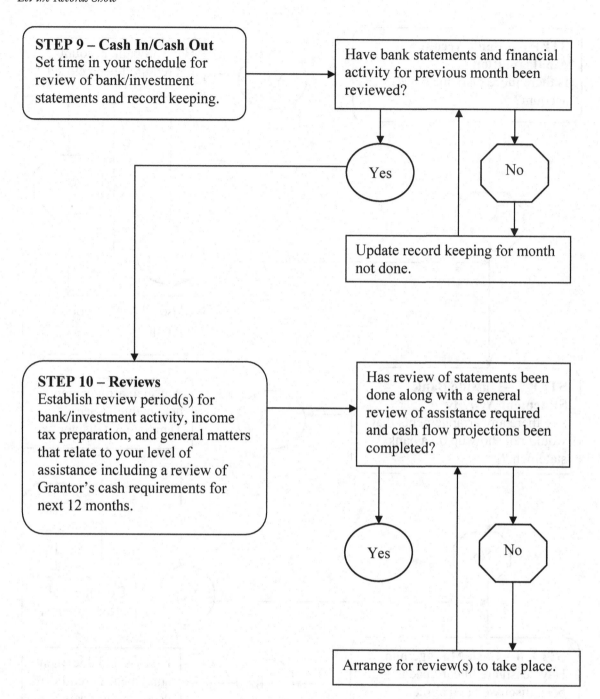

STEP 9 – Cash In/Cash Out
Set time in your schedule for review of bank/investment statements and record keeping.

Have bank statements and financial activity for previous month been reviewed?

Yes

No

Update record keeping for month not done.

STEP 10 – Reviews
Establish review period(s) for bank/investment activity, income tax preparation, and general matters that relate to your level of assistance including a review of Grantor's cash requirements for next 12 months.

Has review of statements been done along with a general review of assistance required and cash flow projections been completed?

Yes

No

Arrange for review(s) to take place.

Appendix II

Ontario Regulation 26/95

Made under the *Substitute Decisions Act, 1992*
ONTARIO REGULATION 26/95
GENERAL

1. For the purposes of subsection 40 (1) of the Act, a guardian of property or an attorney under a continuing power of attorney shall be entitled, subject to an increase under subsection 40 (3) of the Act or an adjustment pursuant to a passing of the guardian's or attorney's accounts under section 42 of the Act, to compensation of,

(a) 3 per cent on capital and income receipts;

(b) 3 per cent on capital and income disbursements; and

(c) three-fifths of 1 per cent on the annual average value of the assets as a care and management fee. O. Reg. 26/95, s. 1; O. Reg. 159/00, s. 1.

Appendix III

Ontario Regulation 100/96

Substitute Decisions Act, 1992
ONTARIO REGULATION 100/96
ACCOUNTS AND RECORDS OF ATTORNEYS AND GUARDIANS

APPLICATION

1. This Regulation applies to attorneys under continuing powers of attorney, statutory guardians of property, court-appointed guardians of property, attorneys under powers of attorney for personal care and guardians of the person. O. Reg. 100/96, s. 1.

FORM OF ACCOUNTS AND RECORDS

2. (1) The accounts maintained by an attorney under a continuing power of attorney and a guardian of property shall include,

(a) a list of all the incapable person's assets as of the date of the first transaction by the attorney or guardian on the incapable person's behalf, including real property, money, securities, investments, motor vehicles and other personal property;

(b) an ongoing list of assets acquired and disposed of on behalf of the incapable person, including the date of and reason for the acquisition or disposition and from or to whom the asset is acquired or disposed;

(c) an ongoing list of all money received on behalf of the incapable person, including the amount, date, from whom it was received, the reason for the payment and the particulars of the account into which it was deposited;

(d) an ongoing list of all money paid out on behalf of the incapable person, including the amount, date, purpose of the payment and to whom it was paid;

(e) an ongoing list of all investments made on behalf of the incapable person, including the amount, date, interest rate and type of investment purchased or redeemed;

(f) a list of all the incapable person's liabilities as of the date of the first transaction by the attorney or guardian on the incapable person's behalf;

(g) an ongoing list of liabilities incurred and discharged on behalf of the incapable person, including the date, nature of and reason for the liability being incurred or discharged;

(h) an ongoing list of all compensation taken by the attorney or guardian, if any, including the amount, date and method of calculation;

(i) a list of the assets, and value of each, used to calculate the attorney's or guardian's care and management fee, if any. O. Reg. 100/96, s. 2 (1).

(2) An attorney under a continuing power of attorney and a guardian of property shall also keep, together with the accounts described in subsection (1), a copy of the continuing power of attorney, certificate of statutory guardianship or court order constituting the authority of the attorney or guardian, a copy of the management plan, if any, and a copy of any court orders relating to the attorney's or guardian's authority or to the management of the incapable person's property. O. Reg. 100/96, s. 2 (2).

3. (1) The records maintained by an attorney under a power of attorney for personal care and a guardian of the person shall include,

(a) a list of all decisions regarding health care, safety and shelter made on behalf of the incapable person, including the nature of each decision, the reason for it and the date;

(b) a copy of medical reports or other documents, if any, relating to each decision;

(c) the names of any persons consulted, including the incapable person, in respect of each decision and the date;

(d) a description of the incapable person's wishes, if any, relevant to each decision, that he or she expressed when capable and the manner in which they were expressed;

(e) a description of the incapable person's current wishes, if ascertainable and if they are relevant to the decision;

(f) for each decision taken, the attorney's or guardian's opinion on each of the factors listed in clause 66 (4) (c) of the Act. O. Reg. 100/96, s. 3 (1).

(2) An attorney under a power of attorney for personal care and a guardian of the person shall also keep a copy of the power of attorney for personal care or court order appointing the attorney or guardian, a copy of the guardianship plan, if any, and a copy of any court orders relating to the attorney's or guardian's authority or the incapable person's care. O. Reg. 100/96, s. 3 (2).

CONFIDENTIALITY AND DISCLOSURE OF ACCOUNTS AND RECORDS

4. An attorney or guardian shall not disclose any information contained in the accounts and records except,

      (a) as required by section 5 or permitted by section 6;

      (b) as required by a court order;

      (c) as required otherwise under the Act or any other Act; or

      (d) as is consistent with or related to his or her duties as attorney or guardian. O. Reg. 100/96, s. 4.

5. (1) An attorney under a continuing power of attorney shall give a copy of the accounts and records he or she keeps in accordance with section 2 to any of the following persons who requests it:

    1. The incapable person.

    2. The incapable person's attorney for personal care or guardian of the person. O. Reg. 100/96, s. 5 (1).

(2) A guardian of property shall give a copy of the accounts and records he or she keeps in accordance with section 2 to any of the following persons who requests it:

    1. The incapable person.

    2. The incapable person's attorney for personal care or guardian of the person.

    3. If the Public Guardian and Trustee is the guardian of property, the incapable person's spouse, except a spouse from whom the incapable person is living separate and apart within the meaning of the Divorce Act (Canada), or the incapable person's partner, child, parent, brother or sister.

    4. The Public Guardian and Trustee, if he or she is not the incapable person's guardian of property or guardian of the person. O. Reg. 100/96, s. 5 (2).

(3) An attorney for personal care shall give a copy of the records he or she keeps in accordance with section 3 to any of the following persons who requests it:

    1. The incapable person.

    2. The incapable person's attorney under a continuing power of attorney or guardian of property. O. Reg. 100/96, s. 5 (3).

(4) A guardian of the person shall give a copy of the records he or she keeps in accordance with section 3 to any of the following persons who requests it:

1. The incapable person.

2. The incapable person's attorney under a continuing power of attorney or guardian of property.

3. The Public Guardian and Trustee, if he or she is not the incapable person's guardian of property or of the person. O. Reg. 100/96, s. 5 (4).

RETENTION OF ACCOUNTS AND RECORDS

6. (1) Every attorney and guardian shall retain the accounts and records required by this Regulation until he or she ceases to have authority and one of the following occurs:

1. The attorney or guardian obtains a release of liability from a person who has the authority to give the release.

2. Another person has acquired the authority to manage the incapable person's property or make decisions concerning the incapable person's personal care, as the case may be, and the attorney or guardian delivers the accounts or records to that person.

3. The incapable person has died and the attorney or guardian delivers the accounts or records to the incapable person's personal representative.

4. The attorney or guardian is discharged by the court on a passing of accounts under section 42 of the Act and either the time for appealing the decision relating to the discharge has expired with no appeal being taken or an appeal from the decision relating to the discharge is finally disposed of and the attorney or guardian is discharged on the appeal.

5. A court order is obtained directing the attorney or guardian to destroy or otherwise dispose of the accounts or records. O. Reg. 100/96, s. 6 (1).

(2) Subsection (1) applies, with necessary modifications, to former attorneys and guardians. O. Reg. 100/96, s. 6 (2).

Appendix IV

Substitute Decisions
Act, 1992—s. 42

Substitute Decisions Act, 1992, S.O. 1992, c.30

42. (1) The court may, on application, order that all or a specified part of the accounts of an attorney or guardian of property be passed. 1992, c. 30, s. 42 (1).

Attorney's accounts

(2) An attorney, the Grantor or any of the persons listed in subsection (4) may apply to pass the attorney's accounts. 1992, c. 30, s. 42 (2).

Guardian's accounts

(3) A guardian of property, the incapable person or any of the persons listed in subsection (4) may apply to pass the accounts of the guardian of property. 1992, c. 30, s. 42 (3).

Others entitled to apply

(4) The following persons may also apply:

1. The Grantor's or incapable person's guardian of the person or attorney for personal care.

2. A dependant of the Grantor or incapable person.

3. The Public Guardian and Trustee.

4. The Children's Lawyer.

5. A judgment creditor of the Grantor or incapable person.

6. Any other person, with leave of the court. 1992, c. 30, s. 42 (4); 1994, c. 27, s. 43 (2).

Appendix V

Rules of Civil Procedure

RULES OF CIVIL PROCEDURE, R.R.O. 1990, Reg. 194

FORM OF ACCOUNTS

74.17 (1) Estate trustees shall keep accurate records of the assets and transactions in the estate and accounts filed with the court shall include,

(a) on a first passing of accounts, a statement of the assets at the date of death, cross-referenced to entries in the accounts that show the disposition or partial disposition of the assets;

(b) on any subsequent passing of accounts, a statement of the assets on the date the accounts for the period were opened, cross-referenced to entries in the accounts that show the disposition or partial disposition of the assets, and a statement of the investments, if any, on the date the accounts for the period were opened;

(c) an account of all money received, but excluding investment transactions recorded under clause (e);

(d) an account of all money disbursed, including payments for trustee's compensation and payments made under a court order, but excluding investment transactions recorded under clause (e);

(e) where the estate trustee has made investments, an account setting out,

   (i) all money paid out to purchase investments,

   (ii) all money received by way of repayments or realization on the investments in whole or in part, and

   (iii) the balance of all the investments in the estate at the closing date of the accounts;

(f) a statement of all the assets in the estate that are unrealized at the closing date of the accounts;

(g) a statement of all money and investments in the estate at the closing date of the accounts;

155

(h) a statement of all the liabilities of the estate, contingent or otherwise, at the closing date of the accounts;

(i) a statement of the compensation claimed by the estate trustee and, where the statement of compensation includes a management fee based on the value of the assets of the estate, a statement setting out the method of determining the value of the assets; and

(j) such other statements and information as the court requires. O. Reg. 484/94, s. 12.

(2) The accounts required by clauses (1) (c), (d) and (e) shall show the balance forward for each account. O. Reg. 484/94, s. 12.

(3) Where a will or trust deals separately with capital and income, the accounts shall be divided to show separately receipts and disbursements in respect of capital and income. O. Reg. 484/94, s. 12.

Appendix VI

Types of Trusts

At the time of writing, the following is a list of trust types as categorized by the Canada Revenue Agency. The list along with more detailed information regarding the preparation of the T3 Trust and Information Return can be found at www.cra-arc.gc.ca/E/pub/tg/t4013/. The reader is encouraged to visit this site at least annually to update themselves on rules and/or requirements that have changed.

Type of trust	General information
Personal trust	This is either: • a testamentary trust; or • an inter vivos trust in which no beneficial interest was acquired for consideration payable either to the trust, or a person who contributed to the trust. The person or related persons who create an inter vivos trust may acquire all the interests in it without the trust losing its status as a personal trust. After 1999, a unit trust is not a personal trust.
Alter ego trust	This is an inter vivos trust created after 1999 by a settlor who was 65 years of age or older at the time the trust was created, for which the settlor is entitled to receive all the income that may arise during his or her lifetime, and is the only person who can receive, or get the use of, any income or capital of the trust during the settlor's lifetime. A trust will **not** be considered an alter ego trust if it so elects in its return for its first tax year.
Specified trust	This is a trust that is: an amateur athlete trust; an employee trust; a master trust; a trust governed by a deferred profit sharing plan, an employee benefit plan, an employees profit sharing plan, a foreign retirement arrangement, a registered education savings plan, a registered pension plan, a registered retirement income fund, a registered retirement savings plan, or a registered supplementary unemployment benefit plan; a related segregated fund trust; a retirement compensation arrangement trust; a trust whose direct beneficiaries are one of the above mentioned trusts; a trust governed by an eligible funeral arrangement or a cemetery care trust; a communal organization; and a trust where all or substantially all of the property is held for the purpose of providing benefits to individuals from employment or former employment.

Joint spousal or common-law partner trust ▲	This is an inter vivos trust created after 1999 by a settlor who was 65 years of age or older at the time the trust was created. The settlor and the settlor's spouse or common-law partner are entitled to receive all the income that may arise from the trust before the later of their deaths. They are the only persons who can receive, or get the use of, any income or capital of the trust before the later of their deaths.
Spousal or common-law partner trust	A **post-1971 spousal or common-law partner trust** includes both a testamentary trust created after 1971, and an inter vivos trust created after June 17, 1971. In either case, the living beneficiary spouse or common-law partner is entitled to receive all the income that may arise during the lifetime of the spouse or common-law partner. That spouse or common-law partner is the only person who can receive, or get the use of, any income or capital of the trust during his or her lifetime. A **Pre-1972 spousal trust** includes both a testamentary trust created before 1972, and an inter vivos trust created before June 18, 1971. In either case, the beneficiary spouse was entitled to receive all the income during the spouse's lifetime, and no other person received, or got the use of, any income or capital of the trust. These conditions must be met for the period beginning on the day the trust was created, up to the **earliest** of the following dates: • the day the beneficiary spouse dies; • January 1, 1993; or • the day on which the definition of a Pre-1972 spousal trust is applied.
Deemed resident trust	This is a trust resident in another country, but which is considered resident in Canada for certain tax purposes. Usually, such a trust has received a contribution from a resident or former resident of Canada. A trust is a deemed resident if: • a resident of Canada transferred property to the trust and is either beneficially interested in the trust (for example, as a beneficiary of the trust), or is related to such a person (including an aunt, uncle, nephew, or niece of the beneficiary); or • the beneficiary acquired an interest in the trust by way of purchase or as a gift or inheritance from a Canadian resident who transferred property to the trust.

	Under proposed changes, a trust will generally be considered to be a deemed resident if it acquired property from a person who is resident in Canada or if any of the beneficiaries are resident in Canada and a contribution of property was made by a resident or former resident of Canada. If you need help in determining whether the trust is a deemed resident of Canada, call one of the telephone numbers listed in "Non-resident trusts and deemed resident trusts" [section found in T3 Trust Guide].
Unit trust	This is an inter vivos trust for which the interest of each beneficiary can be described at any time by referring to units of the trust. A unit trust must also meet one of three conditions as described in subsection 108(2) of the Act.
Communal organization	We consider an inter vivos trust to exist when a congregation: • has members who live and work together; • follows the practices and beliefs of, and operates according to the principles of, the religious organization of which it is a part; • does not permit its members to own property in their own right; • requires that its members devote their working lives to the congregation's activities; and • carries on one or more businesses directly, or manages or controls the businesses through a business agency, such as a corporation or trust, to support or sustain its members or the members of another congregation. The communal organization has to pay tax as though it were an inter vivos trust. However, it can elect to allocate its income to the beneficiaries. For more information, see Information Circular IC78-5, *Communal Organizations* [www.cra-arc.gc.ca/E/pub/tp/ic78-5r3/README.html].
Retirement compensation arrangement (RCA)	This arrangement exists when an employer makes contributions for an employee's retirement, termination of employment, or any significant change in services of employment. For more information, see the Publication T4041, *Retirement Compensation Arrangements Guide* [www.cra-arc.gc.ca/tx/bsnss/tpcs/pyrll/clcltng/spcl/rrngmnt-eng.html]. **Note:** You have to file a T3 return for the portion of an RCA that is treated as an employee benefit plan. A T3-RCA, *Part XI.3 Tax Return—Retirement Compensation Arrangement (RCA)*, has to be filed to report the income of the other portion of the plan.

Mutual fund trust	This is a unit trust that resides in Canada. It also has to comply with the other conditions of the Act, as outlined in section 132 and the conditions established by *Income Tax Regulation* 4801.
Employee benefit plan	Generally, this is any arrangement under which an employer makes contributions to a custodian, and under which one or more payments will be made to, or for the benefit of, employees, former employees, or persons related to them. For more information, and for details on what we consider to be an employee benefit plan and how it is taxed, see Interpretation Bulletin IT-502, *Employee Benefit Plans and Employee Trusts*, [www.cra-arc.gc.ca/E/pub/tp/it502/README.html] and its Special Release [www.cra-arc.gc.ca/E/pub/tp/it502sr/README.html]. **Note:** An employee benefit plan has to file a return if the plan or trust has tax payable, has a taxable capital gain, or has disposed of capital property. Because the allocations are taxed as income from employment to the beneficiaries, report the allocations on a T4 slip, not on a T3 slip. For more information, see the Publication RC4120, *Employers' Guide—Filing the T4 Slip and Summary* [www.cra-arc.gc.ca/E/pub/tg/rc4120/README.html].
Salary deferral arrangement	Generally, this is a plan or arrangement (whether funded or not) between an employer and an employee or another person who has a right to receive salary or wages in a year after the services have been performed. For more information, see Interpretation Bulletin IT-529, *Flexible Employee Benefit Programs* [www.cra-arc.gc.ca/E/pub/tp/it529/README.html]. **Note:** If a salary deferral arrangement is funded, we consider it a trust, and you may have to file a T3 return. The deferred amount is deemed to be an employment benefit, so you report it on a T4 slip, not a T3 slip. The employee has to include the amount in income for the year the services are performed. The employee also has to include any interest, or other amount earned by the deferred amount. For more information, see the publication RC4120, *Employers' Guide—Filing the T4 Slip and Summary*.

Insurance segregated fund trust	This is a related segregated fund of a life insurer for life insurance policies and is considered to be an inter vivos trust. The fund's property and income are considered to be the property and income of the trust, with the life insurer as the trustee. **Note:** You have to file a separate return and financial statements for each fund. If all the beneficiaries are fully registered plans, complete only the identification and certification areas of the return and enclose the financial statements. If the beneficiaries are both registered and non-registered plans, report and allocate only the income that applies to the non-registered plans.
Employee trust	This is an inter vivos trust. Generally, it is an arrangement established after 1979, under which an employer makes payments to a trustee in trust for the sole benefit of the employees. The trustee has to elect to qualify the arrangement as an employee trust on the trust's first return. The employer can deduct contributions to the plan only if the trust has made this election and filed it no later than 90 days after the end of its first tax year. To maintain its employee trust status, each year the trust has to allocate to its beneficiaries all non-business income for that year, and employer contributions made in the year. Business income cannot be allocated and is taxed in the trust. For more information, see Interpretation Bulletin IT-502, *Employee Benefit Plans and Employee Trusts*, and its Special Release. **Note:** An employee trust has to file a return if the plan or trust has tax payable, has a taxable capital gain, or has disposed of capital property. Because the allocations are taxed as income from employment to the beneficiaries, report the allocations on a T4 slip, not a T3 slip. For more information, see the publication RC4120, *Employers' Guide—Filing the T4 Slip and Summary*.
Non-profit organization	This is an organization (for example, club, society, or association) that is usually organized and operated exclusively for social welfare, civic improvement, pleasure, recreation, or any other purpose except profit. The organization will generally be exempt from tax if no part of its income is payable to, or available for, the personal benefit of a proprietor, member, or shareholder. For more information, see Interpretation Bulletin IT-496, *Non-Profit Organizations* [www.cra-arc.gc.ca/E/pub/tp/it496r/README.html].

	If the main purpose of the organization is to provide services such as dining, recreational, or sporting facilities to its members, we consider it to be an **inter vivos trust**. In this case, the trust is taxable on its income from property, and on any taxable capital gains from the disposition of any property that is not used to provide those services. The trust is allowed a deduction of $2,000 when calculating its taxable income. Claim this on line 54 of the T3 return.
	For more information, see Interpretation Bulletin IT-83, *Non-Profit Organizations—Taxation of Income From Property* [http://www.cra-arc.gc.ca/E/pub/tp/it83r3/README.html].
	Note: A non-profit organization may have to file Form T1044, *Non-Profit Organization (NPO) Information Return* [www.cra-arc.gc.ca/E/pbg/tf/t1044/README.html]. For more information, see Publication T4117, *Income Tax Guide to the Non-Profit Organization (NPO) Information Return* [http://www.cra-arc.gc.ca/E/pub/tg/t4117/README.html].
Master trust	This is an inter vivos trust. A trust can elect to be a master trust if during the entire time since its creation it met **all** of the following conditions: • it was resident in Canada; • its only undertaking was the investing of its funds; • it never borrowed money except for a term of 90 days or less (for this purpose, the borrowing cannot be part of a series of loans or other transactions and repayments); • it has never accepted deposits; and • each of its beneficiaries is a registered pension plan or a deferred profit sharing plan. **Note:** A master trust is exempt from Part I tax. A trust can elect to be a master trust by indicating this in a letter filed with its return for the tax year the trust elects to become a master trust. Once made, this election cannot be revoked. However, the trust must continue to meet the conditions listed above to keep its identity as a master trust. After the first T3 return is filed for the master trust, you do not have to file any further T3 returns for this trust. If a future return is filed, we will assume the trust no longer meets the above conditions. The trust will not be considered a master trust and must file yearly returns from then on.

RRSP, RRIF, or RESP trust	**Note:** An RRSP, RRIF, or RESP trust has to complete and file a T3 return if the trust meets **one** of the following conditions: • the trust has borrowed money and paragraph 146(4)(a) or 146.3(3)(a) of the Act applies; • the RRIF trust received a gift of property and paragraph 146.3(3)(b) of the Act applies; or • the last annuitant has died and paragraph 146(4)(c) or subsection 146.3(3.1) of the Act applies. If this is the case, claim an amount on line 43 of the T3 return **only** if the allocated amounts were paid in accordance with paragraph 104(6)(a.2) of the Act. If the trust does not meet one of the above conditions and the trust held non-qualified investments during the tax year, you have to complete a T3 return to calculate the taxable income from non-qualified investments, determined under subsection 146(10.1) or 146.3(9). If the trust is reporting capital gains or losses, it has to report the full amount (that is, 100%) on line 01 of the return. If the trust does not meet one of the above conditions and the trust carried on a business, you have to complete a T3 return to calculate the taxable income of the trust from carrying on a business. **Do not** include the business income earned from the disposition of qualified investments for the trust.
Specified investment flow-through trust (SIFT)	This is a trust (other than a trust that is a real estate investment trust for the tax year) that meets the following conditions at any time during the tax year: • the trust is resident in Canada; • investments in the trust are listed or traded on a stock exchange or other public market; and • the trust holds one or more non-portfolio properties.

163

Appendix VII

Summary of Assets & Liabilities

Date POA Effective: _____ (the date you begin acting as the POA) OR
Date of Death: _____ (if acting as an Estate Trustee)
Bank Accounts and Credit Cards

Item	Location	Identification No.	Contact Person	Value @ date of POA

164

Date POA Effective: _____ (the day you begin acting as the POA) OR

Date of Death: _____ (if acting as an Estate Trustee)

Investments

Item	Location	Identification No.	Contact Person	Value @ date of POA

Date POA Effective: _____ (the day you begin acting as the POA) OR

Date of Death: _____ (if acting as an Estate Trustee)

Other Items

Item	Location	Identification No.	Contact Person	Value @ date of POA

Sample Worksheet Completed With Details

Date POA Effective: June 15, 2007 (this is the date you begin acting as the POA)

Date of Death: _____ (if acting as an Estate Trustee)

Bank Accounts and Credit Cards

Item	Location	Identification No.	Contact Person	Value @ date of POA
Chqing	TD Canada Trust, Fairview Mall 416-491-0667 (f)	Acct No. 1245-1546854	Jane Doe – Branch Manager 416-491-0567 (p)	Bal in acct: $25,460.43
TD CT Credit Card	TD Canada Trust, Fairview Mall 416-491-0667 (f)	12546359775	Jane Doe – Branch Manager 416-491-0567 (p)	Owing $253.63, due July 2, 2007
High Interest Savings	Scotia – Yonge & Sheppard	125875689	Ms XXXX	$53,256.25
Chqing	Scotia – Yonge & Sheppard	56985698	Ms XXXXX	$256.36
Chqing	BMO – Front and University	5986987	Mr YYYYY	$1,236.63
Savings	ING	14364154	No specific person; 1-800-464-3473	$33,256.85

Date POA Effective: June 15, 2007
Date of Death: _____ (if acting as an Estate Trustee)
Investments

Item	Location	Identification No.	Contact Person	Value @ date of POA
GIC	TD Canada Trust, Fairview Mall 416-491-0667 (f)	Acct No. 1245-5649877/10	Jane Doe – Branch Manager 416-491-0567 (p)	Principal: $20,000
1,000 Bell Telephone shares	Safety deposit box at TD CT Fairview Mall	Serial no:	Jane Doe – Branch Manager 416-491-0567	Bought in 1953 – cost unknown
Various bonds and stocks	ScotiaMcLeod – 2300 Yonge Street	Investment Acct: 123456	John Smith – Acct manager, 416-932-3033	History with brokerage house

Date POA Effective: June 15, 2007

Date of Death: _____ (if acting as an Estate Trustee)

Other Items

Item	Location	Identification No.	Contact Person	Value @ date of POA
Loans Receivable	Lent niece $20,000 Sept 2004 for schooling, interest free until she graduates	See detailed note in this file setting out terms & niece's signature acknowledging agreement to terms.		
Mortgage	N/A			
Loans payable	N/A			
Gov't Pension Income	CPP, OAS – direct deposit into TD CT			
Survivor's Pension	Direct deposit monthly into TD CT	No. 9876 from OTSF	Mrs White 416-654-5698 at OTSF	
Insurance policy – Blue Cross Life Insurance	185 The West Mall, Etobicoke	No. 8547 – proceeds from Husbands life insurance policy	Dean Gray 416-626-1688	
Insurance policy – life, health, car, home	Home – 63 Alice Court, Toronto	154326 – with ING Insurance	416-341-1464	$40.63 deducted from TDCT monthly; renews May 10 each yr

Summary of Assets & Liabilities

Appendix VIII

Templates found in Chapter Five

Template 1—Safety Deposit Box Locations and Inventory List (Step 3)

Location(s)

Bank	
Address	
Contact Person	
Phone Number	
E-mail	

Bank	
Address	
Contact Person	
Phone Number	
E-mail	

Inventory of SDB

Location of SDB: _____.

Item	Original Location of Item

Template 2—List of People/Companies to Contact (Step 5)

Company	Person	Date Contact Made	Date CPOAP Copy Delivered	Other Notes

Template 3—Arrangements Outside of the Bank Statements (Step 7)

Does an arrangement outside the bank statements exist?	
Identify the person(s) benefiting from the arrangement (e.g., Charlie, grantor's nephew) and whether they are "dependent" upon the grantor:	
If so, describe the general nature of arrangement (e.g., remaining in the grantor's home although the grantor has now moved to a nursing home):	
Describe the payment obligations of each (e.g., house insurance covering house, property and contents and property taxes will be paid by the grantor, all other expense to be paid by nephew:	
What is the term of the arrangement? (e.g., until nephew finishes post-secondary education or by December 31, 2010 whichever is earlier)	
Describe any conditions that if they occur would mean the immediate conclusion of this arrangement (e.g., if nephew drops out of post-secondary education and is unemployed for more than two months or upon the death of the grantor):	

Appendix IX

Templates found in Chapter Six

Template 4—Annuity

Is annuity income received?	
Is the annuity registered or non-registered?	
What financial company is it received from?	
What is the identification/account number?	
Name and contact of account manager:	
Is the annuity a fixed term? If so, when does the term end?	
Have you made a note in your personal diary of the end date of this income stream to ensure the cash flow assessments properly reflect the cash available to the Grantor?	

Template 5—Bank Accounts

Account Number:	
Bank/Trust Company:	
Street address:	
Mailing address, (if different from street):	
Phone number:	
Fax number:	
Account manager:	
Direct phone line of account manager:	
E-mail address:	
Name of account manager's boss:	
Alternative contact, if account manager unavailable:	
Value at Date of commencing to act as attorney:	

Template 6—Business and/or Partnership Agreement

Does a business or partnership agreement exist?	
Has a copy been located and either filed with the attorney or with the grantor's important papers in a secure place? Indicate where it is filed:	
Is the business/partnership still active? If yes, address of place of business:	
Are there any potential liabilities that need to be planned for when determining the grantor's cash requirements? If so, describe and estimate amount if possible:	
Are there any potential windfalls that should be considered when determining the grantor's cash requirements? If so, describe and estimate amount if possible:	
Who are the other parties that signed the agreement? Provide contact details for each person:	
What are the relationships between the parties who signed the agreement?	
Name and contact information of the business/partnership's lawyer:	
Name and contact information of the business/partnership's accountant:	

Template 7—Contents of House, Condo and/or Cottage

Use the chart below to list the contents of the grantor's residences:

Item Description	Location	Estimated Value	Beneficiary

Template 8—Credit Cards

Have all credit cards been listed on the summary sheet found in Appendix VII?	
Does anyone other than you and the grantor have access to these cards?	
If so, who and for what purpose?	
What system has been agreed upon for keeping track of receipts that support purchases charged to the cards?	

Template 9—Dependents

List any dependents of the grantor, include their relationship to the grantor (e.g., child, parent, aunt):	
Describe the extent of the dependence (e.g., daughter with Downs Syndrome, lives in group home during week but comes home on the weekends and holidays; father is in nursing home):	
Is there a CPOAP document in place for any of the dependents?	
Has contact been made with the attorney identified in such document?	
Record the contact details of the attorney:	
Is the grantor acting as attorney for another party?	
If so, record name and contact information:	
Has contact been made with that person and/or their lawyer to discuss alternative arrangements?	

Template 10—Insurance Policies

Business/Partnership Insurance	
Insurance Broker	
Insurance Company	
Policy Number	
Period of Coverage	
Premium Due	$ (monthly, quarterly, annually)
Car Insurance	
Insurance Broker	
Insurance Company	
Policy Number	
Period of Coverage	
Premium Due	$ (monthly, quarterly, annually)
Apartment/Condo Insurance	
Insurance Broker	
Insurance Company	
Policy Number	
Period of Coverage	
Premium Due	$ (monthly, quarterly, annually)
Cottage Insurance	
Insurance Broker	
Insurance Company	
Policy Number	
Period of Coverage	
Premium Due	$ (monthly, quarterly, annually)
Critical Illness Insurance (Private or Group)	
Insurance Broker	
Insurance Company	
Policy Number	
Period of Coverage	
Premium Due	$ (monthly, quarterly, annually)
Benefits Provided	
Disability Insurance (Private or Group)	
Insurance Broker	

Insurance Company	
Policy Number	
Period of Coverage	
Premium Due	$ (monthly, quarterly, annually)
Benefits Provided	
Health Insurance	
Insurance Broker	
Insurance Company	
Policy Number	
Period of Coverage	
Premium Due	$ (monthly, quarterly, annually)
Benefits Provided	
House Insurance	
Insurance Broker	
Insurance Company	
Policy Number	
Period of Coverage	
Premium Due	$ (monthly, quarterly, annually)
Life Insurance	
Insurance Broker	
Insurance Company	
Policy Number	
Period of Coverage	
Premium Due	$ (monthly, quarterly, annually)
Beneficiaries and contact information:	
Pet Insurance	
Insurance Broker	
Insurance Company	
Policy Number	
Period of Coverage	
Premium Due	$ (monthly, quarterly, annually)

Template 11—Investments

Bonds	
Part of registered or non-registered plan?	
Self-managed or brokerage house?	
If brokerage house, which one?	
Name and contact of brokerage house account manager:	
Institution/Municipality/Company:	
Maturity date:	
Are interest payments:	
a) Received by cheque quarterly/semi annually/annually/upon maturity	
b) Direct deposit (frequency, to what account—current account or brokerage cash account)	
c) Rolled into investment	
Current instructions on file:	

GICs / Term Deposits	
Part of registered or non-registered plan?	
Self-managed or brokerage house?	
If brokerage house, which one?	
Name and contact of brokerage house account manager:	
Institution/Municipality/Company:	
Maturity date:	
Are interest payments:	
a) Received by cheque quarterly/semi annually/annually/upon maturity	
b) Direct deposit (frequency, to what account—current account or brokerage cash account)	
c) Rolled into investment	
Current instructions on file:	

Limited Partnership	
Part of registered or non-registered plan?	
Self-managed or brokerage house?	

If brokerage house, which one?	
Name and contact of brokerage house account manager:	
Operating name of partnership:	
Main contact name at business:	
Phone number of main contact:	
E-mail address of main contact:	
Initial investment amount:	
Further amounts to be contributed:	
Form of revenue stream: percentage of net income, dividend, other:	
Date(s) return of contributions or income expected to be received:	

Mineral Titles and Leases

Part of registered or non-registered plan?	
Self-managed or brokerage house?	
If brokerage house, which one?	
Name and contact of brokerage house account manager:	
Name of mining project:	
Location of project:	
Date purchased:	
Amount invested:	
Date of last income receipt:	
Amount received:	

Mortgage-Backed Securities

Part of registered or non-registered plan?	
Self-managed or brokerage house?	
If brokerage house, which one?	
Name and contact of brokerage house account manager:	
Name/identity of property:	
If shares held in a pool, name of fund:	
Maturity date (if applicable):	
Are interest payments:	
a) Received by cheque	
b) Direct deposit	
c) Other arrangements (if so, describe)	
Current instructions on file:	

Mutual Funds / Income Trusts

Part of registered or non-registered plan?	
Self-managed or brokerage house?	
If brokerage house, which one?	
Name and contact of brokerage house account manager:	
Name of fund:	
Number of units purchased:	
Initial investment amount:	
Activity Statement available?	

Real Estate

Rental property owned?	
Address of property:	
Owner-managed or management company?	
Name/address/contact information of management company (if applicable):	
Number of tenants:	
Location of books and records (leases, financial statements, mortgage information):	
Has equity interest?	
Address of property:	
Name of corporation/partnership holding title to property:	
Contact details:	

Shares – Public

Part of registered or non-registered plan?	
Self-managed or brokerage house?	
If brokerage house, which one?	
Name and contact of brokerage house account manager:	
Name of company:	
Country of incorporation:	
Number of shares held:	
Original cost (if available):	
History of changes to Adjusted Cost Base (ACB) if available (attach separate sheet):	
Current ACB:	
Are dividend payments:	
a) Cash and paid by cheque	

quarterly/semi annually/annually, only periodically	
b) Cash and direct deposit (frequency, to what account—current account or brokerage cash account)	
c) Shares, increasing the number of shares held by shareholder	

Template 12—Line of Credit

Financial institution:	
Limit:	
Interest rate:	
Amount outstanding and date:	
Terms (minimum payment amount and frequency):	
Unsecured or secured:	
If secured, what property/assets have been assigned?	

Template 13—Loan Guarantees

End of the loan period:	
Amount guaranteed (this may not necessarily be the full amount of the loan):	
Name and address of the debtor:	
Grantor's relationship to the debtor:	
Nature of debt:	
Are there any other guarantors and how does their existence affect the possible financial obligations of the grantor?	
Any events that would release the grantor from this agreement:	

Template 14—Loans Payable

Who has lent money to the grantor/deceased?	
Does a promissory note exist?	
Term of the loan (If a promissory note, it can be for a specified fixed length of time or payable "on demand" whenever the lender demands repayment of the amount loaned to the borrower.):	
Amount of the loan:	
Interest rate:	
Interest payment dates:	
Any terms regarding the right to pre-pay the loan before the due date:	
What happens if the borrower misses a payment or fails to pay when payment is demanded:	
Does a personal guarantee exist as part of the loan document?	
Are there any assets that have been put up as collateral for any loan payables that exist? If so, list them:	

Template 15—Loans Receivable

Has any money been lent to business colleagues, friends, or more likely, family members?	
If so, who?	
Has the money been lent for a specific purpose? Describe:	
If so, has either the section on Business or Partnership Agreements or Investments—Limited Partnerships been reviewed and relevant information collected and documented?	
Is there an expectation that interest should be paid?	
If interest is to be received, what is the frequency?	
When is the amount expected to be paid back?	
Is it expected to be paid back or taken out of the person's share of the estate upon the grantor's death?	
Does a formal promissory note exist, and where is it filed (e.g., in grantor's SDB)?	
Is there any property of the grantor's that has been provided as security?	
If yes, what property and what are the specific details:	

Template 16—Maintenance Agreement

Does a maintenance agreement exist?	
Are payments being made or being received?	
Amount and frequency of payment?	
Interest penalties should payments not be paid/received on time:	
Recourse by the receiver should payments not be received within a reasonable period of due date?	
Duration of payments:	
Events, if any, that will result in payments no longer being made/received:	
Are payments required to be paid to or from the estate when one party dies?	
Name of ex-spouse and contact details (either personal or legal representative):	
Name and contact details of grantor's lawyer who represented them:	

Template 17—Miscellaneous Amounts

Describe the general nature of any miscellaneous amounts not recorded elsewhere, including the name and contact details of the other party and their relationship to grantor:	
What is the anticipated frequency and/or date when payment is expected to be received or made?	
What is the approximate amount of money to be received or paid out each time?	
Does a formal agreement exist, and if so, where is it filed?	
Are there any circumstances that would cancel the expectation to pay back any money owed or to receive any money due? If so, describe:	
Are there any verbal agreements that should be formalized into a written agreement? If so, describe:	

Template 18—Mortgage Payable

Is there still a mortgage on the house, condo or cottage?	
Address of each property covered by the mortgage:	
What financial institution holds the mortgage?	
Contact details of loan manager:	
What bank account are payments being made from? (Perhaps a bank account has been missed in the initial review.)	
What are the immediate plans for this/these properties? That is, are they to be sold in the short-term or held?	
Are either property held jointly? If so, with whom?	
Is the mortgage fixed rate or variable rate?	
Have you obtained a statement of mortgage dated on or near the date of you beginning your attorney role?	
Have you made a note in your personal diary in February to obtain a statement of mortgage as of December 31 each year if one has not yet been received?	
Are property taxes being paid to the mortgage funder?	
If not, have these amounts been recorded in the cash flow statement?	
Is the property with the mortgage used to produce income?	
If so, has the section on Real Property been referred to?	

Template 19—Pensions—private, government, survivor benefits, foreign

Is pension income received?	
List the companies and/or governments that pension income is received from:	
Are any of these from foreign countries?	
If so, describe requirements of the specific pension funds for the pensioner to confirm their entitlement:	
Have you made a note in your personal diary to ensure any deadlines with respect to the requirements noted above are met?	

Template 20—Real Property

Condo	
Address:	
Original purchase price:	
Cost and description of any renovations/maintenance, (e.g., new roof):	
Date of purchase:	
Is there a mortgage outstanding?	
Who is the lending institution/party?	
What are the plans for the property?	
Is it held jointly, if yes, with whom?	
Is it being used as security against any lines of credit, loan facilities or other investments? If so, specify:	
If property is located outside Canada, has appropriate advice been obtained from a relevant professional? If so, provide contact information of professional	
Has information obtained from the professional been filed with CPOAP and incorporated into the asset management plan?	
Is it used or has it been used at any time since it was purchased, to produce income? If so, list specific time periods when it was used to produce income?	
Describe any instructions in the will with respect to this property:	

Cottage	
Address:	
Original purchase price:	
Cost and description of any renovations/maintenance, (e.g., new roof):	
Date of purchase:	
Is there a mortgage outstanding?	
Who is the lending institution/party?	
What are the plans for the property?	
Is it held jointly, if yes, with whom?	
Is it being used as security against any lines of credit, loan facilities or other investments? If so, specify:	
If property is located outside Canada, has appropriate advice been obtained from a relevant professional? If so, provide contact information of professional	
Has information obtained from the professional been filed with CPOAP and incorporated into the asset management plan?	
Is it used or has it been used at any time since it was purchased, to produce income? If so, list specific time periods when it was used to produce income?	
Describe any instructions in the will with respect to this property:	
Farm	
Address:	
Original purchase price:	
Cost and description of any renovations/maintenance, (e.g., new roof):	
Date of purchase:	
Is there a mortgage outstanding?	
Who is the lending institution/party?	

What are the plans for the property?	
Is it held jointly, if yes, with whom?	
Is it being used as security against any lines of credit, loan facilities or other investments? If so, specify:	
If property is located outside Canada, has appropriate advice been obtained from a relevant professional? If so, provide contact information of professional	
Has information obtained from the professional been filed with CPOAP and incorporated into the asset management plan?	
Is it used or has it been used at any time since it was purchased, to produce income? If so, list specific time periods when it was used to produce income?	
Describe any instructions in the will with respect to this property:	

House

Address:	
Original purchase price:	
Cost and description of any renovations/maintenance, (*e.g.,* new roof):	
Date of purchase:	
Is there a mortgage outstanding?	
Who is the lending institution/party?	
What are the plans for the property?	
Is it held jointly, if yes, with whom?	
Is it being used as security against any lines of credit, loan facilities or other investments? If so, specify:	
If property is located outside Canada, has appropriate advice been obtained from a relevant professional? If so, provide contact information of professional	
Has information obtained from the professional been filed with CPOAP and incorporated into the asset management plan?	

Is it used or has it been used at any time since it was purchased, to produce income? If so, list specific time periods when it was used to produce income?	
Describe any instructions in the will with respect to this property:	

Undeveloped Land

Address:	
Original purchase price:	
Cost and description of any renovations/maintenance, (e.g., new roof):	
Date of purchase:	
Is there a mortgage outstanding?	
Who is the lending institution/party?	
What are the plans for the property?	
Is it held jointly, if yes, with whom?	
Is it being used as security against any lines of credit, loan facilities or other investments? If so, specify:	
If property is located outside Canada, has appropriate advice been obtained from a relevant professional? If so, provide contact information of professional	
Has information obtained from the professional been filed with CPOAP and incorporated into the asset management plan?	
Is it used or has it been used at any time since it was purchased, to produce income? If so, list specific time periods when it was used to produce income?	
Describe any instructions in the will with respect to this property:	

Template 21—RRSP/RRIF

Does an RRSP or RRIF exist?	
Self-managed or brokerage house?	
If brokerage house, which one?	
Name and contact of brokerage house account manager:	
Name of fund(s):	
Number of units purchased:	
Initial investment amount:	
Activity statement available?	
Are there other investments held within the RRSP (e.g., GIC)?	
Types:	
Amount invested:	
Financial institution purchased from:	
Interest being earned:	
Maturity date:	

Template 22—Shares—Private Company

Are shares held in a private company?	
Name of company:	
Briefly describe the business activities:	
Is it still active?	
Have most recent financial statements been obtained and filed with CPOAP?	
Does a Shareholder Agreement exist?	
If so, has a copy been obtained and filed with the CPOAP?	
Who holds the other shares?	
From reading the Shareholder Agreement and discussions with grantor and/or other shareholders, record any financial obligations or windfalls that need to be included in the cash flow statement:	
Does a shareholder loan exist?	
Is it a loan to or from the company?	
What are the terms of repayment and are there any conditions that the loan is to be forgiven?	

Template 23—Tax-Free Savings Account (TFSA)

Does the grantor have a TFSA?	
If so, what is the account number and at which bank is it held?	
If one exists, what are the details of the investment?	
If other than a savings account, what are the maturity dates of investments?	
Have these dates been recorded in your personal diary?	
Have the annual investment amount been included when considering the grantor's cash flow requirements?	
Has the interest being earned been included in the grantor's cash receipts when reviewing cash availability?	
If a TFSA does not exist, has consideration been given to setting one up?	

Template 24—The Will

Does the grantor have a will?	
Where is it kept?	
If not and the grantor is not incapacitated, have plans been made to ensure a will is made?	
If one exists, upon reading, make notes about any instructions that will impact decisions made as the grantor's property is managed?	

Appendix X

Cash Flow—Annual Basis

Bank Account # _____

For the period _____

	Estimated Amount	# of times during yr	Total
Cash in bank account at beginning of period **(A)**			
Cash In			
OAS			
CPP			
Company pension			
Survivor's pension			
Investment income:			
GIC #			
GIC #			
GIC #			
Term Deposit			
Term Deposit			
Term Deposit			
Dividends			
Dividends			
Dividends			
Other			
Other			
Other			
Investment maturities:			
GIC #			
GIC #			
GIC #			
Term Deposit			
Term Deposit			
Term Deposit			
Other			
Other			
Other			
Other:			
Loan payback			
Inheritance			
Other			

Cash Flow—Annual Basis (continued)

	Estimated Amount	# of times during yr	Total
Total Cash In (B)			
Cash Out			
Monthly rent			
Mortgage pymts:			
Condo			
Cottage			
Farm			
Home			
Undeveloped Land			
Property Taxes			
Condo			
Cottage			
Farm			
Home			
Undeveloped Land			
Utilities:			
Gas			
Electricity			
Water			
Phone – land-line			
Cable TV service			
Cell Phone			
Maintenance (snow removal/ grass cutting)			
Medical expenses			
Dental expenses			
Insurance premiums:			
Car			
Condo			
Cottage			
Farm			
Home			
Undeveloped Land			
Business/Partnership			
Disability			
Critical Illness			
Health			
Life			
Pet			
Loan payments			
Line of credit payments			

Cash Flow—Annual Basis (continued)

	Estimated Amount	# of times during yr	Total
Automobile costs			
Insurance			
Maintenance			
Petrol			
Living Expenses			
Clothing			
Groceries			
Transportation (other than car)			
Gift/donations			
Travel			
Recreation – theatre, movies, club memberships			
Newspapers/magazines/books			
Weekly/monthly cash allowance			
Tax instalments			
Other			
Total Cash Out (C)			$
Cash over/(shortfall) for the year (B – C = D)			
Net Cash Position at end of Period before investing decisions made (A + / - D = E)			
Investments to be rolled over/invested (Cash out):			
GIC #			
GIC #			
GIC #			
Term Deposit			
Term Deposit			
Term Deposit			
Other: (specify)			
Other: (specify)			
Other: (specify)			
Total money re-invested (F)			
Cash expected to be in bank account at end of year (E – F)			

When you subtract your total of cash outs from cash ins you may find yourself with a negative number. This means that you are planning to spend more money this year than you plan on earning or receiving into the bank account. Depending on the amount of the money in the bank account at the beginning of the period, this may not be a cause for concern. However, it may cause you to reconsider the expense amounts—both in light of the type of expenditure as well as the amount. It will also indicate whether you need to re-arrange GIC and/or term deposit maturity dates when they next come due for renewal.

Your **Net Cash Position at end of Period before investing decisions made** will help you determine the amount of cash reserves you have for investing purposes.

Although some pension income is increased each year, being attached to the CPI (Consumer Price Index), for the purposes of this cash flow projection, use the amount that is being received currently. This will understate your revenues by a small amount but it is better to understate your cash in and end up with a little more cash at the end of the period, than overstate what you expect to receive and end up with insufficient funds to meet regular living expenses due to locking up cash in investments because you didn't think you would need it.

Appendix XI

Cash Flow—Monthly Basis

Bank Account # _____

For the period: _____

	MONTH												
	1*	2	3	4	5	6	7	8	9	10	11	12	Total
Cash in bank account at beginning of period **(A)**													
Cash In													
OAS													
CPP													
Company pension													
Survivor's pension													
Investment income:													
GIC #													
GIC #													
GIC #													
Term Deposit													
Term Deposit													
Term Deposit													
Dividends													
Dividends													
Dividends													
Other													
Other													
Other													
Investment maturities:													
GIC #													
GIC #													
GIC #													
Term Deposit													
Term Deposit													
Term Deposit													
Other													
Other													

Cash Flow – Monthly Basis (continued)

	MONTH 1*	2	3	4	5	6	7	8	9	10	11	12	Total
Other													
Other:													
Loan payback													
Inheritance													
Other													
Total Cash In (B)													
Cash Out													
Monthly rent													
Mortgage pymts:													
Condo													
Cottage													
Farm													
Home													
Undeveloped Land													
Property Taxes													
Condo													
Cottage													
Farm													
Home													
Undeveloped Land													
Utilities:													
Gas													
Electricity													
Water													
Phone – land-line													
Cable TV service													
Cell Phone													
Maintenance (snow													

Cash Flow – Monthly Basis (continued)

	MONTH												
	1*	2	3	4	5	6	7	8	9	10	11	12	Total
removal/ grass cutting)													
Medical expenses													
Dental expenses													
Insurance premiums:													
Car													
Condo													
Cottage													
Farm													
Home													
Undeveloped Land													
Business/Partnership													
Disability													
Critical Illness													
Health													
Life													
Pet													
Loan payments													
Line of credit payments													
Automobile costs													
Insurance													
Maintenance													
Petrol													
Living Expenses													
Clothing													
Groceries													
Transportation (other than car)													
Gift/donations													
Travel													

Cash Flow – Monthly Basis (continued)

MONTH	1*	2	3	4	5	6	7	8	9	10	11	12	Total
Recreation – theatre, movies, club memberships													
Newspapers/magazines/books													
Weekly/monthly cash allowance													
Tax instalments													
Other													
Total Cash Out (C)		$											
Cash over/(shortfall) for the year (B – C = D)													
Net Cash Position at end of Period before investing decisions made (A + / - D = E)													
Investments to be rolled over/invested (Cash out):													
GIC #													
GIC #													
GIC #													
Term Deposit													
Term Deposit													
Term Deposit													

Cash Flow – Monthly Basis (continued)

	MONTH												
	1*	2	3	4	5	6	7	8	9	10	11	12	Total
Other: (specify)													
Other: (specify)													
Other: (specify)													
Total money re-invested (F)													
Cash expected to be in bank account at end of year (E – F = G)													

* The beginning balance will be taken directly from the bank statement/passbook, adjusted for cheques written and not cashed yet. From the 2nd month onwards, the opening balance will be the previous month's closing, i.e., cash expected to be in bank account at end of period (G).

Note that the columns have not been labelled. This will allow you the flexibility to look at any 12 month period going forward that best suits your requirements.

References

The following are suggested sources and links for additional information. The authors neither warrant nor guarantee the accuracy of the information contained therein. It is not meant to be exhaustive. The reader is invited to explore further resources contained in these materials.

Books

A Practical Guide to Estates and Trusts, 2nd edition
Ouellette, Laurie, TEP, FCGA
CCH Canadian Limited, 2005

Duties of Estate Trustee, Guardians and Attorneys
Jenkins, Jennifer J., Scott, H. Mark
Canada Law Book Inc., Aurora 2008

Essential Estate Administration in Ontario
Morton, James C., Stone, Risa M.
CCH Canadian Limited, Toronto, 2002

Power of Attorney Litigation
Hull, Ian M.
CCH Canadian Limited, Toronto 2000

Protect Your Elderly Parents: Become your Parents' Guardian or Trustee
Butler, Lynne, Lawyer,
Self-Counsel Press, Canada, 2008

So You've Been Appointed Executor, 2nd edition
Carter, Tom
Self-Counsel Press, Canada, 2007

The Complete Canadian Eldercare Guide
Tapp-McDougall, Caroline
John Wiley & Sons Canada, Ltd., 2004

The Executor's Handbook, 2nd Edition
Greenan, Jennifer A.
CCH Canadian Limited, Toronto 2003

You Can't Take It With You: Common-Sense Estate Planning for Canadians, 5th edition
Foster, Sandra E.,
John Wiley & Sons Canada, Ltd., 2007

Web sites

Shares and Stock Information
Computershare (www.computershare.com)
CIBC Mellon (www.cibcmellon.com)
www.bloomberg.com
ca.finance.yahoo.com
finance.sympatico.msn.ca

Government Web Sites

Tax Matters:
www.cra-arc.gc.ca

Pension Matters:
www.hrsdc.gc.ca

Elder Care Matters:

Province/Territory	Web Site	Email address	Phone number(s)
British Columbia	www.gov.bc.ca/health	EnquiryBC@gov.bc.ca	1-800-663-7867 (BC)
			604-660-2421 (outside of BC)
	www.seniorsservicessociety.ca/	info@seniorsservicessociety.ca	604-520-6621
Alberta	www.health.alberta.ca	health.ahinform@gov.ab.ca	780-427-7164
	www.seniors.alberta.ca/	Alberta.Seniors@gov.ab.ca	1-877-644-9992 (toll free in Alberta)
			780-644-9992 (Edmonton area only)
Saskatchewan	www.socialservices.gov.sk.ca/seniors	socialservicesinquiry@gov.sk.ca	306-787-3700
	www.skseniorsmechanism.ca/	info@skseniorsmechanism.ca	306-359-9956
			1-888-823-2211 (toll fee)
Manitoba	www.gov.mb.ca/health		204-287-8827
			For calls outside Winnipeg area: 1-866-COM-INFO (266-4636)
	www.seniors.cimnet.ca/cim/19.dhtm	info@crm.mb.ca	204-949-2565
Ontario	www.health.gov.on.ca	Use "Service Ontario" link found on Contact Us page of website under "General Information"	1-866-532-3161
	www.losingourparents.com	mbart@losingourparents.com	905-939-2931

Elder Care Matters: (continued)

Province/Territory	Web Site	Email address	Phone number(s)
Quebec	www.msss.gouv.qc.ca	Use "send email" option found on Contact Us page of website.	Montréal area: 514 644-4545 Elsewhere in Québec : 1 877 644-4545 (toll free)
	www.aines.info.gouv.qc.ca/en/	Use "send email" option found on Contact Us page of website.	Montréal area: 514 644-4545 Elsewhere in Québec : 1 877 644-4545 (toll free)
New Brunswick	www.gnb.ca/0051/index-e.asp	Health_Sante@gnb.ca	506-457-4800
	www2.gnb.ca/content/gnb/en/departme nts/ social_development/seniors.html	sd-ds@gnb.ca	506-453-2001
Nova Scotia	www.gov.ns.ca/health	DoHweb@gov.ns.ca	1-902-424-5818 1-800-387-6665 (toll free in Nova Scotia)
	www.gov.ns.ca/seniors/	seniors@gov.ns.ca	902-424-0065 1-800-670-0065 (toll free)
Prince Edward Island	www.gov.pe.ca/sss/		902-620-3777
	www.seniorssafety.ca/	Use "send email" option found on Contact Us page of website	902-566-0737
Newfoundland & Labrador	www.health.gov.nl.ca/health/	healthinfo@gov.nl.ca	709-729-4984
	www.seniorsresource.ca/	info@seniorsresource.ca	709-737-2333 1-800-563-5599 (toll free)

Elder Care Matters: (continued)

Province/Territory	Web Site	Email address	Phone number(s)
Yukon	www.hss.gov.yk.ca/	hss@gov.yk.ca	1-800-661-0408 (toll free in Yukon)
	www.gov.yk.ca/services/people_seniors.html		1-800-661-0408 (toll free in Yukon)
Northwest Territories	www.hlthss.gov.nt.ca/english/health/default.htm	Use "send email" option found on Contact Us page of website.	1-800-661-0830
	www.hlthss.gov.nt.ca/seniors/default.asp	seniors@yk.com	867-920-7444 1-800-661-0878 (toll free)
Nunavut	www.gov.nu.ca/health/		

Institute of Chartered Accountant Offices across Canada

Institute	Web Site	Phone Contact	Toll-Free Phone Contact	Email Contact
Canadian Institute of Chartered Accountants	www.cica.ca	416-977-3222		Contact Us option found on Home page of website.
Institute of Chartered Accountants of British Columbia	www.ica.bc.ca	604-681-3264	1-800-663-2677	Contact Us page of website.
Institute of Chartered Accountants of Alberta	www.icaa.ab.ca	780-424-7391	1-800-232-9406	info@icaa.ab.ca
Institute of Chartered Accountants of Saskatchewan	www.icas.sk.ca	306-359-1010		Contact Us option found on Home page of website.
Institute of Chartered Accountants of Manitoba	www.icam.mb.ca	204-942-8248	1-888-942-8248 (within Manitoba only)	icam@icam.mb.ca
Institute of Chartered Accountants of Ontario	www.icao.on.ca	416-962-1481	1-800-387-0735	custserv@icao.on.ca
Ordre des comptables agrees du Quebec	www.ocaq.qc.ca	514-288-3256	1-800-363-4688	info@ocaq.qc.ca
New Brunswick Institute of Chartered Accountants	www.nbica.org	506-634-1588		nbica@nb.aibn.com
Institute of Chartered Accountants of Nova Scotia	www.icans.ns.ca	902-425-3291		icans@icans.ns.ca
Institute of Chartered Accountants of Prince Edward Island	www.icapei.com	902-894-4290		Contact Us option found on Home page of website.
Institute of Chartered Accountants of Newfoundland	www.icanl.ca	709-753-7566		Contact Us option found on Home page of website.
Institute of Chartered Accountants of the Yukon	www.icayk.ca	904-681-3264	1-800-663-2677	Contact Us page of website.
Institute of Chartered Accountants of the Northwest Territories and Nunavut	www.icanwt.nt.ca	867-920-4404		N/A

List of Law Society Offices across Canada

Society	Web Site	Phone Contact	Toll-Free Phone Contact	Email Contact
The Law Society of British Columbia	www.lawsociety.bc.ca	604-669-2533	1-800-903-5300 (BC only)	information@lsbc.org
The Law Society of Alberta	www.lawsocietyalberta.com	403-229-4700	1-800-661-9003 (limited areas within Alberta)	Contact Us page of website.
The Law Society of Saskatchewan	www.lawsociety.sk.ca	306-569-8242		reception@lawsociety.sk.ca
The Law Society of Manitoba	www.lawsociety.mb.ca	204-942-5571		admin@lawsociety.mb.ca
The Law Society of Upper Canada (Ontario)	www.lsuc.on.ca	416-947-3300	1-800-668-7380	lawsociety@lsuc.on.ca
Chambre des Notaires du Québec	www.cdnq.org	514-879-1793	1-800-668-2473	information@cdnq.org
Barreau du Québec	www.barreau.qc.ca	514-954-3400	1-800-361-8495	information@barreau.qc.ca
Law Society of New Brunswick	www.lawsociety-barreau.nb.ca	506-458-8540		gereral@lawsociety-barreau.nb.ca
Nova Scotia Barristers' Society	www.nsbs.org	902-422-1491		Contact Us page of website.
Law Society of Prince Edward Island	www.lspei.pe.ca	902-566-1666		lawsociety@lspei.pe.ca
The Law Society of Newfoundland and Labrador	www.lawsociety.nf.ca	709-722-4740		Contact Us page of website.
Law Society of Nunavut	lawsociety.nu.ca	867-979-2330		lawsociety@qiniq.com
Law Society of the Northwest Territories	www.lawsociety.nt.ca/	867-873-3828		lawsocnt@lawsociety.nt.ca
Law Society of Yukon	www.lawsocietyyukon.com	867-668-4231		info@lawsocietyyukon.com

Index

review with, 51,55

H
Health insurance, 33, 68, 177
House insurance, 33, 69, 177

I
Income received, 19
Income Tax Act, 38, 102
Income trust, xxv
    identifying, 69-70, 76–77
    template, 77, 180
Individual Consent Form—T1013E, 38
Informal review, litigation and, 134–135
Institute of Chartered Accountant Offices, 206
Insurance
    policies, 67–69
    template, 67–69, 176–177
    premiums, 50
Insurance segregated fund trust, 161
Inventory, 28
    checklist for, 56
    making and gathering the information, 32–35
    preparing, 59–98
    of safety deposit box(es), 35
Investments, 19
    accounts, 50
    identifying, 69–80
    templates, 71–72, 178
    types of, 70
Investment statement, identification of items included on, 21
Invoices/bills/statements/confirmations, to support activities, 21

J
Jewellery, 65
Joint spousal trust, 158
Judgment creditor, 12
Jurisdiction, in Canada, xiii

L
Law society offices, 207
Legal advice, disclaimer, xv
Legislation, for power of attorney, 9

Letters Probate, 101–102*n*3
Liabilities, xxv, 20, 33–34
    benchmarking, 21
    control, 101
    incurred/discharged, 20
    release of, 16
    template, 164–169
Life insurance, 33, 69, 177
Limitation period, 83–84, 83*n*2
Limited liability partnership (LLP), 63
Limited partnership (LP), 63
    identifying, 33, 73
    template, 73–74, 178–179
Line of credit (LOC)
    identifying, 34, 80
    template, 80–81, 181
Litigation, 129–138
    communication/miscommunication, 130–131
    costs of, 136–137
    finding fault, 130–132
    formal review, 135–136
    informal review, 134–135
    negotiations, 133
    preparing a response to, 132–133
    record keeping, 131, 134, 137
    willful conduct, 131–132
LLP *See* Limited liability partnership
Loan guarantees
    identifying, 34, 81
    template, 81, 181
Loans payable
    identifying, 34, 81–82
    template, 82, 182
Loans receivable
    identifying, 34, 82–84
    template, 84, 183
LOC *See* Line of credit
Long-term living, options and planning, 46
LP *See* Limited partnership

M
Maintenance agreement, 34, 84–85
    paying maintenance, 85
    receiving maintenance, 85
    template, 85–86, 184